Grandshaykh's Notes Series

Banquet for the Soul

Fine-Tuning the Seeker's Approach to the Divine Presence

The Miracles and Inspired Wisdom of Shaykhs of the Naqshbandi Golden Chain

Shaykh Muhammad Hisham Kabbani

Institute for Spiritual and Cultural Advancement

Library of Congress Cataloging-in-Publication Data Forthcoming.

Published and Distributed by:
Institute for Spiritual and Cultural Advancement

17195 Silver Parkway, #401
Fenton, MI 48430 USA
Tel: (888) 278-6624
Fax:(810) 815-0518
Email: staff@naqshbandi.org
Web: http://www.naqshbandi.org

First Edition: July 2008
ISBN: 978-1-930409-56-9

Shaykh Muhammad Nazim Adil al-Ḥaqqani (right), world leader of the most distinguished Naqshbandi-Ḥaqqani Sufi Order, with his representative, and author of this book, Shaykh Muhammad Hisham Kabbani.

CONTENTS

بسم الله الرحمن الرحيم

The head of every association is:

A‘ūdhū billāhi min ash-Shayṭān ir-rajīm

Bismi’l-Lāhi ‘r-Raḥmāni ‘r-Raḥīm

Nawaytu ’l-arbā‘īn, nawaytu ’l-‘itikāf, nawaytu ’l-khalwa, nawaytu ‘l-‘uzla, nawaytu ’r-riyāḍa, nawaytu ’s-sulūk, lillāhi ta‘ala fī hādhā ’l-masjid

Ati‘ Allāh wa ati‘ ar-Rasūla wa ūli ‘l-amri minkum

I seek refuge in Allah from Satan the rejected,

In the name of Allah the Merciful, the Compassionate.

I intend the forty (days of seclusion); I intend seclusion in the mosque; I intend seclusion; I intend isolation; I intend discipline (of the ego); I intend to travel in God’s Path for the sake of God in this mosque.

Obey Allah, Obey the Prophet and obey those in authority among you. Sūratu ’n-Nisā (Women), 4:59.

ABOUT THE AUTHOR

Shaykh Muhammad Hisham Kabbani is a world-renowned author and religious scholar. He has devoted his life to the promotion of the traditional Islamic principles of peace, tolerance, love, compassion and brotherhood, while opposing extremism in all its forms. The shaykh is a member of a respected family of traditional Islamic scholars, which includes the former head of the Association of Muslim Scholars of Lebanon and the present Grand Mufti[1] of Lebanon.

In the U.S., Shaykh Kabbani serves as Chairman, Islamic Supreme Council of America; Founder, Naqshbandi Sufi Order of America; Advisor, World Organization for Resource Development and Education; Chairman, As-Sunnah Foundation of America; Chairman, Kamilat Muslim Women's Organization; and, Founder and President, The Muslim Magazine.

Shaykh Kabbani is highly trained, both as a Western scientist and as a classical Islamic scholar. He received a bachelor's degree in chemistry and studied medicine. In addition, he also holds a degree in Islamic Divine Law, and under the tutelage of Shaykh ʿAbd Allāh Daghestani ق, license to teach, guide and counsel religious students in Islamic spirituality from Shaykh Muhammad Nazim ʿAdil al-Qubrusi al-Ḥaqqani an-Naqshbandi ق, the world leader of the Naqshbandi-Ḥaqqani Sufi Order.

His books include: *Illuminations* (2007), *Universe Rising* (2007), *Symphony of Remembrance* (2007), *A Spiritual Commentary on the*

---

[1] Arabic: *muftī*—The highest Islamic religious authority in the country.

Chapter of Sincerity (2006), *Sufi Science of Self-Realization* (Fons Vitae, 2005), *Keys to the Divine Kingdom* (2005); *Classical Islam and the Naqshbandi Sufi Order* (2004); *The Naqshbandi Sufi Tradition Guidebook* (2004); *The Approach of Armageddon? An Islamic Perspective* (2003); *Encyclopedia of Muhammad's Women Companions and the Traditions They Related* (1998, with Dr. Laleh Bakhtiar); *Encyclopedia of Islamic Doctrine* (7 vols. 1998); *Angels Unveiled* (1996); *The Naqshbandi Sufi Way* (1995); *Remembrance of God Liturgy of the Sufi Naqshbandi Masters* (1994).

In his long-standing endeavor to promote better understanding of classical Islam, Shaykh Kabbani has hosted two international conferences in the United States, both of which drew scholars from throughout the Muslim world. As a resounding voice for traditional Islam, his counsel is sought by journalists, academics and government leaders.

Preface

The manuscript upon which the following lectures are based is extremely rare and was written (dictated) by Sayyidina Shaykh Sharafuddīn ad-Daghestani ق, the 38th shaykh in the Naqshbandi Golden Chain. It consists of more than 4000 pages.

Explanations from this manuscript which comprise this book are particularly directed to those seekers who understand the Sufi Way (*ṭarīqah*); who have accompanied *awlīyā* (saints) for a long time; who are willing to open their minds and hearts to the deep love of Allah, His Messenger, and the spiritual guides (*maḥabat-Allah, maḥabat ar-Rasūl, maḥabat al-mashaykh)*; and who seek complete Oneness with them (*fanā'un fillāh, fanā'un f 'il-ḥabīb, fanā'un f 'il-mashaykh)*.

For those who hope to experience the high spiritual states of the centuries-old sciences of Knowledge of Sincerity, Vision of Sincerity, and Reality of Sincerity (*'ilm al-yaqīn, 'ayn al-yaqīn, ḥaqq al-yaqīn)*, these lectures may perchance open the seeker's heart to a horizon of clarity.

Shaykh Muhammad Hisham Kabbani

Representative of Shaykh Nazim Adil al-Haqqani, fortieth Shaykh of the Naqshbandi-Haqqani Golden Chain

Introduction

This book represents a landmark in the publication of rare, hidden, spiritual secrets more precious than all the gold stored in Fort Knox, the sum total of African-mined diamonds, or the volume of stock trades on NASDAQ. As such, the preservation of these secrets for more than fifteen centuries is a mission appointed to the most trusted souls of all humanity.

What on earth could be so valuable?

In ancient times, rulers and the elite believed they could transport all their precious possessions to the hereafter. Archeological digs have discovered the extent of these lavish burials, which are testament to the fact that we cannot take worldly wealth with us to the next life—not our bank balances, real estate, jewels, stock portfolios, liquid assets, titles, academic achievement, or social rank.

Just as financial institutions, high-end retail outlets, and in fact our very identities are heavily safeguarded by sophisticated security systems, what about a strategy to accumulate wealth that lasts for all eternity, that can never be reduced in value? Wouldn't that be safeguarded, as well, by the highest level of security?

The secrets revealed in this book are a foolproof strategy preserved over time, protected against thieves whose only goal is to rob you of your divine right to achieve excellence on all levels. As such, you should understand this book has not come into your possession by accident.

On some level, you have sought this information, these guidelines, to make sense of a world turned upside down, wherein wrong is the new right, wherein "integrity" was the number one

Googled word of 2006, a world in which previously unknown human atrocity and natural disasters fill our nightly news broadcasts.

These ancient teachings have remained hidden to protect them from the taint of political and social greed. They are transmitted from master to student and cannot exist in universities, for there is no degree or title by which to measure them. In this discipline, students graduate only when the master acknowledges their preparedness, and thereafter they join the hierarchy of the Unseen world.

The author has inherited the trust of spiritual secrets handed down from one master to the next, dating back to the earliest prophets. Shaykh Muhammad Hisham Kabbani is authorized by his master, Shaykh Muhammad Nazim al-Ḥaqqani of Cyprus, who is authorized by his master, Grandshaykh ق ʿAbd Allāh al-Fa'iz ad-Daghestani of Damascus. Masters in the Naqshbandi Sufi Order have been chosen to preserve these secrets for every subsequent generation dating back to seventh century Arabia, when Prophet Muhammad ﷺ continued and completed the sequence of divine transmission that began with Adam, through all the prophets and messengers, including Abraham ﷷ, Moses, and Jesus Christ, peace be upon them all.

This guarded knowledge cannot be mass produced or mass consumed. It is published by permission of those masters unto whom it is entrusted, with the understanding that it can only truly reach those who will accept it. These guardian masters have waited for the current era, in which hearts have become so destitute they are now prepared to hear and follow the "language of the heart".

One may read this book and take no benefit from it, if their spiritual receiver is not tuned to what is being transmitted. Perhaps this knowledge is intended for them at some point in the future, when they will remember this book, or perhaps they will give this book to someone who is ready to start their journey now. For those who have started their journey, sitting at the feet of the master is their dearest worldly destination that far exceeds any tropical vacation.

The content of the this book is taken from the treasure trove of notes of Grandshaykh ق 'Abd Allāh that, upon his death, were bequeathed to his deputy Shaykh Nazim al-Ḥaqqani, who has put them in the trust of his representative, Shaykh Hisham Kabbani.

Shaykh Hisham interpreted these notes in daily talks during the holy month of Ramadan—"the month of the community"—thirty days of fasting in which God's favor and bounty is limitless.

At the simplest level, the fast involves a substantial physical undertaking wherein no food or drink is consumed from before dawn until sundown. One must also avoid anger, contemplate their mortality, give charity, feed the poor, and reconnect with family and community. At a higher level, the fast of Ramadan purifies our hearts and replaces the negative characters greed, anger, and jealousy with the positive characters generosity, contentment, and a desire to serve others.

Through the purification of fasting and the mentoring of their spiritual master, students are prepared to receive the guarded secrets. In predawn hours they sit at Shaykh Hisham's feet, observing the time-honored meditation and reciting chants of remembrance that sanctify the gathering, ushering it into the spiritual realm, where secret knowledge is transmitted.

This book is a transcript of those precious talks from the Ramadan of October 2006. You may choose to accept or reject what is contained in these pages. If you accept, perhaps you will be on your way to learning the language of the heart.

If you are a first-time reader of Shaykh Kabbani's work, you may be struck by his extemporaneous style of discourse, which contains sidebars, anecdotes, and numerous footnotes, all generously intended to help us grasp what he offers and not lose it.

PUBLISHER'S NOTES

This book is specifically designed for laypersons and readers unfamiliar with Sufi terminology. As such, we have often replaced Arabic with English translations, except in instances where Arabic terms are crucial to the tone and substance of the text. In such instances, we have included transliterations or footnoted explanations as well as an extensive glossary.

As the source material is an oral transmission, its language was revised for a written format, and references have been added as appropriate; however, we have tried our best to retain the essence of the author's original talks. We ask the reader's forgiveness for any omissions in this final text.

Quotes from the Qur'an are centered, highlighted in bold, italicized, and chapter number and verse is cited. The Holy Traditions of Prophet Muhammad ﷺ (known as hadith) are offset, italicized and footnoted referencing the books in which they are cited.

Where gender-specific pronouns such as "he" and "him" are applied in a general sense, it has been solely for the flow of text, and no discrimination is intended towards female readers.

The following symbols are universally recognized by Muslims and have been respectfully included in this work:

The symbol ﷻ represents *subḥānahu wa taʿala*, (may His Glory be Exalted) praise customarily recited after reading or pronouncing the name "Allah" and any of the Islamic names of God.

The symbol ﷺ represents *sall-Allāhu ʿalayhi wa sallam* (God's blessings and greetings of peace be upon him), which is customarily recited after reading or pronouncing the holy name of Prophet Muhammad.

The symbol ﷺ represents *ʿalayhi 's-salām* (peace be upon him/her), which is customarily recited after reading or pronouncing the holy names of the other prophets, family members of Prophet Muhammad, the pure and virtuous women in Islam, and the angels.

The symbol ؓ represents *raḍī-Allāhu ʿanh* (may God be pleased with him/her), which is customarily recited after reading or pronouncing the holy names of companions of the Prophet ﷺ.

The symbol ق represents *qaddas-Allāhu sirrah* (may God sanctify his secret), which is customarily recited after reading or pronouncing the name of a saint.

Transliteration

To simplify reading the Arabic names, places and terms are not transliterated in the main text. Transliteration is provided in the section on the spiritual practices to facilitate correct pronunciation and is based on the following system:

Symbol	Transliteration	Symbol	Transliteration	Vowels: Long	
ء	’	ط	ṭ	آ ى	ā
ب	b	ظ	ẓ	و	ū
ت	t	ع	‘	ي	ī
ث	th	غ	gh	**Short**	
ج	j	ف	f	َ	a
ح	ḥ	ق	q	ُ	u
خ	kh	ك	k	ِ	i
د	d	ل	l		
ذ	dh	م	m		
ر	r	ن	n		
ز	z	ه	h		
س	s	و	w		
ش	sh	ي	y		
ص	ṣ	ة	ah; at		
ض	ḍ	ال	al-/’l-		

1: THE HEARTS OF THE FRIENDS OF GOD

Ascensions of the Prophet

There is a special quality carried by the words of the saints.[2] Saints know things and say things that God, the Exalted, has revealed to them alone. They see a range of realities beyond what we see. As a result, they don't necessarily speak with the language of the tongue, but rather with the language of the heart. Their hearts send vibrations to the tongue which, in turn, can express what is originally in their hearts that was sent by God, the Exalted.

They speak to us in an encrypted form, and just as computer languages need decoders to translate the coded messages, some people are able to decode part of the message, while others might decode other parts. What flows through the hearts of the gnostic Friends of God, *awlīyāullāh*, are inspirations that come from heavenly sources, and the heart and the mind try to decode this knowledge and pass it through to the tongue.

Because of this unique communication process, throughout history people have often been surprised at the actions and words of the Friends of God. Laymen and scholars generally cannot understand what the Friend of God is saying because not all hearts can interpret or hold these meanings.

The notes I am referring to are from lectures given by Grandshaykh ق and translated by Mawlana Shaykh Nazim, may God, the Exalted, grant him a long life. The notes I took may be

---

[2] *Awlīyāullāh/awlīyā*: Friends of God; saints (singular, *walī*).

understandable to some, and not others; it is in the nature of the messages that come through the Friends of God.

God, the Exalted, has dressed his beloved Prophet ﷺ with the light of God's Greatest Name.[3] He also dressed him with the light of the Paradise river *al-Kawthar*, the light of which first purifies each member of the community and then adorns them. Whoever says, "O Allah! Shower us from the river al-Kawthar in Paradise."[4] will be adorned by those Divine manifestations, *tajallīs*, and receive those blessings.

Grandshaykh ق said:

> God, the Exalted, gave the authority to the Prophet ﷺ by giving him all these levels at his birth. Immediately upon birth, the Prophet ﷺ was able to see all the things that God, the Exalted, had granted to him. He went into prostration[5], saying, "My Community, My Community—*Ummatī*."[6]
>
> God, the Exalted, gave him authority:
>
> وَسَخَّرَ لَكُم مَّا فِي السَّمَاوَاتِ وَمَا فِي الْأَرْضِ جَمِيعًا مِّنْهُ إِنَّ فِي ذَلِكَ لَآيَاتٍ لِّقَوْمٍ يَتَفَكَّرُونَ

---

[3] The Sufis believe that God has 99 Beautiful Names and Attributes, and the greatest Divine Name (Arabic *ismallāh al-ʿaẓam*) is a secret revealed only to a select few individuals. It is said that whoever knows this Name, will be given the power to "*say to a thing 'Be!' and it will be.*" Sūrah Yāsīn, 36:82.

[4] Arabic: *Allāhumma asqinā min nahr al-Kawthar.*

[5] Arabic: *sajda*—Ritual prostration, during prayer or supplication.

[6] "My community—*ummatī*": from the moment Prophet ﷺ appeared in this world, he was preoccupied with the welfare of his people. Sent as a "Mercy to all Humanity", we can assume all human beings are a part of his nation, not only Muslims.

And He has subjected to you, as from Him, all that is in the heavens and on earth: Behold, in that are Signs indeed for those who reflect.[7]

As soon as he went into prostration, he went into ascension[8]. He asked for the light with which to dress his Community. That is why Friends of God[9] say that the Prophet ﷺ did not have just one ascension, but that every moment in his life and every moment in his holy grave he is in ascension and taking what God, the Exalted, grants him from the Divine Presence; in turn, the Prophet ﷺ dresses the Community with these lights.

God, the Exalted, has given the Prophet ﷺ incomparable gifts and has made him the Seal of the Messengers. He was granted the strongest power of prophecy and is able to adorn his Community from this attribute. If we are able to accept the Prophet ﷺ and his teachings, we might, in some degree, share in these attributes and be dressed with his image. Those who follow in his footsteps become *Muhammadiyūn*—Muhammadan in appearance, and they will merge with that light[10] on Judgment Day. They will resemble the Prophet Muhammad ﷺ and, therefore they will resemble one another. This is not due to their ingenuity, but is a reward for having sought to follow the example of the Prophet ﷺ. They will shine with his light and appear to be his twin. Someone who is not dressed with that light, deniers of spirituality, will be surprised, saying, "How many people look like the reflection of Sayyidina Muhammad ﷺ and his light shines from their faces!"

---

[7] Sūratu 'l-Jāthīya (Crouching), 45:13.

8 *Miʿrāj*: ascension through the seven heavens to the Divine Presence, made by Prophet Muhammad ﷺ in the eleventh year of his prophecy.

[9] Arabic: *awlīyāullāh/awlīyā*: saints, literally "God's friends".

[10] Arabic: *nūr*: divine light; in this case, the light of Prophet Muhammad's essence.

قُلْ إِن كُنتُمْ تُحِبُّونَ اللَّهَ فَاتَّبِعُونِي يُحْبِبْكُمُ اللَّهُ

Say (O Muhammad)! Follow me and then God will love you.[11]

Who is God's Beloved? Sayyidina Muhammad ﷺ. And by a special authority given to Prophet ﷺ, he can reflect that light to anyone who loves him.

The Three Lights

As soon as the Prophet ﷺ was born he fell on knees in prostration. Then God, the Exalted, showed him the reality of the three lights from which He created the universe. God, the Exalted, wove the heavens and the earth from these lights, and they are related to the Divine Name "the Light," an-Nūr[12]. From that light, God created the light of Prophet Muhammad ﷺ, and from that light He created the light of the first human, Adam عليه السلام.

Grandshaykh ق, speaking in the language of the Friends of God, related that God said to the Prophet ﷺ:

> Because there is no change in My reality, I am not going to change the way I have dressed My servants with these three lights. I have dressed them for your sake, O Muhammad. On Judgment Day, your Community is going to come to My Presence with these three lights that will help them deserve to be in Paradise.
>
> May God, the Exalted, make us believers in the Prophet ﷺ!

In many places in Holy Qur'an, God, the Exalted, expresses Divine Anger with those who harm others. He cursed oppressors

---

[11] Sūrat Āli-'Imrān (the Family of 'Imrān), 3:31.

[12] From among the 99 Beautiful Names and Attributes of Allah, meaning "The Light".

and tyrants[13], describing the severity of His punishment for them and for those who refused to follow the ways of faith. Grandshaykh ق said that while this curse appears in the Holy Qur'an, it did not apply to the realities of the souls and the bodies of human beings, because they are made from the three lights. Rather that curse was directed to their characters. It is not the body which is the oppressor, and it is not the soul that receives the curse—it is the character. The wisdom of cursing it is to change it from a negativity and darkness to positivity and light.

This is why recitation of the Holy Qur'an[14] will purify us of the negative traits that have burdened our characters and our souls. It is crucial to read the Holy Qur'an, for that will help punishment bypass you. God, the Exalted, will lift the curse and bestow His rewards on you.

When God, the Exalted, sent these curses, He did it to help transform our characters from evil to good, both in our souls and in our bodies. In his notes Grandshaykh ق closes with this Sacred Tradition:

يقول الله : ما وسعني أرضي ولا سمائي ولكن وسعني قلب عبدي المؤمن

God, the Exalted, said, "Neither heavens nor earth contained Me, but the heart of My believing servant contained Me."[15]

---

[13] Arabic: *ẓālimīn*—oppressors, tyrants.

[14] Reciting the Holy Qur'an in Arabic (not its transliteration) opens secrets hidden in the original words, which the *awlīyāullāh*, Friends of God, then reveal.

[15] Al-Ghazālī mentioned it in his *Revival of the Religious Sciences*. It is similar to the Israelite tradition Āḥmad has related in *al-Zuhd* from Wahb bin Munabbih who said that God opened the heavens for Ezekiel until he saw the Throne, so Ezekiel said, "How Perfect are You! How Mighty are You, O Lord!" So God said, "Truly, the heavens and the earth were too weak to contain Me, but the soft, humble heart of my believing slave contains Me."

This means the hearts of Friends of God are controlled by the Prophet ﷺ, the one whose heart can truly contain his Lord.

Tonight is the anniversary of the Prophet's Night Journey and Ascension.[16] No one knows what God, the Exalted, gave his beloved Prophet Muhammad ﷺ from His Divine Knowledge on that night. All that the Friends of God have received over the centuries is the result of what God, the Exalted, poured into the heart of the Prophet ﷺ that night.

The Friends of God are of many different levels: some are always in the presence of Prophet Muhammad ﷺ while others are not always in that state, but receive information from time to time, while some receive information from another Friend of God, but not directly from Prophet Muhammad ﷺ.

When you visit a waterfall, or the tumbling streams of a mountain, there is often foam floating on the surface of the waves. The foam bubbles up out of the water in frustration. There is an intense energy contained in the water that seeks to come out and be seen. It seeks to quench the thirst of the people standing at the water's edge. These waterfalls obtain their tremendous power from the height of the mountains as they rush in torrents off their cliffs.

The Friends of God, the saints, are similar. There are some Friends of God who receive immense, flowing oceans of knowledge from the Prophet ﷺ. These oceans pour upon them like great waterfalls of knowledge. This Divine Knowledge carries so much energy that people would not be able to understand what is being related to them. Ideas and meanings of such intensity and

---

[16] Arabic: *Laylat al-Isrā wa 'l-Mi'rāj.* the night Prophet Muhammad ﷺ traveled with Archangel Gabriel ﷺ on the heavenly steed Burāq from Mecca to Jerusalem in the blink of an eye, and ascended to the highest heaven.

speed pour into them in a form beyond what most minds can accept.

There are other Friends of God who receive knowledge less strongly, like a gentle river that flows without the foam and spray of rapids. This is a different level. Every drop of such "water" is in reality an ocean of knowledge in itself. That is why when a great Friend of God—such as Shaykh Nazim or Grandshaykh ق 'Abd Allāh ad-Daghestani—says one word, it is like an ocean for us. The more deeply you go into even one of their words, the more knowledge you can take from it. Such knowledge cannot be restricted because it is from the Divine Presence:

فَوَجَدَا عَبْدًا مِّنْ عِبَادِنَا آتَيْنَاهُ رَحْمَةً مِنْ عِندِنَا وَعَلَّمْنَاهُ مِن لَّدُنَّا عِلْمًا

So they found one of Our servants, on whom We had bestowed Mercy from Ourselves and whom We had taught knowledge from Our own Presence.[17]

Our Grandshaykh ق relates:

God, the Exalted, showed the Prophet ﷺ the three lights from which He created humanity. God wove the heavens and the earth from these lights and they are related to the Beautiful Divine Name an-Nūr, the Light. The first is God's own light—from that light He created the light of Muhammad ﷺ. Then from the light of Muhammad ﷺ He created Adam's light, and from these three lights He created humanity. After creating them Allah showed the Prophet ﷺ these lights and said, "O Muhammad ﷺ! I am giving these to you pure and clean; they are My servants. I will give them to you as a trust to return to Me on Resurrection Day."

---

[17] Sūratu 'l-Kahf (the Cave), 18:65.

The Prophet ﷺ answered, "I accept!"and God gave the lights to him.

Then God, the Exalted, showed him how mankind would behave, and what each person would do after being sent from the heavenly dominion to this worldly life, *dunyā*—the abode of affliction.[18] When the Prophet ﷺ saw all the sins of human beings, he was distressed.

Unchanging Attributes

God said to the Prophet ﷺ, "O Muhammad ﷺ! See how My Generosity and Greatness never change; I am The Greatest, I am The Most Powerful, I am The Merciful and I am The Most Generous. Because these Attributes do not change in Me, I am not changing the lights I gave to human beings. I am not taking that honor away. No matter what they have done, I am keeping My Word with them."

This means God, the Exalted, wants his Prophet ﷺ to feel tranquil and to relax. The Lord reaffirmed that He does not change and He is not like us.

If we humans get upset with someone, even someone whom we have been helping, we suddenly stop helping them. That is a sign of bad character. If someone says something bad about you, don't stop helping him; instead, redouble your efforts.

Some illnesses are difficult to treat. The very medicine for the cure may simply build up the ego. In spirituality, most of the seekers on the Path possess various sorts of ego illnesses. If, as a spiritual teacher, in the course of treating them, you come against their egos, they will resist and fight back. Therefore you must

[18] Arabic: *dār al-ibtilā*—the abode of affliction.

always make sure to protect yourself. If someone is acting like a donkey, pet him like a lion—then he will be happy.

That is a characteristic in every one of us. Therefore you cannot go to someone and accuse him of being a donkey, as then his "donkeyness" will obstinately resist and in the process contaminate everyone.

God, the Exalted, wanted to make sure that the Companions[19] would follow the Prophet ﷺ. How many times in the Holy Qur'an does Allah say to the companions of the Prophet, "If you go forth supporting My Prophet against the aggressors who are persecuting him, I will grant you many paradises."

What did the Arabs treasure at that time? Remember, they lived in a desert empty of rivers and greenery. So, they valued rivers and Allah gave them rivers in Holy Qur'an. They also loved wine, but while Allah prohibited wine in the Holy Qur'an, nevertheless, He said that in Paradise they would be given wine. He was building them up. They also liked beautiful women. So Allah said, "I am giving you heavenly maidens."[20] Even though Allah gave the Companions the highest level of perfection, far above anything any of us will ever reach, His method of dealing with them illustrates the nature of our egos quite well.

So Grandshaykh ق said:

> When Allah says "God cursed the idolaters; God cursed the disbelievers, God cursed the tyrants," that curse is directed against their bad characteristics, but as Sons of Adam it does not come against our essences[21].

---

[19] Arabic: *Ṣaḥāba*—Companions of Prophet Muhammad ﷺ who lived in his lifetime and followed his guidance.

[20] Arabic: *ḥūr al-ʿayn* - Pure, beautiful heavenly maidens who live in Paradise.

[21] Arabic: *Dhawāt*-The essences from which we were created.

This is because the creation of human beings brought together the three different lights: the light of the God; the light of the Prophet ﷺ and the light of Adam ؑ, all blended together. So Allah's curse is only against our deficient and harmful characteristics, not our essential selves.

That is why Grandshaykh ق and Mawlana Shaykh Nazim ق often said:

> A Friend of God is happiest when he can shout at the disciple who remains loyal even under fire. The shaykhs cannot yell at everyone, as most of us would simply run away. The shaykh can shout at only two or three of his followers, those who can carry it without becoming angry.
>
> Sometimes problems arise when disciples misinterpret what is being said by the shaykh.

And here Grandshaykh ق said something big, something that might shock the reader. He said:

> God, the Exalted, cannot be a god, *ilāh*,[22] if He curses the lights from which He created human beings. In truth, He only curses our actions[23], while our essences remain clean. When He dressed us at the time of our creation, God, the Exalted, put these three different lights in our hearts. That is why He said:
>
> *Neither the heavens nor earth contain Me, but the heart of my believing servant contains Me.*
>
> Because the believer has these three lights. This refers not only to the believers, rather everyone is a believer. Why?

---

[22] The concept of a deity, a lord, or a god and does not necessarily refer to Allah; as in, "Satan is a god to his worshippers." "Allah" is the personal name of the One Supreme God.

[23] Arabic: *'amāl* - Deeds; actions (sing. *'amal*).

Because everyone is a servant, but bad actions veil our belief. However, the lights Allah dressed us with are in continuous worship in the Divine Presence, from where they are never absent.

In the Heart of the Servant

That is why Grandshaykh ق said, "Everyone is a believer." So if everyone is a believer, how can you speak against anyone? You cannot. Try to cover the faults of others. Does anyone willingly expose his sin? No one does. Why then do we feel compelled to expose the sins of others?

God, the Exalted, has said, "Nothing contained Me except the heart of My servant." That is the station of the most hidden, *maqām al-akhfā*.

There are five levels within the heart: Heart, Secret, Secret of the Secret, Hidden, Most Hidden[24]. That most hidden station is where these secrets reside. Friends of God are trying to bring these out, but not every Friend of God can bring this kind of knowledge. These secrets have never been printed, because they are lost.

People see the heart like flesh, or as a piece of meat, but in reality it is not a piece of meat. It has four chambers: right atrium, left atrium, left ventricle, left atrium. There are four levels of secrets, but they are veiled by what we call the heart. The Friends of God go inside these four levels.

Allah said:

وَنَحْنُ أَقْرَبُ إِلَيْهِ مِنْ حَبْلِ الوريد

[24] Arabic: *qalb, sirr, sirr as-sirr, khafa, akhfā.*

I am nearer to you than your jugular vein.[25]

These four different chambers are four different universes. Each chamber of the heart is a universe. Don't think it is a small, cramped chamber. These chambers are so vast, if you throw the universe into one of these chambers it will disappear, according to the Friends of God. This our minds cannot grasp, but the Friends of God understand.

All these four chambers are covered by the outer shape of the heart, veiled. In open-heart surgey they open the heart, and then you can see these four chambers. That is why these knowledges are veiled because they are veiled by the heart, which is the level of Satan, and he can go inside that level. He is able to go around within the heart and he tries to cover it more and more so that no one can see what is inside.

But the shaykh makes surgery on the servant's heart. That is the duty of the shaykh, to perform open-heart surgery on the disciple.[26] He opens the heart and exposes the four chambers, and then the heart can begin to receive heavenly information.

Grandshaykh ق gave an example of this with the story of a Friend of God who lived in the Meedan District of Damascus. His name was Bāshā Shukrī al-Majnūn[27].

He relates:

During the 1940's there was a war in Syria involving British and French forces. One day in Damascus the time for the Ẓuhr[28] prayer came and the Syrian soldiers wanted a place to

---

[25] Sūrah Qāf, 50:16.
[26] Arabic: *murīd*—Student, disciple, seeker on the spiritual path.
[27] Arabic: *Shukrī* the one thankful to Allah; *Bāshā* (Pasha) is a high rank in Turkish times, like a lord; and *al-majnūn* means "the crazy one."
[28] Arabic: *Ẓuhr*—Midday; noon.

pray where the rockets wouldn't fall on them. So Bāshā Shukri suggested they go to his *zāwīya*[29] which was carved out of a large rock. That place provided a perfect place of his seclusion; there he lived alone, and never went out. He survived off the milk from his single goat.

He told everyone, "Let us pray inside." They looked at him as though he was insane. He repeated more forcefully, "Let us go and pray inside—move!" One after the other, the entire group of 1000 men entered his cave. They all fit inside that *zāwīya* without making the *zāwīya* bigger or making the people smaller. And so, they prayed their Ẓuhr prayer in that small room.

Grandshaykh ق said:

That rock was like a small room and it was able to take 1000 people in it without increasing the size of the room. When your faith is strong, everything becomes possible. But when your faith is not strong, everything becomes opposite.

If your faith and belief is that you are doing well, regardless, it is not your opinion that counts. It is the shaykh that confirms whether you are doing well or not. There are many people who think they are doing well, and their faith is strong. In reality they have slight doubts.

For example, if a doctor tells you to take one medicine, but you self-prescribe and take another medicine to speed your recovery, you may kill yourself. Mixing prescriptions is a dangerous practice. By doubting the first medicine and adding a second, your ego can finish you. When God's saints give you

---

[29] Arabic: *zāwīya*—designated place of prayer and meditation independent of a mosque.

something, don't doubt them. If you doubt, then you will poison yourself.

> Due to their faith in the Friend of God, Bāshā Shukri al-Majnūn, that small, narrow, tight space of his *zāwīya* became wide enough to hold a large congregation, and the whole regiment was able to enter there and pray.

If you encounter hardships in your finances, your health, employment, or in family matters, meet the difficulties with faith. Hardships cannot be carried without faith. If you have faith in God, the Exalted, your hardships will disappear. Don't use your mind to find a solution. If you use your mind alone you will only meet with further hardship.

In times of hardship keep faith, just as those 1,000 soldiers kept faith in Bāshā Shukrī al-Majnūn. They entered the cave and all were safe. They did not say, "How can we enter that cave? It cannot hold more than two or three people." God will increase it as needed. God, the Exalted, can shape space and time, and never sends us anywhere without His provision.[30]

For example, you came from New York and you stayed here. Did you sleep one day hungry? No. God never made any of us to sleep hungry. Look how many people are living and dying in the rubble and ruins of wartorn cities. It is said that 15 million children will die from AIDS this year. We must consider these facts and thank our Lord for the good condition we are in.

Grandshaykh ق said:

> Imagine how many people on earth now will be gathered in Shām ash-Sharīf. People will be gathered from around the globe, because Shām ash-Sharīf is *Kinanatullah*, the place that

---

[30] Arabic: *rizq* – sustenance, provision, ordained by God.

is safe, where nothing bad will happen, and where there is no bloodshed. *Kinānatullāh* will save everyone.[31]

He said:

Not a million and not hundreds of millions of people, but one billion people will be in Damascus, and that small city will accommodate all of them without increasing its borders and without diminishing the amount of people. That will be in the time of Mahdi ﷺ."

قال رسول الله صلى الله عليه وسلم :... ألا وإن الإيمان حين تقع الفتن بالشام

The Prophet ﷺ said: Indeed when the trials and tribulations befall safety is in Shām.[32]

How many people are in and around Mecca and Madinah and around the whole world war will enter every home across the globe. But Shām will remain safe, because on the Resurrection Day it—and it alone—is the place of resurrection.

Grandshaykh ق said:

I am hearing that, ringing in my ear. The war is going to be stronger and stronger. Sometimes a trance comes to me at night and I drop everything, and I take my prayer beads[33] and

[31] Shām is a name for the whole Levant or "Greater Syria" region that today contains Syria, Jordan, Lebanon, Israel, and the Palestinian territories (sometimes excluding the Jazira region in the north-east of modern Syria). The term linguistically comes from "land of the left hand", referring to the fact that for someone in the Hijaz (Mecca or Madina), facing east, north is to the left (so the name Yemen correspondingly means "land of the right hand"). The region is sometimes defined as the area that was dominated by Damascus, long an important regional centre — in fact, the Arabic word al-Shām الشام standing on its own can refer to the city of Damascus.

[32] Ṭabarānī.

[33] Arabic: *tasbīḥ:* rosary.

my *miswāk*[34] and by reciting, "with the name of God, the Merciful, the Compassionate"[35] I travel to Madinah, the City of the Prophet ﷺ. Once in this trance state, when I reached Madinah, there I saw Imām at-Ṭarīqah[36] Shah Bahauddin Naqshband with something in his hand.

We leave that to next time to continue.

Wa min Allāhi 't-tawfiq, bi ḥurmati 'l-Fātiḥah.

[34] Arabic: *miswāk* —toothstick made of bitter wood for cleaning the teeth.
[35] Arabic: *"Bismi'l-Lāhi 'r-Raḥmāni 'r-Raḥīm"*—In the Name of Allah, the most Benificent, the Most Merciful." This powerful supplication is recited often.
[36] Leader of the Sufi Way.

2: When God's Friends Speak

A Pail of Mercury

K*alām al-awlīyā,* the words of saints, are always living. There is a spiritual light in their words. When ordinary people speak, their ego drives their tongues and there is only ego in their words. They write their speeches beforehand. Friends of God don't write their speeches before addressing a group; they take from the heart of Sayyidina Muhammad ﷺ, and their words contain letters made of Divine Light. Like a newscaster's teleprompter, the letters dance before them and lead them through the broadcast.

Friends of God receive that light from the heart of the Prophet ﷺ and pass it on to us. So when we repeat Grandshaykh's words, there are many deep meanings. Some people might not understand, while others may. When Friends of God speak, the majority of people cannot understand. For example, the works of Muḥyīdīn ibn ʿArabī ق[37] are difficult to understand, but are widely read around the world by Muslims and non-Muslims alike. Interestingly, many non-Muslims are enlightened by his books; such is the power of his writing.

This is a drop from that knowledge that Grandshaykh ق is opening to us. We will not go into all the details, but wherever there is permission we will mention it.

So he said, "I took my rosary and went to Madinah, and by reciting *'Bismi'l-Lāhi 'r-Raḥmāni 'r-Raḥīm,* in the name of God,

---

[37] Muḥyīdīn ibn ʿArabī, 13th century Sufi mystic, poet, and scholar from Andalusia.

the Compassionate, the Merciful,' I was in the masjid of Prophet ﷺ in front of his holy grave.[38] There I saw Sayyidina Shah Naqshbandi from Bukhara, the renowned imam for which the Naqshbandi Sufi Order was named. He gave me a large bucket full of mercury and said, 'By the order of the Prophet ﷺ, I brought you this pail of mercury.'"

The pail being full of mercury has significance. If you drop mercury on the floor, it scatters and breaks. You cannot hold it like other liquids, so they call it "quicksilver."

Friends of God know that there is wisdom in everything. They don't foolishly question the message. They know that it is something with benefit because there is nothing on earth that God created that has no benefit. This is why everything they say and any word that comes from their mouth also contains benefit.

This is why sometimes disciples come to them and say, "I want to do this; what do you think?" Then the Friend of God prays for the disciple. When he says, "I pray for you," it means there is a benefit in what you are proposing and he will present the matter to the Prophet ﷺ. Or he says, "I will ask my shaykh to pray for you," and with the blessing[39] of Mawlana Shaykh it will happen. This means he has made a petition or notified the highest authorities of sainthood of what you are asking. You could ask for nothing better than the shaykh to pray for you.

To continue the story:

Grandshaykh ق took the bucket, put it on his head, and kissed it. He said, "I am still standing in that presence. Ever since

---

[38] Arabic: *rawḍat ash-sharīfa*—the space before the holy grave of Prophet ﷺ in Madinah.

[39] Arabic: *baraka*—Divine blessing.

that time when I was seven years old, I have been praying to my Lord on behalf of the Community."[40]

By this Grandshaykh ق is showing his heart has never been veiled—he is always in that state of Intimate discourse with the Divine Presence and the presence of Prophet ﷺ.[41] On behalf of the Friends of God, he is responsible in the Divine Presence to carry the responsibility and difficulty of the entire Community.

Grandshaykh ق said:

> O my Lord, from my age of seven years I am in that position, asking for the benefit of Ummat an-Nabī. And hear me today, I am asking for Imam Mahdi ؑ[42] to appear, and till today Mahdi ؑ did not appear. And also my master, Shaykh Sharafuddīn, often said, "Today Mahdi ؑ will appear" or "Tomorrow Mahdi ؑ will appear." With all this, Mahdi ؑ did not appear. All Friends of God are asking for Mahdi ؑ to appear, and all of them are saying, "Today he is appearing," and when today passes they then say, "Mahdi ؑ will appear tomorrow." All this time I have been asking, and now I have this bucket and what do I with it?

And he said even though Mahdi ؑ did not appear, anyone who attempts to analyzes or weigh statements of the Friends of God with their intellect, and then develops even the slightest doubt regarding them, have left the realm of the Friends of God, and will be thrown from their presence.

---

40 Arabic: *Ummat an-Nabī* - the Community of the Prophet ﷺ.

41 Arabic: *munājāt* - Intimate discourse with the Divine Presence and the presence of Prophet ﷺ.

42 Mahdi, the Messiah; the appointed one who has yet to come, who will save believers and kill the anti-Christ, yielding world peace before the Last Day.

Truth and Belief

Grandshaykh ق said, "My shaykh is saying and I am saying, doubts lead away from the circle of the Friends of God. No one can understand the Friends of Gods' words, any more than they can hold mercury in their hands, because it always runs through your fingers. You may feel better when you listen to them, but you won't necessarily understand much of what is being said."

Remember how they killed the great Friend of God Manṣūr al-Ḥallāj ق. He said, "There is nothing in my cloak except Allah."[43] Friends of God understood this statement, but a mob objected violently and killed al-Ḥallāj ق on the spot.

Grandshaykh ق said that once Gabriel عليه came to the Prophet ﷺ and told him, "Yā Rasūlullāh, yā Muhammad ﷺ! Call all the Companions."

This is how Friends of God speak. They don't say "so-and-so said that so-and-so said". They don't need to attribute words to ʿAlī, Said, Mustafa or Yasser. They take from the heart of the Prophet ﷺ directly, so they say, "The Prophet ﷺ said." That is their way of receiving knowledge. That is not a chain of transmission from one person to the next and then to the next. That system is used in Shariʿah,[44] which we accept fully. But in ṭarīqah, we also acknowledge the station of perfected character[45] and we draw knowledge from both Shariʿah and ṭarīqah.

The archangel Gabriel عليه told the Prophet ﷺ to call all the Companions. And this is a famous hadith from the Signs of the

---

[43] There is no union with His existence, ittiḥād; there is only His Existence, His Presence; there is no "I" or "me".

[44] Islamic jurisprudence.

[45] Arabic: maqām al-Iḥsān - Station of the perfect character, moral excellence.

Last Days.[46] Prophet ﷺ told about a valley in the land beyond Shām, in the land ruled by the Romans called "Wādī 'Umuq."

The Story of Habib an-Najjar

This place is mentioned in Surah Yāsīn

وَجَاءَ مِنْ أَقْصَى الْمَدِينَةِ رَجُلٌ يَسْعَى قَالَ يَا قَوْمِ اتَّبِعُوا الْمُرْسَلِينَ

And there came a man running from the farthest part of the town. He said, "O my people! Obey the Messengers."[47]

Prophet Jesus ﷺ sent his apostles to that valley, to the people of the city of Antioch, who were idol-worshippers. When the people rejected and cursed these messengers, a devout local man, named Ḥabīb an-Najjār, came running from outside the city affirming to the people the message the apostles came with. They began to stone him while he was saying, "O God, guide my people for they do not know," and they kept stoning him and despite that he never stopped praying for them, until finally they killed him.

Even after his death, his concern remained for his people, for God granted him to enter Paradise directly as a martyr, after being killed so violently. He did not consider how they harmed him, rather he forgave, and further wished that his people could know what he was seeing with his own eyes of the honor God granted him so that they would change their ways and turn to God.

Ibn 'Abbās ؓ,[48] the cousin of the Prophet ﷺ, said, "He was sincere towards his people during his lifetime by saying:

---

[46] Arabic: *'alamāt as-sā'at* - Signs of the Last Hour.
[47] Sūrah Yāsīn, 36:20.

$$\text{يَقَوْمِ اتَّبِعُوا الْمُرْسَلِينَ}$$

'O my people! Obey the Messengers.'[49]

and after his death by saying:

$$\text{قِيلَ ادْخُلِ الْجَنَّةَ قَالَ يَلَيْتَ قَوْمِى يَعْلَمُونَ – بِمَا غَفَرَ لِى رَبِّى وَجَعَلَنِى مِنَ}$$
$$\text{الْمُكْرَمِينَ}$$

"If only my people knew that my Lord has forgiven me, and made me among the honored ones! Because of my faith in my Lord and my belief in the Messengers."[50]

He meant that if they could see the great reward and eternal blessings he had attained, it would have lead them to follow the messengers. This sacrifice he made in the hope that his people would be guided.

The Prophet ﷺ predicted that there will come a time when the Mahdi ﷺ will appear in that area of Antioch, as will the Anti-Christ and Jesus. Near the valley of 'Umuq, there will be a great battle in the time of the Mahdi ﷺ.[51]

This didn't happen yet, but can you say the Prophet ﷺ did not speak the truth? Anyone who could say that is completely outside

---

[48] 'Abd Allāh ibn 'Abbās, son of the Prophet's uncle al-'Abbās ؓ, was confirmed by the Prophet ﷺ as one of the foremost people in understanding and interpreting the Holy Qur'an.

[49] Sūrah Yāsīn, 36:20.

[50] Sūrah Yāsīn, 36:27.

[51] This is why in his book *Al-'Aqīdah Murshidah*, Imām Ibn 'Asākir mentioned that the Prophet ﷺ told his Sahaba that the Anti-Christ was coming from behind the date trees, and the Sahaba were looking behind the date trees, fully expecting him to appear in their time.

the realm of belief. If he said that the Companions will see it, they will; Allah will send them to see it. The predictions of the Prophet ﷺ will always come true.

Grandshaykh ق said:

The Companions will see the Anti-Christ, Jesus ؑ, and Mahdi ؑ through our eyes, and we are the children of the Companions, their descendents. When the Prophet ﷺ was talking to the Companions, by order of Gabriel ؑ he was talking to us. We were sitting behind the Companions, we were listening to the Prophet ﷺ with our ears, and that is how the Friends of God hear and see, just as the Companions did.

That means if they tell you that you will see Mahdi ؑ, and it doesn't happen in your lifetime, then your offspring will see him. Don't question or doubt. Your descendents will see these things even if you don't. These predictions are addressed to the entire human race: past, present and future. We too will see those tremendous events, including that great battle, and we will receive the rewards.

Grandshaykh ق said:

وَقُلْ جَاءَ الْحَقُّ وَزَهَقَ الْبَاطِلُ إِنَّ الْبَاطِلَ كَانَ زَهُوقًا

And say: "Truth has (now) arrived, and Falsehood perished;"[52]

What I am saying is based on truth and not falsehood."

He said that decision was taken by God, the Exalted, and God gave authorization to the Prophet ﷺ, that all Muslims will be under the power of non-Muslims. He mentioned this 35 years ago, as if it was going to happen then. Today we see the truth

---

[52] Sūratu 'l-Isrā (The Night Journey), 17:81.

of it, that Muslims are suffering oppression because of their bad behavior. However, this is going to change.

This is from the knowledge of the bucket of mercury that Shah Naqshband ق showed to Grandshaykh ق, and he is speaking from that knowledge.

To continue, Grandshaykh ق said:

O my Lord, send the Mahdi ﷺ to us and save the Community, al-Ummah. Change the unbelievers to believers."

He said, "He is The Most Merciful of those who show mercy, *Hūwa arḥam ar-Raḥīmīn*. When I made that prayer I was asking the Lord to put everyone under that mercy in the time of Mahdi ﷺ, without distinguishing between Muslim, Jew, Buddhist or Hindu."

He said, at that moment the bucket of mercury began to move in his hand. It was not a dream, but a reality. The bucket moved and the mercury started to drip and shake. It splashed and sprayed, the way a can of Coke sprays when it is shaken. The mercury began to release its power. Its black color holds its power and the silver its purity. The mercury splashed everywhere and then it began to speak, saying, "I am the Mahdi ﷺ. Because of your prayer and intimate discourse with God, He made me appear and allowed you to see this vision."[53]

Grandshaykh ق is pure. He is the Sultan of the Saints.[54] His prayers will never be rejected. Immediately it happened.

He continues, "Imam Mahdi ﷺ said to me, 'You opened for me that door through which I will come and serve human

---

[53] Arabic: *Anta fattaḥta hādha al-bāb bi munājātik.*

[54] Arabic: *Sulṭānu 'l-Awlīyā*—King of saints.

beings. Before my appearance there will be a lot of explosive calamities on earth.'"[55]

There is more to come. This means, "There will be great geological disturbances around the world involving water and volcanoes before my appearance."

He said to me, "The only place that is safe will be Shām. Sit in Shām and do not move!" He said that he asked God, the Exalted, for the sake of our master Muhammad ﷺ that nothing would happen to all of our students around the world. Therefore, the Naqshbandis will be safe and they will not leave this world without seeing Mahdi عليه السلام. Even if they don't see him with their physical eyes, they will see the coming of Mahdi عليه السلام as the inheritors of the Companions did, by virtue of the Prophet's description."

Grandshaykh ق also said one of the signs of the Mahdi عليه السلام's appearance is that there will be a huge mountain in Turkey, in Bursa, three hours drive from Istanbul, that will erupt. Under this mountain there is a huge volcano of fire and that is going to explode. It was supposed to erupt seventy years ago, but it was delayed in order that many of the believers who live in that area would have time to gradually move away. They are carrying the children who are to see Mahdi عليه السلام.

The appearance of Mahdi عليه السلام was delayed several decades from the time it was written, and that *suhbat* was over thirty years ago. Counting the years from that time, we have a short time left in front of us. You must believe that Mahdi عليه السلام is coming in only a few years. If not, then you will not see it. Don't have doubts! Even if you don't understand this, believe it!

---

55 Arabic: *tatafajjar ad-dunyā*—areas where the earth will explode, producing tsunamis, without earthquakes.

The Most Patient

God, the Exalted, is aṣ-Ṣabūr, the Most Patient.[56] He does not rush. Therefore in everything, be patient! The meaning of patience is to carry difficulties.

God, the Exalted doesn't carry difficulty, but He is "carrying" us and we are enough difficulty. He is merciful with us, so learn to be patient with others. Be patient with your country, with your neighbors, with your sisters and brothers. Be patient with your leaders. Don't involve yourself in any fight or struggle. When you are patient, God will send the best for you.

Don't say, "I need this, I need that." God knows better. No one can give you something if God doesn't want you to have it. Many obstacles will come to block the things that God has not decreed for you.

Say, "O my Lord, I am giving up what I want; I am in Your hands and I am a student of that sincere servant, my shaykh, who takes me to the presence of the Prophet ﷺ, who in turn takes me to Your Divine Presence."

If you remain patient, you will be dressed by God with His Beautiful Name, the Patient, aṣ-Ṣabūr, and He will then give you the power and light of that Divine Name.

Who walks in that journey and seeks the Divine Presence and bears with the difficulties and obstacles, he is the one who will be with God and with His Prophet ﷺ. And whoever doubts a lot and questions a lot and seeks to be something and someone, will lose greatly. Be nothing! When they asked Shah Naqshband ق, "How do you like students to behave?" He said, "I like them to submit; not as the submission of a dead person."

---

[56] Among Allah's 99 Beautiful Names and Attributes is aṣ-Ṣabūr, the Patient.

A corpse still retains some of its original power. The shaykhs do not want such submission, nor the submission like that of a person under anesthesia, who can still hear and respond to some stimulus, nor the "submission" of someone who complains constantly.

Shah Naqshband ق said:

> I want students who are like the leaf in autumn that becomes brittle, and the wind takes it left and right; even if the wind takes it into the fire it does not complain. If they submit like that, they will be with God and His Prophet ﷺ.

From God is all success, we ask for the sake of the Opening Chapter of Qur'an.

3: THE UNIQUE PATH

Mistakes are our Nature

Human nature is built up on mistakes and if it was not built on mistakes then Sayyidina Adam ﷺ would never have made the mistake of listening to Iblees' whispering in his ear after which he ate from the Forbidden Tree. And Adam ﷺ was a prophet. But he was pure of sin, *m'aṣūm*, so he repented and Allah forgave him.

So our nature is to always be committing sins. That is not part of our essential nature, *fiṭrah*, for in our nature God created us perfect and revealed to us what is good and what is bad:

فَأَلْهَمَهَا فُجُورَهَا وَتَقْوَاهَا

And He inspired us to do the good and to avoid the bad.[57]

We know we are defective when we realize that we like mistakes. We run towards the bad quickly and we never run towards the good. That is why we are mistake-makers[58]. To eliminate these mistakes from ourselves we must follow a guide.

Without a guide it is impossible to learn about our internal natures, to be able to understand and to change. You can learn the theory but you will not have the practice. Only with a guide can you practice the reality of taste of eliminating sins and evil from the self. That is why we see that many wise men would put their

---

[57] Sūratu 'sh-Shams (the Sun), 91:8.

[58] Arabic: *khaṭā'ūn*—those who always make mistakes.

followers through severe training in order to teach them the real life of the journey that they ask to follow.

Bayazid 's Beginning

The example of that difficult journey of following a shaykh in order to guide you on the Path, is when Bayāzīd al-Bistāmī ق[59] was young and his mother sent him away to study. On the first day in school, the teacher was reciting the verse of Surah Luqmān:

وَوَصَّيْنَا الْإِنسَانَ بِوَالِدَيْهِ حَمَلَتْهُ أُمُّهُ وَهْنًا عَلَى وَهْنٍ وَفِصَالُهُ فِي عَامَيْنِ أَنِ اشْكُرْ لِي وَلِوَالِدَيْكَ إِلَيَّ الْمَصِيرُ

And We have enjoined on man (to be good) to his parents: in travail upon travail did his mother bear him, and in two years was his weaning: (hear the command), "Show gratitude to Me and to your parents: to Me is (your final) Goal."[60]

Here Luqmān was teaching his son that Allah advised human beings to look after their parents and to care for them.

Here Allah honored the mother for what she experiences of the difficulties during pregnancy and childbirth. For that reason men are going to be questioned more than women, for women experience the difficulties of giving birth and raising their children, while men experience only pleasure; they don't experience the difficulties.

As soon as young Bayāzīd ق heard this verse he left the school immediately and went back to his mother. She said to him, "Why are you coming back early?" He said, "I cannot

[59] A great saint of Persia who is fifth in succession of the Naqshbandi-Haqqani Sufi Golden Chain after the Prophet ﷺ.
[60] Sūrah Luqmān, 31:14.

continue now." She asked, "Why? Did the teacher scold you, beat you, or do anything to you?"

Bayāzīd ق replied, "No," and then he recited the verse from Surah Luqmān. He said, "To me Allah is saying to take care of you. Now I am confused, I don't know what to do." She said, "Why?" He said, "Because Allah mentioned in that Surah:

And We have enjoined on man (to be good) to his parents.

God is asking me to do observe my responsibility towards my parents and He is also asking me to fulfill my responsibility towards Him. Now I have you and I have Him and I cannot be protector to two homes. I have only one heart. I can protect only one place."

In today's language: "I am not ADT—Advanced Defense Technology, or *Awlīyā* Defense Technology. I cannot protect two places."

He said, "I am coming to you, O my mother, asking you to release me from my responsibility towards you; then I will be able to concentrate on my responsibility to my Lord. So ask your Lord on my behalf to release me from my responsibility to you so I can focus on my duties towards Him."

That is what we call a spiritual state, *ḥāl*. He went into that state when he was young. Who can think like that?

When she saw that in him, she began to cry. She said, "O my son I am releasing you from responsibility towards me. Go in your way and feel free to protect your house, the House of God, where God said:

ما وسعني أرضي ولا سمائي ولكن وسعني قلب عبدي المؤمن

My sky could not contain Me nor My earth, but the heart of My believing servant contained Me.

"You are right. You cannot divide your attention between two; your focus must be one."

Who among us has had such an experience as Bayāzīd ق? He was feeling the magnitude of that responsibility. That is why he did not want to be away from his Lord for even one moment. That is a perfect guide. That is what we need—to accompany a perfect guide.

يَا أَيُّهَا الَّذِينَ آمَنُواْ اتَّقُواْ اللّهَ وَكُونُواْ مَعَ الصَّادِقِينَ

O you who believe be pious and accompany trustworthy people.[61]

We cannot be like them, but we can accompany them.

From that moment Sayyidina Bayāzīd al-Bistāmī was able to direct his heart completely to God. Before that he was not able to go seeking his Lord, in order to make his mother happy.

Who among us is seeks to make his or her mother happy? When a young person reaches sixteen he says, "I am leaving and going to live in the dorms."

If his mother did not say, "I am releasing you," he would never have left her. Look how much the respect for the mother in the heart of God's friends, *awlīyā*. That is as the Prophet ﷺ said:

الجنة تحت اقدام الامهات

Paradise lies under feet of mothers.[62]

He knew that if you make your mother happy and you will end in Paradise. And she knows her responsibility to her Lord also. She will say "Yes, go find your way to the Lord." It does not

---

[61] Sūratu 't-Tawbah (Repentance), 9:119.

[62] Al-Qadīb in his *Jami'a*, and al-Qudā'ī in his *Musnad*, ad-Daylamī and al-Khatīb.

make a mother happy if her child goes to discos and nightclubs. Make her happy by directing yourself to your Lord.

Dedicated Prior to Birth

So young Bayāzīd ق went in the Way of God, like the Virgin Mary[63], when her mother described in the Qur'an as the daughter of 'Imrān, said:

إِذْ قَالَتِ امْرَأَةُ عِمْرَانَ رَبِّ إِنِّي نَذَرْتُ لَكَ مَا فِي بَطْنِي مُحَرَّرًا فَتَقَبَّلْ مِنِّي إِنَّكَ أَنْتَ السَّمِيعُ الْعَلِيمُ

"O my Lord! I do dedicate unto You what is in my womb for Thy special service: So accept this of me: For You hear and know all things."[64]

فَلَمَّا وَضَعَتْهَا قَالَتْ رَبِّ إِنِّي وَضَعْتُهَا أُنْثَى وَاللَّهُ أَعْلَمُ بِمَا وَضَعَتْ وَلَيْسَ الذَّكَرُ كَالْأُنْثَى وَإِنِّي سَمَّيْتُهَا مَرْيَمَ وَإِنِّي أُعِيذُهَا بِكَ وَذُرِّيَّتَهَا مِنَ الشَّيْطَانِ الرَّجِيمِ وَإِنِّي أُعِيذُهَا بِكَ وَذُرِّيَّتَهَا مِنَ الشَّيْطَانِ الرَّجِيمِ

Then when she delivered her (child Mary), she said:

"Oh my Lord! I have delivered a female child,"- and Allah knew better what she delivered. "And the male is not like the female, and I have named her Mary, and I seek refuge with you (Allah) for her and for her offspring from Satan, the outcast."[65]

---

[63] Although the name of her mother is not mentioned in the Qur'an, it is accepted as Ḥannah bint Qāfūdā.

[64] Sūrat Al-'Imrān (the Family of 'Imrān), 3:35.

[65] Sūrat Al-'Imrān (the Family of 'Imrān), 3:36.

Her mother's name was Ḥannah bint Qāfūdā. She made an oath dedicating the child that was in her womb to God's service, without seeking any payment. She knew that vow was accepted, so when she delivered a girl she exclaimed in surprise, "I gave birth to a girl," for in those times, only boys were given to the service of God, as devotees in the Great Temple in Jerusalem.[66] Despite this she fulfilled her vow and gave her child, even though she was a girl, in the service of God. Hannāh then took Maryam to stay in the temple with the other devotees where she would learn and practice with them. Of course, this being the first occasion of a girl being entered in Divine service, the rabbis and priests rejected her, but, then her uncle, the Prophet Zakarīyya[67] عليه السلام, stepped forward and said he would accept her into his trusteeship.

فَتَقَبَّلَهَا رَبُّهَا بِقَبُولٍ حَسَنٍ وَأَنْبَتَهَا نَبَاتًا حَسَنًا وَكَفَّلَهَا زَكَرِيَّا

So her Lord (Allah) accepted her with goodly acceptance. He made her grow in good manner and put her under the care of Zakarīyya.[68]

Allah made that blessed girl the mother of the Prophet Jesus عليه السلام. When she grew older she spent her time in seclusion in a prayer niche. There she was received her provision directly, without seeking it and without any human action.

---

[66] Ibn Kathīr, in his *Commentary* says, regading this verse: "This meant that she dedicated the child (Maryam) to the service of the Masjid of the Sacred House (in Jerusalem). Thus, they (Zakarīyya, Maryam's mother and Maryam) were similar in that aspect." (*Tafsīr Ibn Kathīr*).

[67] Zakarīyya—Zechariah in the New Testament.

[68] Sūrat Āli-'Imrān (the Family of 'Imrān), 3:37.

كُلَّمَا دَخَلَ عَلَيْهَا زَكَرِيَّا الْمِحْرَابَ وَجَدَ عِندَهَا رِزْقًاقَالَ يَا مَرْيَمُ أَنَّى لَكِ هَـذَا

قَالَتْ هُوَ مِنْ عِندِ اللّهِ إنَّ اللّهَ يَرْزُقُ مَن يَشَاء بِغَيْرِ حِسَابٍ

Every time he entered the prayer-niche to (visit) her, he found her supplied with sustenance. He would ask: "O Mary, whence came this unto thee?" She would answer: "It is from God; behold, God grants sustenance unto whom He wills, beyond all reckoning."[69]

The commentators of Qur'an among the Successors said it means, "He would find with her the fruits of the summer during winter, and the fruits of the winter during summer."[70]

So when Sayyidina Bayāzīd al-Bistāmī reached that level, and obtained his mother's permission to devote himself to the service of his Lord, he was always looking for the best way to make his Lord happy.

And to make his Lord happy he said, "O my Lord. I am coming to Your door."

At the beginning of his life, he said, "Allah made me to be standing at the door of scholars," for he was a great religious scholar[71] in his early life. He said, "I accompanied the scholars for along time and I learned from them every different kind of Shariah knowledge, until my egoistic self began to tell me 'now you reached the highest level of knowledge and you don't need more than that. And you became a gnostic in the highest level of Divine Knowledge.' As I continued in that

---

[69] Sūrat Āli-'Imrān (the Family of 'Imrān), 3:37.

[70] The Successors (*Tabi'īn*) relating this are: Mujāhid, 'Ikrimah, Sa'īd bin Jubayr, Abū Ash-Sha'tha, Ibrāhīm An-Nakha'i, ad-Dahhak, Qatadah, ar-Rabī' bin Anas, 'Atīyah al-'Awfī and aṣ-Ṣuddi.

[71] Arabic: *'alim*—religious scholar.

> ascension of knowledge and gnosticism, I reached a place where I saw many like myself, standing at the door to the Divine Presence, waiting for it to open. There were countless scholars and gnostics, all standing in the same place. He said, "It was too crowded before that door, and I could not find a way to reach it through the masses of seekers."

The Crowd of Seekers

That is like when you go some place and you see a long queue—you cannot reach the door before closing time. However, there was no queue there. Rather all of them were crowding in front of that door to be the first to enter.

> "I didn't find a place to put my feet due to their great number. I said it is impossible to get in."

What do people do when they find a long queue, a line, or when there is traffic jam? They look for a back route. Already that way was filled with heavy traffic, many scholars, all of them fighting to reach that door. All of them were like big roosters, strutting like peacocks.

We are explaining how to be a perfect shaykh. This leads to the understanding that one must follow a perfect one. *Alḥamdūlillāh* that Allah guided us to Shaykh Nazim the perfect guide and *walīullāh,* Friend of God.

> I did not find a way to reach and I left and did not reach the Divine Presence. So I realized that *ḥikmah,* wisdom, *ʿilm,* knowledge and *maʿrifah,* gnosticism, divine understanding, without a reality or a taste in it, is not considered anything. Because I was thinking that reality is found in knowledge and endeavor, *ijtihād,* but I discovered that is not the truth. Because I found that what I was doing is like what everyone is doing and still the door was shut with too many seekers standing before it.

So I realized I had not reached the truth and reality of certainty: the Knowledge of Certainty, the Vision of Certainty or the Reality of Certainty.[72]

I knew there must still be another way. So I began to hit the backroads. I found myself following those people who are worshippers, who constantly pray in congregation—*al-Mūṣālīn fil-jamaʿat.* They come to every prayer and I never missed even the opening *takbīr* of my five prayers in congregation for a long time. Before the imam says "*Allāhu Akbar,*" I am there, five times a day. Finally I had a vision that I am with a huge crowd at a similar door to that of the *ʿulamā,* scholars of religion, and all were in prostration at that door and I was in prostration with them and the door didn't open either and I couldn't find a place to put my head.

Now again, there were too many praying their five prayers behind the imam, standing, bowing, sitting and making prostration. I found no place to put my head and I could not enter. When I saw that I turned away and I left them, knowing I would never reach that door.

So I said to myself "I will go with the *ṣāimūn,* those who fast." So I began to fast every day of the year and I began to eat and drink with them at *ifṭār,* the fast-breaking at sunset Maghrib and at the early morning meal, *sahūr* before dawn, at Fajr until I found myself before the door of the pre-dawn risers and found a huge crowd of fasting people and I could not find a place to put my feet.

Those who were fasting days and continuing in the night, but I found many and I did not find a place to put my feet and I began slowly to move away until I left.

---

[72] Arabic: *ʿilm al-yaqīn, ʿayn al-yaqīn, ḥaqq al-yaqīn*—Knowledge of Certainty, the Vision of Certainty, the Reality of Certainty.

I went to Mecca, and began to make *tawāf* circumambulating around the Ka'ba, for many many years, with every pilgrim and with every visitor that comes there. I was making *tawāf* with every pilgrim for a long time, until I had a vision where I found myself standing before a similar door, with all these pilgrims standing in line before it, and I found no place to put my feet among all the pilgrims standing at that door asking for it to open.

In that vision Allah showed me, they were standing at that door crying, "*Labayk Allāhuma labayk, labayk la sharīk laka labayk*—At Your service, O our Lord, at Your service. You have no partner. I am here at Your service!" They came from every farthest place, *min kulli fajin 'amīq,* dressing in the pilgrim's unstitched garb, *iḥrām,* and coming to the House of God beseeching Him. I saw them at that door and they were a huge crowd. So I withdrew and I didn't reach the Divine Presence of my Lord. That door never opened.

Then God put me with those who are struggling against their lower selves, *jihād an–nafs,* and I was struggling along with the others who struggle, sitting in their company trying to reach as far as possible. And then I found myself at a similar door, with all of them standing there, carrying their spiritual swords against their egos, but there were too many of them so I retreated and I did not reach my Lord's Divine Presence.

Then I realized this is not going to be the way, that there is something else destined for me. I went into the prayer niche of my room, and I said, "O my Lord; send Your mercy on me. I am confused and I do not know what to do. Put me in a situation where there is no competition, as I cannot compete."

Competition is difficult for competing with others requires building up your arrogance to reach the goal you seek.

> I cried out to God: "I cannot compete with all these different kinds of people we have mentioned already. Put me in a place where there is not too much competition; in a place where there is not too much traffic. Do not put me in a place where people have already surpassed me, being stronger than me; who moved forward quickly and whom I cannot pass."
>
> I was asking with a burning heart, until I heard a voice, saying, "O Bayāzīd ق. No one can approach Me with something that belongs to Me; something that relates to Me. You have to come with something that does not relate to My Qualities."

The Door of Poverty

That means one must approach the Divine Presence by means of something that belongs only to creation, to human beings; something which is unbefitting Lordship, which God transcends utterly.

> I said: "O Allah what is that thing that is not for you by which I can come to You with it, and You will not let anyone reach You without coming by its means? Teach me!"
>
> Then I heard a voice saying, "O Bayāzīd , There is nothing I am in need of from creation and I have nothing to do with poverty.[73]. If anyone wants to come to Me, then come to Me through these attributes."
>
> I said, "O Lord, show me these people of poverty and need while You are not in need of them."

God is the Rich, al-Ghanī. *Faqr,* poverty cannot be used to describe the Lord, only Richness. He cannot be described with

[73] Arabic: laysa lī fakatun wa lā faqrun.

fāka, needfulness. One must come to the Lord through these characteristics.

It is as if God is saying, "Prayers are for Me, fasting is for Me, extra worship is for Me. You have to come to Me through the attributes of creatures, the attributes of weakness, humility and neediness. Only through such taste and experience can you approach Me."

> I looked and I saw they are very few people standing at the door of poverty and very few coming to their Lord through their need.
>
> I reached them and found them standing at a door similar to the other doors, but their numbers very few and there was much space for me to stand there.
>
> So I was thinking, is that what is meant by poverty, *faqr*? Does *faqr* mean spiritual poverty or physical poverty?
>
> I saw no one by that door, so I realized *faqr* cannot be physical poverty for there are many poor around the world; rather it is the spiritual poverty. I came crying, "I am poor, O my Lord. I am coming with complete helplessness to Your door, not like the peacockish scholars, nor like the people of prayers, nor like the fasting people; nor like pilgrims who come and write Hajj before their names. Of all those there are multitudes."

God wants someone who throws everything to the side and comes to the Lord with poverty. Poverty here has two meanings.

At the physical level, it means not carrying anything from this world, *dunyā*. But people don't want to be poor. They always want to be rich. That is why the destitute don't approach God for Shaytan is playing with their minds them saying, "You have to be rich."

At the spiritual level it means coming to God in a state of utter helplessness, expressing utter humility and need and complete dependence on God. This can only be achieved by those with utter purity of heart.

> I didn't find many at the door of poverty. I am happy now, there are not too many standing at this door.
>
> Then I heard a Divine Voice: "Now you have to experience poverty. To express utter poverty is in theory only. Go and make yourself a dumpster to My servants; carry their difficulties and their garbage."

Poverty teaches humbleness. Homeless people go in garbage cans in street, just like cats. They are happy with whatever they find. These homeless people Allah gave them that no pride no arrogance. They go and eat from the garbage and Allah gives them immunity to all the illnesses from what is there. We cannot eat that, we are very delicate. If anyone ate from a spoon we cannot eat form it. If anyone touched it they can eat from it.

These people are immune from all these sickness. Through experiencing poverty Allah gives them immunity from sickness, and at the level of spirituality, immunity from Shaytan. See how they go and find a piece of apple in the garbage; they clean it off and then eat it. It is as if God is sayin, "Go and be dumpster, show your complete humbleness and poverty to Me then I open My door."

> From that moment that I decided to be a dumpster for all human beings and I gave my promise to my Lord that "O Allah I will come to you from poverty and weakness to you, from that moment every movement became a *karamah*, a miracle. No one can reach such miracles except someone who accepts to show weakness and helplessness and to show he is poor to his Lord and show patience on it.

This shows us how much a perfect guide has to go through experiences in order to reach Allah's door.

هَاأَنتُمْ هَؤُلَاء تُدْعَوْنَ لِتُنفِقُوا فِي سَبِيلِ اللَّهِ فَمِنكُم مَّن يَبْخَلُ وَمَن يَبْخَلْ فَإِنَّمَا يَبْخَلُ عَن نَّفْسِهِ وَاللَّهُ الْغَنِيُّ وَأَنتُمُ الْفُقَرَاء وَإِن تَتَوَلَّوْا يَسْتَبْدِلْ قَوْمًا غَيْرَكُمْ ثُمَّ لَا يَكُونُوا أَمْثَالَكُمْ

But Allah is free of all wants, and it is you that are needy. If you turn back (from the Path), He will substitute in your stead another people; then they would not be like you![74]

Allah is rich and you are poor and if you are not happy to serve, Allah will take you away and replace you with another people. It is not up to you to accept.

So Bayāzīd al-Bistāmī ق accepted that and that is why he became a perfect guide. Spiritual poverty is what makes you reach your Lord through humility. Not with a head that is always up but with a head that is always down. This is the importance of reaching a perfect guide to guide you to what is needed and what is wanted from you in order to reach a door similar to that which they reached before.

You don't want to be waiting at a door where you cannot find space to put your feet. And while you observe the five pillars, that is not sufficient. Those doing *shahāda* were standing at the door of *shahāda*. Then those doing *ṣalāt* were standing at the door of *salāt*. Those fasting stood at the door of fasting. Those who perform hajj were standing at the door of pilgrimage. But these doors don't open. The only door that is accessible is the door of humility.

May Allah help us and bless us and bless this meeting.

Bi-ḥurmati 'l-Fātiḥah.

---

[74] Sūrah Muhammad, 47:38.

4: LEVELS OF ANNIHILATION

Bayazid Makes Himself a Dump

Finally Bayāzīd al-Bistāmī heard a voice saying, "O Bayāzīd , you must be a dump[75] for My servants."

Who can be a garbage dump for humanity? No one can, except the the prophets and messengers, the Companions, and the Friends of God. For us ordinary people, if someone says one word that we don't like, we disappear, leaving whatever community we were in. If someone says anything to upset us, we fight and create confusion for nothing.

You cannot say to someone, "May God forgive you!" We should say, "O my Lord, if I was not bad that person would not have said something bad against me." That is even better than saying, "O God forgive me!"

You must say, "O my Lord! That person was right to say that about me, because I am a bad person." Humble yourself.

Mawlana Shaykh Nazim ق said:

> Bayāzīd al-Bistāmī ق was trying to humble himself by accepting to be the worst of people, by accepting the role of a dump for others. He said to himself, "I am a dirty one; no one else is dirty."

Today if you say to someone, "You are dirty!" he will beat you and run away. You won't see him until you go and apologize.

---

75 Meaning he must carry difficulties, sins, and anything that is a burden to others, and come to Allah without complaint.

Sayyidina Bayāzīd al-Bistāmī ق did not say anything except, "O my Lord! I am submitting to what You are asking of me."

What happened? He reached the level of *fanā*, annihilation—he sees only the existence of God, and nothing exists of himself. It means he was absent from his self and from his own existence[76]—there is no more of him. His ego became nothing and disappeared from his own desire. If existence is solely for God, the Exalted, how can you be upset by whatever transpires?

> When Bayāzīd ق disappeared from existence, he said, "O my Lord, are You the—owner of this kingdom?[77] Is Your kingdom this huge universe and everything You have created? Is that it, O Lord?"
>
> And he heard an answer (inspiration came to his heart), "Yes, My servant—this My kingdom."
>
> Bayāzīd ق replied, "O my Lord, this kingdom of Yours is poor. My kingdom is bigger than Your kingdom."

For us to say this would be heresy, unbelief,[78] and we will become unbelievers, because we still have egos, we still exist, and in such a case we would be liars. We cannot say this, but Bayāzīd ق said it! Why? Because he has no more ego, so in his case the meaning is, "O my Lord! Your kingdom is this world and paradises, which You said in Your eyes doesn't even have the weight of the wing of a mosquito. So what is this kingdom—the wing of a mosquito? But my kingdom is You, O Lord! There is no Bayāzīd ق; there is only You. So I desire and I love that kingdom that is You, which is better than this whole universe."

---

[76] Arabic: *ghāba 'an nafsihi wa 'an wujūdihi.*

[77] Arabic: *malik al-mulk*—king of kings.

[78] Arabic: *kufr*: unbelief; the opposite of faith.

He is saying this out of real belief and acceptance. There is no cheating. If we were to say such things, we would be cheating. Why are we cheating? Because if someone comes behind you and slaps you on the back, you will run after him to beat him. Think how much they slapped Bayāzīd ق when he made himself a dumpster for humanity, and all the time he said nothing.

That is the station of Friends of God.

> He said, "Your kingdom is whatever is other than God.[79] But my kingdom is You, so of course it is greater than Your kingdom. *Allāhu Akbar*! You are the Greatest."

> And further, Bayāzīd ق said, "O my Lord! You have put a bridge[80] over hellfire[81] for people to pass to enter Paradise. O my Lord! Why are You playing with people, telling them they must pass over that bridge while You make it finer as a hair? How are they going to pass? Why are You wasting Your time and our time? You asked us to pass over it. How are we going to pass? Of course we will fall! But since You own us all and we are Your creation, when You own something You don't want it to disappear from Your hands."

This utterance Bayāzīd ق spoke from the station of annihilation, *fanā*.

Abd al-Qadir Jilani Extracts His Disciples

> When war was declared on Sultan Harūn al-Rashīd,[82] many in Baghdad were the disciples of the great saint 'Abd al-Qādir

---

[79] Arabic: *mā siwā-Allāh:* Whatever is other than Allah.
[80] Arabic: *Ṣirāt al-mustaqīm.*
[81] Arabic: *Jahannam*—Hellfire.
[82] The fifth Abbasid Caliph.

Jilānī ق.[83] Harūn al-Rashīd could not find one soldier. So he went to Shaykh ʿAbd al-Qādir Jilānī to request his support.

The shaykh said, "I will show you how many disciples I have." He called all his disciples and told Harūn al-Rashīd, "I am going to give you a big army."

Sayyidina ʿAbd al-Qādir Jilānī ق called all of his disciples to an open area, and from the top of a hill called down saying, "Today is the day of slaughtering." They were all happy, saying, "Our shaykh is going to slaughter sheep and goats, and give them to us to eat."

The shaykh said, "Whoever loves me the most, come to the tent; I am going to slaughter him." He brought a butcher with a big knife to cut their necks. He saw one skinny man to whom no one gave much regard, and selected him.

There is a lesson here. When you seek importance and respect from people, God does not grant you that, because genuine respect is only from the Almighty. Don't run after the respect of people—they will never give it. You only need the Lord's respect.

So that person who had no value in anyone's eyes, went into the tent with ʿAbd al-Qādir Jilānī ق, and lay down, with only legs sticking out. The shaykh shouted, "*Bismi 'l-Lāh, Allāhu Akbar!*"[84] Privately he told the butcher, "Don't slaughter him; slaughter the goat instead."

The butcher slaughtered as he was told, but the man squirmed around as if he was dying. When that happened,

---

[83] Shaykh ʿAbd al-Qādir Jilānī ق, known as *Ghawth al-ʿAdham*, the Supreme Helper, whom God empowers to bring succour to suffering humanity, in response to His creatures' cry for help in times of extreme adversity.

[84] Arabic: "*Bismillāh, Allāhu Akbar*!—In the name of God, God is Greater," words pronounced to sanctify the sacrifice of livestock for use as meat, much like the kosher method of sacrifice.

half of the disciples watching below ran away! The shaykh shouted, "Who is next?" Then the wife of the skinny man stepped forward, someone whom no one gave any respect as well. The lesson is, when people don't give you attention it is better. You know Satan is playing with someone when they attract too much attention.

Once again, the butcher pretended to slaughter her and the remaining disciples ran away.

Sayyidina ʿAbd al-Qādir Jilānī ق then turned to Harūn al-Rashīd and said, "This one man and his wife are my disciples. As for all the rest, you may take them—they are your army!"

It is very difficult to be in the level of annihilation.

Returning to the story of Bayāzīd ق, he said, "O my Lord! You put hellfire under the Bridge and said, 'Pass over it.' Who is going to be on that bridge? You created us, and we don't own ourselves. We are Your shadow, and when You take what You own, You take it with You. You own the bridge, so first show us how to pass over it. When You pass over it, we are with You, and we are Your kingdom."

For example, a good general will never leave his soldiers behind. Do you think God, the Exalted, the Creator will leave His servants in the hands of Satan?

So Bayāzīd al-Bistāmī ق is pleading, "You go first, O Lord! We will go with You, because You own us."

It is very difficult to understand the words of the Friends of God. Many scholars refuse to accept the ecstatic utterances of Shaykh Muḥīyddīn ibn ʿArabī. Some scholars condemn his books. If the words of the Friends of God are not understood, what do you think of the words of the prophets? Think of all the hidden meanings in what the Prophet ﷺ says. What do you think of God's Words? If normal words of the Friends of God cannot be understood, what the words of the Prophet ﷺ or the words of God Himself. Imagine these difficulties.

Bayāzīd 's meaning is, "O my Lord! To You the past, present, and future are all equal. So when You move, we are present with You; we will be with You. Don't look at our deeds, for they are useless. Your Mercy is what counts. You are the One that can give us safety."

Don't expect that we can give ourselves safety by doing something good. No one can do anything. That is why the Friends of God are always supplicating: "O God, bless Your servants. They don't know what they are doing. We don't know what we are doing."

> Ponder what Bayāzīd ق is saying. "I am absent, and there is no more existence for my ego or for myself. O my Lord! There is no more will for ourselves. Everything is in Your hands. If You want us to be here, we will be here. If You want us to be there, we will be there. It is Your Will[85] that counts, not our will. O God, you have put the Scale to weigh the deeds of mankind. What have we done? Everything is from Your Will. Why must You weigh us? Weigh Your Will and You will find us inside it, in that power,[86] inside that knowledge, in Your Attributes, because everything is in Your Hands."

مَا أَصَابَ مِن مُّصِيبَةٍ إِلَّا بِإِذْنِ اللَّه

Nothing of hardship occurred without Allah's permission.[87]

فَأَلْهَمَهَا فُجُورَهَا وَتَقْوَاهَا

[85] Arabic: *Irāda*—will.

[86] Arabic: *qudrah*—power.

[87] Sūratu 't-Taghābun (Loss and Gain), 64:11.

He inspired the self with its good and its bad. [88]

لا حركة ولا سكون إلا بمشيئة الله

Every movement and every stillness is from Allah.[89]

This explanation supports Bayāzīd 's plea.

Stillness and movement are from Allah. All that affects, its good and its bad, *khayrihi wa sharrihi,* are from that Will, *irāda,* "*and He inspired the self with its good and its bad,*" and "and there is no movement and no stillness except by Allah's order," and as the Prophet ﷺ said, "*Al-khayru fimā waqaʿa*—the good is in what occurred."

> So Bayāzīd 's argument was: "O my Lord! Since it is Your Will, then weigh Your Will and all will pass to heaven. When You weigh Your Will, there is nothing to ask from us, because Your *irāda* is complete (*irādat al-kullīyah*) and ours is partial (*irādat al-juz'īyya*)."

Uwais al-Qarani

God, the Exalted, gave us partial *irāda* (will) in this world, as something to play with. The only importance is the main one, which is fully in His Hands.

> At the age of 63 years, Sayyidina Muhammad ﷺ was asked by Gabriel ﷺ, "O Muhammad ﷺ, Allah sends His greetings of peace[90] and asks if you would like to leave this world and return to Him, or would you like to stay?"

Our death and birth are under the absolute will of Allah; you cannot change them. But as a sign of honor to the Prophet ﷺ, God

---

[88] Sūratu 'sh-Shams (The Sun), 91:8.

[89] This is part of the *ʿaqīdah,* doctrine, of God's Attributes.

[90] Arabic: *salām*—peace.

granted this choice to the Prophet ﷺ exclusively. That is he was granted complete freewill, *al-irādat al-kullīyah*.

The Prophet ﷺ replied, "O my Lord! I prefer to return to You. Your message is completed."

When Prophet ﷺ chose voluntarily to return to God, the Exalted, he began to sweat profusely, until his clothes were soaked. He called Sayyidina 'Alī ؓ and Sayyidina 'Umar ؓ, gave them his clothes soaked with his sweat, and instructed they be given to Sayyidina Uwais al-Qaranī[91] as a trust.

When Prophet ﷺ made the decision to return to God, the Exalted, he entered a spiritual state where he entered the Divine Presence, pleading forgiveness for every single human being of his Community. As each acceptance was granted, his body sweat one drop. He ﷺ then asked on behalf of one person, then another and another, until the entire Community had been accounted for.

Grandshaykh ق said:

Allah has forgiven everyone for the sake of the Prophet ﷺ and that every drop of the sweat represents a human being, and if you count them they number as the Community of the Prophet ﷺ, who sent that trust to Uwais al-Qaranī, to preserve that secret and build it up.

When Sayyidina 'Alī and Sayyidina 'Umar ؓ gave Prophet's clothes to Uwais al-Qaranī, with love and respect he put them on his head and on his chest, at which time he was given knowledge

---

[91] Uwais al-Qaranī —a man living in Yemen in the time of the Prophet ﷺ whose elderly mother was ill for which he requested to stay with her due to his high level of *adab* (etiquette) he did not leave her, and thus was prevented from physically meeting Prophet ﷺ in this world, but was later personally rewarded by Prophet.

of the original heavenly name of every single human being.[92] With these names we appeared to Uwais as normal human beings. Uwais took us, one by one, accepting and cleaning us. That means it is his responsibility to return us to the Prophet ﷺ clean on Judgment Day.

Grandshaykh ق said the total of our sins, mistakes, crimes, and bad characteristics entered in that drop of sweat from Prophet ﷺ, and water always cleans and renews.

وَجَعَلْنَا مِنَ الْمَاء كُلَّ شَيْءٍ حَيٍّ أَفَلَا يُؤْمِنُونَ

And We have created from water every living thing.[93]

That sweat obliterated all of our crimes. The Prophet ﷺ asked forgiveness from Allah on our behalf, and that water was changed into the water of youth. We all pass through that moment in front of Sayyidina Uwais al-Qaranī and in so doing, we become clean and young again.

Prophet Muhammad ﷺ carried all these bad characteristics and sins. He took mountains of them from the Community. He carried these things from Allah's servants on behalf of the Community and gave this as a trust to Sayyidina Uwais al-Qaranī.

We know the *du'a* of Prophet ﷺ:

اللهم لا تَكِلْني الى نفسي طَرْفة عين، ولا تنزع مني صالحَ ما اعطيتَني.

O my Lord! even with that power you gave me, don't leave me to my ego for a blink of an eye, or I will fail.

---

[92] We are all named by our parents, but Allah also named each soul with a name in Paradise.

[93] Sūratu 'l-Anbīyā (the Prophets), 21:30.

So what about us? Are we going to say we are clean and we want everyone to respect us? Prophet ﷺ is always exponentially expanding in ascension, in every blink of an eye.

Grandshaykh ق said:

> If you put all power of Friends of God and Companions's power together they cannot reach, *lā yumkin lahum idrāk min hādha at-tarakī,* they cannot grasp the meaning or reality of even one of these exponential ascensions. If even one moment of this ascension cannot be understood, what do you think about all the other moments? The great ascension continues at every moment. With all their power, they could not grasp what the Prophet ﷺ was receiving, even for one moment.

That is why Friends of God's knowledge never ends. Even one moment's drop is too much. The Friends of God take less than drops.

May Allah forgive us and may Allah keep us on track of real love to Him, and to Prophet ﷺ, and to Friends of God.

Wa min Allāhi 't-tawfiq, bi ḥurmati 'l-Fātiḥah.

5: Divine Inspiration

Sayyida Fatima's Choice

Whatever the Prophet ﷺ wants, will happen. God, the Exalted, created the whole universe for the sake of Sayyidina Muhammad ﷺ.

لولاك لولاك ما خلقت الأفلاك.

If not for you, [O Muhammad], I would not have created the heavenly bodies.[94]

Allah will never say to the Prophet ﷺ "no." And the Prophet ﷺ never spoke except what was revelation:

وَمَا يَنطِقُ عَنِ الْهَوَى إِنْ هُوَ إِلَّا وَحْيٌ يُوحَى

He does not speak from his own desires, that (which he conveys to you) is but a divine inspiration with which he is being inspired.[95]

Even with all this authority, the Prophet ﷺ asked his daughter if she would marry Sayyidina ʿAlī ؓ. He asked her if she would accept him, even though his words were spoken from revelation.

Grandshaykh ق said that today there are people who force their daughters to marry for a handful of money, and if they don't marry who they choose, they beat them.

---

[94] While this particular wording is not authenticated to the Prophet ﷺ, the meaning is true, and there are many ahadith to this effect.

[95] Sūratu 'n-Najm (the Star), 53:3-4.

The Prophet ﷺ upholds *makārim al-akhlāq,* the highest character; thus, he doesn't need to ask. He has the best manners and did not command his daughter to marry Sayyidina ʿAlī ؓ. Instead, he asked, "Would you like to marry Sayyidina ʿAlī ؓ?"

Surprisingly, she answered, "no", but of course she had a good reason. Grandshaykh ق has added some details to this story:

> When Sayyida Fāṭima ؓ declined, the Prophet ﷺ turned red. This is a very important point. He became embarrassed. He thought that the reason was because Allah had given Sayyidina ʿAlī ؓ long eyebrows that were connected across his forehead like a visor. This is because he was an expert warrior, and equipped with these eyebrows he could keep the sweat from his eyes during battle. The Prophet ﷺ thought that perhaps she preferred Sayyidina ʿUmar ؓ because he was more attractive than Sayyidina ʿAlī ؓ.

Consider this point carefully! We say the Prophet ﷺ knows everything and some say that the Friends of God know everything. Don't say "the shaykh knows everything." If Allah wants His Prophet ﷺ to know everything then His Prophet ﷺ knows everything. To be sure, Allah gave him *ʿulūm al-awalīn wa 'l-ākhirīn*—the knowledge of the First and the Lasts[96].

Permission to Know

If Allah wants a Friend of God to know certain things, he will inherit them from Prophet ﷺ. If He doesn't want him to know, then He blocks this knowledge. Therefore, Friends of God also may be under a test. Many people today think they reached a high level of spirituality. Allah controls these levels, and will block you where He wishes. That is an important point. Beware! When we

---

[96] Knowledge of who are saints, and the status of souls in the Hereafter.

think we have an inspiration, when we hear a voice in our heads, it might not be the truth.

Today, technology to filter emails is common. Programming on the receiving servers distinguishes and isolates spam from legitimate messages. Similarly, our ears are like this, thousands and thousands of signals come in and we must filter them. If not, then we mix apples and oranges and it becomes like a soup.

Sayyidina Adam ﵇ was a prophet and what happened?

فَوَسْوَسَ لَهُمَا الشَّيْطَانُ لِيُبْدِيَ لَهُمَا مَا وُورِيَ عَنْهُمَا مِن سَوْءَاتِهِمَا وَقَالَ مَا نَهَاكُمَا
رَبُّكُمَا عَنْ هَذِهِ الشَّجَرَةِ إِلاَّ أَن تَكُونَا مَلَكَيْنِ أَوْ تَكُونَا مِنَ الْخَالِدِينَ

Then began Satan to whisper suggestions to them, bringing openly before their minds all their shame that was hidden from them (before). He said, "Your Lord only forbade you this tree, lest you should become angels or such beings as live for ever.[97]

As soon as they listened to Satan, their nakedness became evident. At that point they began to cover themselves with fig leaves.

So don't expose yourself. They thought that what came into their heads was correct. They mistakenly thought that Allah told them not to eat from the tree because He didn't want them to become two angels who would live forever. So they mixed apples and oranges; they mixed the real inspirations of heaven and the ones from Satan. They didn't filter thoughts, and what happened? They fell down. So whenever you are inspired, don't think immediately, "That is the truth", but try to distinguish what enters your mind, especially before speaking about it or acting on it.

---

[97] Sūratu ' l-'Arāf (the Heights), 7:20.

Grandshaykh ق said that sometimes we don't have enough knowledge and are confused by thoughts and inspirations. We must ask ourselves if what we are hearing is permissible in Islam; if so, it is inspiration, and if not, it is a whisper. So we must be on guard against the whispers, and distinguish what comes to our minds (thoughts) and hearts (inspiration).

A Friend of God Who Rejected the Angels

Grandshaykh ق, may Allah bless him, related a story about a *walīullāh*, a Friend of God.

The *walīullāh* said, "O my Lord! I am not happy with Your angels. I am not accepting them; all of them."

Allah said, "If you don't accept them, they are My angels[98]."

He said, "I prefer to go to the Hellfire than to accept them."

Friends of God have *hātif*, like a heavenly telephone, and with that direct line they hear God, the Exalted, through angels. But that Friend of God was not accepting them, even though by means of angels he was hearing heavenly messages.

Allah asked, "Why?"

The Friend of God replied, "Send me to the Hellfire, for I will be happier there than sitting with them."

Allah asked, "Why?"

The Friend of God said, "Because, O my Lord! when You asked them something they criticized and complained."

Allah asked, "What did they complain about?"

The Friend of God quoted the verse:

[98] It means, "You will go to the Hellfire."

وَإِذْ قَالَ رَبُّكَ لِلْمَلاَئِكَةِ إِنِّي جَاعِلٌ فِي الأَرْضِ خَلِيفَةً قَالُواْ أَتَجْعَلُ فِيهَا مَن يُفْسِدُ فِيهَا وَيَسْفِكُ الدِّمَاء وَنَحْنُ نُسَبِّحُ بِحَمْدِكَ وَنُقَدِّسُ لَكَ قَالَ إِنِّي أَعْلَمُ مَا لاَ تَعْلَمُونَ

Behold, your Lord said to the angels: "I will create a vicegerent on earth." They said: "Will You place therein one who will make mischief and shed blood? While we celebrate Your praises and glorify Your holy name?" He said: "I know what you know not."[99]

Look how far the knowledge of Friends of God reaches, what Grandshaykh ق is teaching us! The angels objected that Allah would create a race of creatures that sheds the blood of his creation while all they do is praise God, the Exalted, which should be enough. Yet, Allah tells them they must submit to His will, because He knows best.

وَعَلَّمَ آدَمَ الأَسْمَاء كُلَّهَا ثُمَّ عَرَضَهُمْ عَلَى الْمَلاَئِكَةِ فَقَالَ أَنبِئُونِي بِأَسْمَاء هَـؤُلاء إِن كُنتُمْ صَادِقِينَقَالُواْ سُبْحَانَكَ لاَ عِلْمَ لَنَا إِلاَّ مَا عَلَّمْتَنَا إِنَّكَ أَنتَ الْعَلِيمُ الْحَكِيمُ

And He imparted unto Adam the names of all things; then He brought them within the den of the angels and said: "Declare unto Me the names of these [things], if what you say is true." They replied: "You are limitless in Your glory! No knowledge have we save that which You have imparted to us. Verily, You alone are all-knowing, truly wise."[100]

To show the angels that Adam ﷺ is honored more than them, Allah taught him the names. What names—mine and yours?

---

[99] Sūratu 'l-Baqara (the Heifer), 2:30.

[100] Sūratu 'l-Baqara (the Heifer), 2:31-32.

Adam ﵇ was taught the names for the sake of the light of Sayyidina Muhammad ﷺ. In teaching him the names, Allah gave Adam ﵇ the ability to reach the light of Sayyidina Muhammad ﷺ through the forehead of Sayyidina Adam ﵇. In this fashion, he learned the names of all creation—those that Allah is continuously creating in every moment.

Allah commanded the angels, "Tell Me their names." And they said, "We don't know." And then Allah commanded Adam ﵇ to show them the names.

قَالَ يَا آدَمُ أَنبِئْهُم بِأَسْمَآئِهِمْ فَلَمَّا أَنبَأَهُمْ بِأَسْمَآئِهِمْ قَالَ أَلَمْ أَقُل لَّكُمْ إِنِّي أَعْلَمُ غَيْبَ السَّمَاوَاتِ وَالأَرْضِ وَأَعْلَمُ مَا تُبْدُونَ وَمَا كُنتُمْ تَكْتُمُونَ

Said He: "O Adam, convey unto them the names of these (things)." And as soon as Adam had conveyed unto them their names, (Allah) said: "Did I not say unto you, 'Verily, I alone know the hidden reality of the heavens and the earth, and know all that you bring into the open and all that you would conceal'?"[101]

Then the Friend of God said, "That is why I don't like the angels: they didn't listen and obey you."

Remember, Friends of God are the beloved of Allah.

إِنَّ أَوْلِيَائِي تَحْتَ قِبَابِي لاَ يَعْرِفُهُمْ غَيْرِي

My saints are under My domes; no one knows them except Me.[102]

---

[101] Sūratu 'l-Baqara (the Heifer), 2:33.

[102] Imām Ghazālī's *Ihyā 'ulūm ad-dīn.*

So these inspirations must be filtered. You cannot take everything that comes to mind and begin saying things based on it.

When we were young, Shaykh Adnan and I completely accepted whatever Grandshaykh ق had to say, which is the correct attitude. Sometimes out of love or inspiration a certain whispering would come to our ears, notions that mixed with what Grandshaykh ق was teaching us. Things would become mixed in our heads like oranges and apples, like a soup. Out of love we were saying things and praising Grandshaykh ق in ways that would sometimes go beyond the limits. There would be a discussion of issues and we would speak from our inspiration.

Once we did this in print, and the court called Grandshaykh ق to answer for it. They didn't understand it. We were young. Sometimes Grandshaykh ق would reveal high-level information in private that could not be understood by common folk; sometimes not even by scholars. The authorities, seeing this in print, sought an explanation and called us to court. We had to take Grandshaykh ق to court and stand before a judge. So you must be very careful what you say, and to whom.

Sometimes you must analyze your actions before repeating spiritual issues we heard in a discussion within the Sufi Order. Do not go and post things on the Internet without permission and create a problem with no benefit.

The Dowry

There is a powerful hadith about Sayyida Fāṭima az-Zahrā ﷺ. On Judgment Day, before everything, she will say, "O my Lord! give me my dowry, or else my marriage with Sayyidina ʿAlī ﷺ is not complete." That dowry is the whole community, the Ummah. So God, the Exalted, will protect the entire Community for the sake Sayyida Fāṭima ﷺ.

Consider the importance of one lady. Remember how Allah honored Āhlu 'l-Bayt[103] and honored women because they are women[104].

Grandshaykh ق said:

Allah will make His judgment. The people of Hell will be sent to Hell, and the people of Paradise will be sent to Paradise. Then, Sayyida Fāṭima ﵂ will ask to have her dowry, even before the intercession of Prophet ﷺ. One lady will have the power to pull people out of Hell!

The Prophet ﷺ has the power to intercede. His intercession is to dress the whole Community with the manifestations of mercy that are coming on Judgment Day. Thus by intercession of Sayyida Fāṭima ﵂ they will be taken to Paradise, and with intercession of Prophet ﷺ they will be raised.

الَّذِينَ أَنْعَمَ اللَّهُ عَلَيْهِم مِّنَ النَّبِيِّينَ وَالصِّدِّيقِينَ وَالشُّهَدَاءِ وَالصَّالِحِينَ وَحَسُنَ أُولَٰئِكَ رَفِيقًا

Those on whom is the Grace of Allah: the prophets (who teach), the sincere (lovers of Truth), the witnesses (who testify), and the righteous (who do good). Ah, what a beautiful fellowship![105]

Wa min Allāhi 't-tawfiq, bi ḥurmati 'l-Fātiḥah.

❋

[103] Arabic: Āhlu 'l-Bayt—Family of Prophet; literally, "people of the house".
[104] They carry within them the secret of life.
[105] Sūratu 'n-Nisā (Women), 4:69

6: THREE TREES

Time Scales

*E*very day there is a different *tajallī*, a divine manifestation. No one knows what the manifestation will be in this moment, nor in the second moment or the third. "Every day" means "every moment." Because every moment in heavenly time is a much larger unit in our time; a Divine Moment may amount to the entire life of the planet earth.

$$كُلَّ يَوْمٍ هُوَ فِي شَأْنٍ$$

Every moment He tends to a different matter.[106]

It means: "Every day, Allah's manifestations continuously emerge through His universe and through His creation."

This is a story from Grandshaykh ق:

One time Sayyidina Bilāl ؓ wanted to call *adhān*.[107] Prophet ﷺ said, "Wait", then one moment later he said, "Call it now." The Companions were surprised. Between "wait" and then "call it", was not even one second. And the Prophet ﷺ explained, "From the moment I said to him 'wait' and the time I said to him 'call,' the universe moved 500,000 heavenly years to come to the exact moment of the prayer."

Today we call the prayer according to the turning of earth on its axis, and as it turns the time zones change. But in heaven, the time of *adhān* is based on movement of the entire universe. As

---

[106] Sūratu 'r-Raḥmān (The Merciful), 55:29.
[107] Arabic: *adhān*—the Arabic call to prayer.

time moves forward, changing, the call of the *adhān* is stretching forward, as if you were stretching a straight line from the beginning of creation. Allah ordered Sayyidina Adam ﷺ to pray, and from that time forward, every prayer is timed according to the movement of the universe.

How much is this universe moving in this vacuum? They say it is moving at the speed of light. To where? No one knows. That is the heavenly timing, not the turning of earth around its axis and its orbit around the sun, one circuit equaling one year. The timing of the prayers is measured with this heavenly clock. Imagine how much we are moving through space and we don't know it!

This explains:

Every moment He tends to a different matter.

No one understands this process except Sayyidina Muhammad ﷺ. That is why the Friends of God are standing helpless. Allah made them His friends, but if Allah doesn't will something, it will not happen.

When Sayyidina Muhammad ﷺ told the Companions about the Anti-Christ, they were looking behind the date palms, expecting to see him lurking there at that moment. The Prophet ﷺ said there will be a big struggle in 'Umuq Valley (in Turkey near Adana), and bloodshed will be rampant in the Last Days, after which the Saviour, Imam Mahdi ﷺ will appear. The Companions were looking for that day even in their time. Friends of God are saying day and night, "tomorrow, today, tomorrow, today." Every moment they are expecting those events to take place.

Grandshaykh ق said, "Since I was seven years of age the '*ulamā*[108] said 'it is going to happen this year.'" Grandshaykh's teacher, Shaykh Sharafuddīn, used to say, "today or tomorrow."

---

[108] Arabic: '*ulamā*—Religious scholars (sing. '*alim*).

Mawlana Shaykh Nazim ق says, "today or tomorrow." The most important thing is not to analyze what the Friends of God say. You cannot understand them. When they say something, they are raising you up to that level. Waiting for the Mahdi ﷺ, they are raising you to that expectation, which in turn elevates your level of worship. It adds a certain energy and urgency to one's faith, an "edge." So, don't analyze what they say!

Sayyidina Ali's Vision

Imam Muhammad al-Busayrī ☀, composer the world-renowned poems *Qasīdat al-Burdā* and *al-Mudarrīyya*,[109] said, "We have been given glad tidings of a pillar, of something we can lean on."

Even though there are pitfalls all around you, by leaning on something stable you can keep from falling. These are good tidings for us, Ummat an-Nabī ﷺ, the Community of the Prophet ﷺ, that Allah gave us not only something to lean on, but a very strong pillar, Sayyidina Muhammad ﷺ, the perfect one, to lean on.

Why do we need something to lean on? Because we have a lot of cracks in our lives—our sins. But having that love of Sayyidina Muhammad ﷺ in our heart will help us to be always successful. So Imam al-Busayrī said, "Don't be afraid, *Yā ummata* Muhammad ﷺ." He knew about the special vision of Sayyidina 'Alī ☀:

> One day the Prophet ﷺ called 'Alī ☀ and told him, "Look at me from the belly and up!" and he could not see the Prophet's head, because it rose above the level of the Throne. Then he said, "Look at me from the belly and down!" and he saw the Prophet's legs reaching down such an immense distance that his knees reached the span of seven earths, and he was only able to see to his knees and no farther. Then he said, "Look at

---

[109] *Qasīdas al-Burdā* and *al-Mudarrīyya*: sublime poetic compositions in praise of Prophet Muhammad ﷺ.

the whole of me!" and he saw the Prophet's appearance filling this universe.

Imam al-Busayrī understood that there is no one to be asked about anything regarding matters of the Community, except Sayyidina Muhammad ﷺ. When the Prophet ﷺ is asked and he answers, what more can be said? Sayyida Fāṭima ؓ put us all in her dowry. And the Prophet's *shafa'a,*[110] intercession, is going to raise us to higher stations in Paradise.

Don't think that sins can prevent you from entering Paradise. The Prophet ﷺ was given intercession to erase our sins. But we must not commit sins and whenever we fail, we must repent. Faith is of different levels. You cannot say you don't have *imān,* faith, as you believe in Allah and His Prophet ﷺ. But sometimes the level of faith drops and you sin. Immediately you must repent to restore your spiritual level to what it was before the sin. Instead of letting faith sink to a lower level, try to increase it.

Think how many verses of the Holy Qur'an are about those who make their faith stronger. So many verses begin with the address:

يَا أَيُّهَا الَّذِينَ آمَنُواْ

O you who believe![111]

You already believe, so now go higher in belief, to the levels of *'ayn al-yaqīn, 'ilm al-yaqīn, ḥaqq al-yaqīn.*[112] That is why we say that each day represents a different manifestation.

---

[110] Arabic: *shafa'a*—intercession of the Prophet ﷺ on Judgment Day.

[111] Nearly 90 verses begin with the phrase *"O you who believe!"* compared with about 20 which begin, *"O mankind!"*

[112] In advanced stages on the Sufi Path, these are known as the "Three Stages of Certainty": *'ayn al-yaqīn* (Eye of Certainty), *'ilm al-yaqīn* (Knowledge of Certainty), and *haqq al-yaqīn* (Truth of Certainty).

This Ramadan carries a different manifestation from last Ramadan. This coming year will be filled with heavy burdens. A great many things—too many things—will occur within the span of this year. I am experiencing this myself—at 4:00 p.m. I begin to have no power. My energy seems drained and goes away completely. We don't know what work the Friends of God are doing. We don't see that far—they don't let us know. However, I can tell you they are gathering and reclaiming energy for some special, concentrated effort.

By Maghrib[113] time I cannot raise my head, I cannot stand, it is impossible. That happened last Saturday, first. And it happened again on Sunday. Saturday I managed to hold *dhikr,* Friday was difficult, but yesterday I was completely drained. I could not even stand. That is a sign of the heavy events to appear in the coming year.

Grandshaykh ق, may Allah bless his soul, often said when Shaykh Sharafuddīn needed power, that he took power from him. So when Grandshaykh ق needed more power he said, "I take from Shaykh Nazim's power." We are not that level but we feel that something is going on.

It means this year, from Ramadan to Ramadan, is going to be full of events that might make a way for Sayyidina Mahdi ﷺ to come so that he doesn't need weapons. Sayyidina Mahdi ﷺ doesn't need worldly power to appear; Allah gives him heavenly power. When people look at him, they believe. He doesn't need to come with a sword or a machine gun; he comes with love. He doesn't fight; he stops the war, makes peace, and prepares for the prophet Jesus Christ ﷺ to come.

---

[113] Arabic: *maghrib*—sunset.

If we want to be in that time or we want to be known to those who will be in that time, it would be well to live by the example set by the Prophet ﷺ. Obedience to the Prophet ﷺ is obedience to Allah:

مَّنْ يُطِعِ الرَّسُولَ فَقَدْ أَطَاعَ اللهَ

Whoever is obeying the Prophet is obeying Allah.[114]

On the 15th of the month Shaʿbān this year (2006), the Prophet ﷺ ordered all Friends of God to appear in his presence, to assign their responsibilities for the coming three years. These responsibilities are a three-year plan concerning how they will face and solve the coming problems. Out of their love for humanity, many Friends of God were asking the Prophet ﷺ to delay these difficult years. They hoped Imam Mahdi ؑ could delay such events, but an order is an order. The Friends of God cannot stop anything. They have already been informed that they must be ready to take care of the human race when the time comes. To protect humanity, they have been instructed to pray and to recite through the inspiration in their hearts.

Although they don't come with his power or force, Friends of God are like Sayyidina Mahdi ؑ in that they inherit from Prophet ﷺ. Sayyidina Mahdi ؑ comes with love. The Friends of God inspire their followers what to recite and how to conduct themselves. So when the inspiration comes to you to pray two *rakaʿats,*[115] do it quickly! When it comes to you to do *istighfār,*[116] don't delay! When the thought comes to pray on the Prophet ﷺ, do it! We must all make *duʿa,*[117] always asking God, the Exalted, for protection from difficulties in the coming years.

---

[114] Sūratu 'n-Nisā (Women), 4:80.
[115] Arabic: *rakaʿt*—cycle of the prescribed prayer.
[116] Reciting the supplication *astaghfirullāh,* "I seek forgiveness from God."
[117] Arabic: *duʿa*—Supplication.

The Friends of God will send special messages to our hearts to keep us from the traps of Satan. If it comes into your heart to open the Qur'an and read, do so immediately! Normally, our egos will not let us do it. The ego will make all kinds of excuses to delay prayers or read the Qur'an. This will be especially true over the next three years. This sudden loss of energy I have felt tells me there is something going on. It did not happen last year; only this year. We ask Allah to give us power to fast this month and to bring happiness to people on earth.

We must obey the Prophet ﷺ as much as we can, even though our obedience cannot compare to that of the Friends of God. They obey by *ʿayn al-yaqīn* (Eye of Certainty), *ʿilm al-yaqīn* (Knowledge of Certainty), and *ḥaqq al-yaqīn* (Truth of Certainty). We, ordinary people, don't see things directly; we learn and obey only through imitation. Our inspiration should be the Friends of God. We should try to do as they do. In this way we can be accepted in their presence and they, in turn, will take us to presence of the Prophet ﷺ.

The Sacred Grove

Allah gave us three huge trees, each bearing numerous branches and countless leaves, so we could stand beneath them and be protected in this world. If we care for these trees and water them, the leaves will not fall; they will always be green and in the full bloom of spring, because you are watering them. Protect these trees! Keep them well and in the proper climate. If you change the climate, the leaves will become dry, turn yellow and fall. When these leaves fall to the ground, you will have no more shade to protect you. You need the shade, you need the branches and leaves with their beautiful canopy arching overhead, the leaves and branches covering each other. That shade will save you from the burning sun.

The first tree is *ati' Allah*—obey Allah. The second tree is *wa ati' ar-Rasūl*—and obey the Prophet ﷺ. The third tree is *wa ūli 'l-amri minkum*—and obey those in authority among you.[118]

The first tree is rooted in obedience to Allah.

The second tree spreads its branches in obedience to the Prophet ﷺ.

The third tree stands in obedience to those who are in authority. So:

يَا أَيُّهَا الَّذِينَ آمَنُواْ أَطِيعُواْ اللّهَ وَأَطِيعُواْ الرَّسُولَ وَأُوْلِي الأَمْرِ مِنكُمْ

O you who believe! Obey Allah, obey the Prophet and obey those in authority among you.[119]

is like three trees. The branches and shade of these three trees are connected in such a way as to give us lasting and staunch protection. God, the Exalted, ordered us to obey these three kinds of authority. Authorities provides the various structures in which we live. Some types of authority govern locally, others nationally. It is the proper role of government to take responsibility for the well-being, security and safety of its citizens.

The Friends of God also look after the safety of every individual in each country. They protect us from the enemies who come from inside the country and from beyond its borders, from outside the country. There are two kinds of internal enemies and two kinds of external enemies. These enemies can be characterized in four different levels: *nafs,* the lower self; *dunyā,* this worldly life, *hawā,* lustful desires, and Satan.

---

[118] In the Naqshbandi-Haqqani Sufi Order, we begin every gathering and even chapters of this book with this command from Holy Qur'an, to remind us of our status, and to seek the blessing.

[119] Sūratu 'n-Nisā (Women), 4:59.

Friends of God keep an army standing forever at attention, ready to protect us. All these bad elements are held at bay: the ego, this world, the longing for wealth, and a host of bad desires commanded by the devil. They are monitoring the body and soul in order to reach you in every moment. They are the border guards, looking both ways to hold off internal and external threats.

The Sultan and the Three Gamblers

Grandshaykh ق told us the following story:

> Sultan ʿAbdul Ḥamīd was very pure person, a spiritual emperor, a very good and faithful Ottoman king who carried on a tradition of Sayyidina ʿUmar ﷺ, of going out in the community at night incognito so he could personally attend to any of his subjects who were in need.
>
> He, and many saints like him, do not appear to sleep. They sacrifice their rest for our sake. That is why you must listen and obey the saints and not reject them, because they are looking after you. If you argue with them, they will leave you to your own devices and after that you will find yourself falling apart.

No matter how clever you may be, your cleverness will not protect you. If the saints pull their support away from you, there will be nothing left to hold you up. God, the Exalted, told Sayyidina Adam ﷺ not to eat from the forbidden tree. Nevertheless, when Satan said, "Eat from the tree", he succumbed and ate. Allah let Adam ﷺ eat to show him that, left unsupported, he would fall and commit sin.

Civil authorities work for their citizens and spiritual authorities work for their students. The spiritual guides do not sleep: if they pull their hand from support, the student will have a problem. If the disciple argues and doubts too much, then the guide will stop his support. If that should happen, the disciple will fall, and learn what it means to lose the support of his guide and protector, and lose his way on the spiritual path.

Sultan ʿAbdul Ḥamīd went out and found three people playing gambling. One of them said, "Oh, if only I were the son-in-law of the king, I wish to be the son-in-law of the king."

When he overheard this, Sultan ʿAbdul Ḥamīd said to his companions, "Write his name and address!"

Mawlana Shaykh Nazim said, "Don't think that you are not under surveillance. We are all being observed. That is why it is best to respect authority and abide by the law. Don't think the police can't see you. So be good. God, the Exalted, is al-ʿAfūw.[120] If you do something wrong, He will forgive you. As Allah mentioned in the Holy Qur'an in many verses, he is the one who forgives those who repent. Allah also gave the Prophet ﷺ the power to forgive. Obedience to the Prophet ﷺ follows definite lines.

Prophet ﷺ said:

شفاعتي لاهل الكبائر من امتي

My intercession is for the grave sinners from my nation.[121]

And Allah said:

قُلْ يَا عِبَادِيَ الَّذِينَ أَسْرَفُوا عَلَى أَنفُسِهِمْ لَا تَقْنَطُوا مِن رَّحْمَةِ اللهِ إِنَّ اللهَ يَغْفِرُ الذُّنُوبَ جَمِيعًا إِنَّهُ هُوَ الْغَفُورُ الرَّحِيمُ

Say: "O my Servants who have transgressed against their souls! Despair not of the Mercy of Allah. for Allah forgives all sins: for He is Oft-Forgiving, Most Merciful.[122]

---

[120] Arabic: al-ʿAfūw—One of Allah's Beautiful Names and Attributes, meaning "The Pardoner".

[121] Āḥmad in his *Musnad*, Ibn Mājah, Abū Dāwūd, Ibn Ḥibbān and Ṭabarānī.

However, those who are in authority will take you into custody if you do something that threatens the safety of the country. Friends of God also want to secure your safety. They don't want you to forfeit their guidance through disobedience. You will encounter great difficulties if you lose their support.

Grandshaykh ق continued the story of Sultan ʿAbdul Ḥamīd:

> He immediately had them record the name of the indiscrete gambler. Take heed of the *ūli 'l-amr,* those in authority. He said, *hifẓ al-lisān min salāmāt il-insān.* "To safeguard your tongue is to safeguard yourself." To cut your tongue is better—not physically, but in the sense ceasing its incessant chatter. Every problem comes from the tongue.

عَنْ سَهْلِ بْنِ سَعْدٍ، عَنْ رَسُولِ اللَّهِ صلى الله عليه وسلم قَالَ " مَنْ يَضْمَنْ لِي مَا بَيْنَ لَحْيَيْهِ وَمَا بَيْنَ رِجْلَيْهِ اضْمَنْ لَهُ الْجَنَّةَ

The Prophet ﷺ said:

> *Whoever obeys me and through his good behavior guards what is between his jaws and what is between his legs, I will guarantee a place for him in Paradise.*[123]

The most difficult thing to control is the tongue. It is always barking, always arguing. All of us do this. That is why it is said "if talking is from silver, then silence is from gold."

It is always best to refrain from talking. You will only bring difficulties on yourself with talking. Think how often loose talk has brought people to the attention of the authorities. Talking can also turn the Friends of God against you or make the Prophet ﷺ unhappy

---

[122] Sūratu 'z-Zumar (the Groups), 39:53.
[123] Saḥīḥ Bukhārī.

with you. It is better to talk by saying *subḥanallāh, wa alḥamdūlillāh, Allāhu Akbar,* to make *ṣalawāt* on the Prophet ﷺ and to recite the Qur'an. Speak only when it is necessary, otherwise keep quiet.

We return to the story of Sultan ʿAbdul Ḥamīd and the three gamblers.

> The second man said, "I would like the king to make me the minister of the treasury so that I could take as much as I wished from his treasures. Whatever I wanted, I would take. I'd like that." In so saying, he revealed that his ego liked wealth. The first man didn't like wealth—he said he wanted to marry the king's daughter, which means he wanted to be around the king and present at that happy moment. The second one didn't care about that; he only wanted money.
>
> The third gambler said, "I want to be Sultan ʿAbdul Ḥamīd." The king said, "Take their names and bring them to me tomorrow."
>
> Next morning he sent the police to get them. When the police came to these three men, they were worried but they knew they hadn't done anything wrong. However, they did suspect that their conversation had been overheard and they were puzzled, because as far as they could recall they had said nothing against the sultan.

Today people speak against the government and against the Friends of God. Furthermore, if they don't find anyone else to speak against, they speak against themselves. Anger can bend and twist us when it gets the upper hand. The Prophet ﷺ told Abū Bakr aṣ-Ṣiddīq, "*al-ghadabu kufr*—anger is unbelief." If we are not angry with our government, we are angry with the Friends of God. If we don't like what they do, rather than express our anger, it is better we beat our horse! If we have no horse, and who does not have a horse, his or her ego— let us beat our own selves.

The next morning the three gamblers were presented at the king's court. Sultan 'Abdul Ḥamīd pointed to the gambler who wanted to marry his daughter and said, "That one's heart is clean. Sayyidina 'Umar ❀ married the Prophet's daughter in order to be able to touch a member of the Prophet's Family, Āhl al-Bayt. Because the Prophet ❀ said, "Whoever touches the body of Āhl al-Bayt will enter Paradise," thus demonstrating his love to the Prophet ❀.

The first gambler didn't want wealth or power, he only wanted to be in the sultan's presence. So Sultan 'Abdul Ḥamīd called the Shaykh al-Islam,[124] and told him, "Arrange for a marriage between that man and my daughter." *Allāhu Akbar!* Look how much that man was honored!

The sultan then pointed to the second gambler and said, "It seems what makes you happy are the treasures of this world, the fleeting things of this world that will pass away. Don't long for what others have. We must protect you from jealousy. If Allah didn't give you exactly what they have, what makes you think you could be like them in any event? Some people want spiritual wealth, but you dream of physical wealth. Well, why don't you bring some bags and the guards will take you to the treasury where you can have all the gold and fill them as much as you wish."

The man took his bags, filled them, and was happy with his newfound wealth.

The king turned to the third man and said, "So, you want to be Sultan 'Abdul Ḥamīd?" Calling the guards he said, "Put him on my throne and tie him, make sure his legs are bound

---

[124] Arabic: Shaykh al-Islam—the most highly knowledgable Islamic scholar of the time.

securely." Then he looked into the eyes of the newly enthroned gambler and said, "Look above you!"

The man looked up looked and saw a very sharp sword hanging above the middle of his head. The king explained, "You see, my friend, the sword comes with the chair. This is what it means to be Sultan 'Abdul Ḥamīd. Look closely at the sword. It is suspended from the ceiling by a very fine thread. As sultan, if I do anything wrong, God, the Exalted, and the Prophet ﷺ will see it, and the thread will break."

The man looked up and trembled.

The king said to him, "You will remain here beneath the sword all day. At sundown you may run away or stay; it will be your choice."

Many thoughts ran through the man's head that day. Look how generously the king had dealt with his two companions and how strange were their rewards. Could it be that he would actually become the new sultan? He looked up again at the dangling blade and God, the Exalted, put fear in his heart.

The king looked at the man on his throne and said, "O my son! This is how I work, day and night. I toil ceaselessly for the benefit of the country, its safety, and security. I work to keep our citizens safe from aggressors in neighboring kingdoms and from terrorists who would attack us from within our own borders."

The Sleepless Watch

With this tale, Grandshaykh ق is showing us that authorities do not sleep. You are sleeping, you move here and you move there without any problem. But the authorities are not sleeping; they are constantly on the lookout for any terrorist attacks.

Day and night, we are observed by the authorities. Between the Friends of God and the civil authorities, every aspect of our behavior is known. Even when you are sleeping, the Friends of God are aware of your tossing and turning which, to them, sounds as loud as thunder. They look and send you tests to check you. When a public speaker prepares to address an audience someone checks the microphone first. He taps it and says, "Testing, testing."

Friends of God also have a microphone, "Test, test, test… oh, this is not good." Then they raise the volume to the point that your body will shake. They don't send a weak test, they want to send a test strong enough to break you down and make you surrender, until you say, "I am running away!" Until that moment when they break you down completely, they don't leave you. They like to break you down.

Often I saw Grandshaykh ق testing and retesting all of his followers, including Mawlana Shaykh Nazim ق. In turn, Mawlana Shaykh Nazim ق is testing all of his followers, testing you and me, and this one and that one. He does not say, "This one is my representative" and leave it at that; he gives that one even more hardships! If we fail, what can we do?

In any case, they are protecting us. Their responsibility for us hangs over them like a sword: they are always aware of our difficulties. If any devil or attacker approaches us, they immediately jump on them so that we can avoid that difficulty.

Conscious Action

Allah said in the Holy Qur'an:

وَأَعِدُّواْ لَهُم مَّا اسْتَطَعْتُم مِّن قُوَّةٍ وَمِن رِّبَاطِ الْخَيْلِ تُرْهِبُونَ بِهِ عَدْوَّ اللّهِ وَعَدُوَّكُمْ
وَآخَرِينَ مِن دُونِهِمْ لاَ تَعْلَمُونَهُمُ اللّهُ يَعْلَمُهُمْ وَمَا تُنفِقُواْ مِن شَيْءٍ فِي سَبِيلِ اللّهِ يُوَفَّ
إِلَيْكُمْ وَأَنتُمْ لاَ تُظْلَمُونَ

Make ready for them all you can of (armed) force and of horses tethered, that thereby you may dismay the enemy of Allah and your enemy, and others beside them whom you know not. Allah knows them. Whatever you spend in the way of Allah it will be repaid to you in full, and you will not be wronged. [125]

Allah is telling us to prepare against our four enemies: *nafs,* the bad ego, *dunyā,* this world, *hawā,* lustful desire, and Satan. Gather your strength for the battle! You must learn the art of internal warfare, the struggle against your own desires. A good warrior in this type of combat must learn to handle certain weapons and techniques, just as a master swordsman will practice for years learning his art.

This implies a conscious division within your being—part of you acting and the other part observing the actor. Cultivate this increased awareness and carefully analyze your motives! A blind, heedless individual does not question his own actions, nor does he observe what lies behind them. Be on your guard against such heedlessness! Put your body and soul into the fight, just as a good general will put his horsemen at the battle front to strike fear into the hearts of the enemy soldiers. Inevitably, the enemy will come to each of us and try to turn us against Allah and his Prophet ﷺ. Allah will see your efforts in this battle and reward you accordingly.

This is all about using specialized techniques and preparations. Even though these particular enemies are within, we don't want to destroy ourselves in the process, but rather destroy our enemies. Remember, this is an internal struggle, and not about the domination of others. This makes the struggle much more complicated and difficult than an ordinary battle between two armies engaged on a field in broad daylight. The enemies inside us can assume many forms, blend into the background of our own

---

[125] Sūratu 'l-Anfāl (the Spoils), 8:60.

internal landscape and effectively disguise themselves, wrapped in robes of self-righteousness and self-justification. That is why we must prepare in a certain way for this inner conflict.

Prepare against them all you can of (armed) force and of horses tethered...

Marshal your forces and gather what you can of your power!

Today we don't make these kinds of preparations for the internal battle. Instead, we expend incredible amounts of energy battling others. Perhaps some of the people we oppose are actually better than we are. Leave those kinds of battles behind you and prepare against yourself first! When you are clean inside, then you can clean others.

That is why the Friends of God want you to destroy inwardly first, banishing your bad desires and ego. After that they can give you the authority to find students to bring back to the real shaykh. Anyone who takes *baya*ʿ[126] with the shaykh's representative must renew it when he meets the shaykh. That is why we tell students to go to Mawlana Shaykh and take his hand. Your duty is to greet the owner of the house and pay your respects. Never can the doorman be the owner. He brings people to the door, and the owner will take care of what is needed.

Wa min Allāhi 't-tawfiq, bi ḥurmati 'l-Fātiḥah.

---

[126] Arabic: *bayaʿ*—initiation in the Sufi Order; allegiance.

7: Heavenly Protocol

The Constant Caliph

O Believers! Oh Muslims! God, the Exalted, has honored us in our acceptance of Islam, which He described as:

الإِسْلَامُ وَمَا إِنَّ الدِّينَ عِندَ اللَّهِ

Religion to God, the Exalted, is Islam.[127]

Islam cannot be without Sayyidina Muhammad ﷺ, who God, the Exalted, sent to humanity as the Seal of the Messengers until Judgment Day. He is the last messenger, wrapping all messages within the Islamic religion. God, the Exalted, gave Sayyidina Muhammad ﷺ the authority to be God's Deputy on earth, *khalifatullah 'ala al-ard.* As Allah said in the Holy Qur'an:

إِنِّي جَاعِلٌ فِي الأَرْضِ خَلِيفَةً

I am putting a deputy on earth.[128]

For each period in history, there must be a caliph. In his time, Prophet Abraham ﷷ was the caliph, and Prophet Moses was caliph in his time, as was Prophet Jesus ﷷ caliph in his time. Finally, Prophet Muhammad ﷺ is the caliph.

There is a specific caliph for each time. When one sultan leaves, the next one must come. The caliph of the Ottoman Empire was a good example. You cannot have two sultans at the same

---

[127] Sūrat Āli-'Imrān (the Family of 'Imrān), 3:19.
[128] Sūratu 'l-Baqara (the Heifer), 2:30.

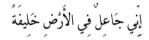

time. They arrive and rule in succession. When his time is finished, then God, the Exalted, takes his soul and the next one comes.

Allah made all prophets His deputies on earth,[129] representing the Divine Message on earth. When one prophet's mission is over, another one comes. For example, the message of Prophet Noah [130] was not over until Prophet Abraham [131] came. In turn, the message of Prophet Abraham was not over until Prophet Moses [132] came.

This means that as long as the Prophet is living, even living in soul, beyond the life of the body, he is still the caliph.

In his holy grave, Prophet Muhammad is observing the deeds of the Community until Judgment Day. He is responsible for the actions of every one of us until then. That his why he said:

عن ابن مسعود رضي الله عنه قال قال رسول الله صلى الله عليه وسلم حياتي

خير لكم تحدثون ويحدث لكم ووفاتي خير لكم تعرض علي اعمالكم فما رايت

من خير حمدت الله وما رايت من شر استغفرت الله لكم

The actions of my Community are displayed to me (in my grave). If I see good I praise God, the Exalted, and if I see other than that, I ask forgiveness for them.[133]

Prophet looks after the deeds of the Community because he is a living caliph, not a dead caliph. Our ordinary notion of death does not apply to Prophet Muhammad. If that were the case, God, the Exalted, would not send Archangel Gabriel to ask him

---

[129] Arabic: *khulafā-ullāh 'ala al-arḍ*—vicegerents of God on earth.

[130] Arabic: Nūḥ

[131] Arabic: Ibrāhīm

[132] Arabic: Mūsā.

[133] Ad-Daylamī.

his own decision regarding this life whether he wanted to leave this world or return to Allah:

...ثم استأذن ملك الموت عليه السلام فقال – يعني جبريل – يا أحمد هذا ملك الموت يستأذن عليك و لم يستأذن على آدمي كان قبلك و لا يستأذن على آدمي بعدك...

"O Āḥmad! This is the Angel of Death, seeking your permission (to take your soul), and he has never sought permission on any human who came before you and will not ask permission on any human to come after you."[134]

Allah gave him this perpetual authority. He is living in his grave, as he said:

عن أبي هريرة رضي الله عنه ـ أن رسول الله قال : ما من أحد يسلم على إلا رد الله على روحى حتى أرد عليه السلام

Whoever sends me salām, *God, the Exalted, sends me back my soul to reply to them.*[135]

Imam Jalāluddīn as-Suyūṭī explained this hadith. He said that these *salāms* flow continuously to the Prophet ﷺ as millions of people across the planet honor him. He asked, "Do you think then that his soul is being sent back to us each time someone gives a *salām*?" In answering his own question he said, "No, his soul is always there. He is observing his Community and he asks forgiveness if he sees anything bad."

---

[134] Bayhaqī in his *Dalā'il* in a long hadith describing the circumstances of the Prophet's final illness and passing from this life.

[135] Abū Dāwūd, Āḥmad, Bayhaqī.

وَمَا أَرْسَلْنَا مِن رَّسُولٍ إِلاَّ لِيُطَاعَ بِإِذْنِ اللّهِ وَلَوْ أَنَّهُمْ إِذ ظَّلَمُواْ أَنفُسَهُمْ جَآؤُوكَ فَاسْتَغْفَرُواْ اللّهَ وَاسْتَغْفَرَ لَهُمُ الرَّسُولُ لَوَجَدُواْ اللّهَ تَوَّابًا رَّحِيمًا

And We have sent no messenger but that he should be obeyed by the command of Allah. And if they had come to you when they had wronged their souls, and asked forgiveness of Allah, and if the Messenger had also asked forgiveness for them, they would have surely found Allah Oft-Returning, with compassion and Mercy.[136]

It means you must go to the representative, not directly to the Creator. Between you and the Creator there are many worldly veils. However, Sayyidina Muhammad ﷺ is here, and he can be reached from this world. He is with you. He is on this planet. That is why he said, "I observe their actions and if I find good I praise Allah, and if I see other, then ask for their forgiveness."

And Allah said:

They ask forgiveness in your presence.

Are you going to the presence of the Prophet ﷺ and repenting to Allah? When we do something wrong we say *"astaghfirullāh"*. But we must go through the Prophet ﷺ. That is why, when we make *du'a*, we must wrap it. You must say *ṣalawāt* on the Prophet ﷺ—that is the perfume, which makes it acceptable as a petition: it acts as an authorized signature.

If you give a petition to someone important, he will look to see who endorsed it. If the endorsement was given by someone important, someone higher than himself in the organization, he will sign it immediately and close his eyes. He easily gives his approval.

---

[136] Sūratu 'n-Nisā (Women), 4:64.

No one is above Sayyidina Muhammad ﷺ. When you come to him and take your endorsement to God, the Exalted, it goes straight up the line. What will be left? He is presenting you and endorsing you. God, the Exalted, will accept it immediately. As God, the Exalted, said in the Qur'an:

> *You ask forgiveness in his presence and Prophet will ask forgiveness on their behalf. Then they would find Allah* tawāban Raḥīma—*Oft-Returning, with compassion and Mercy.*

The Impatient Blind Man

Without coming to Sayyidina Muhammad ﷺ you have no guarantee; no endorsement. You need someone to introduce you. That is why every *'amal,* action,[137] should be sent with *ṣalawāt an-Nabī,* prayers on the Prophet ﷺ in order to be accepted.

وروينا في كتابي الترمذي و ابن ماجه, عن عثمان ابن حنيف ان رجلا ضرير البصر أتي النبي صلي اللّه عليه و سلم فقال: ادع اللّه تعلي ا يعفيني, قال: اي شت دعون, و ان شت صبرت فهو خير لك قال: فادعه, بامره أن يتوضأ فيحسن وضوءه و يدعو بهدا الدعاء:

اللهم اني اسالك واتوجه اليك بنبيك محمد نبي الرحمة يا محمد اني اتوجه بك الى الله في حاجتي هذه لتقضى لي، اللهم فشفعه في.

There is the hadith of blind man who wanted to go to the Fajr[138] prayer. Because he could not see, he could not find his way to the prayers. He asked the Prophet ﷺ, "Please pray for me to be able to see." Prophet ﷺ said, "Can you be patient?"

---

[137] Arabic: *'amal*—good action, or more generally all deeds.
[138] Arabic: *Fajr*—pre-dawn.

The man was definitely not patient. He stood so near the Prophet ﷺ, and yet he could not see him. He might be patient about anything except that. In those times God, the Exalted, poured heavenly love into the hearts of people near the Prophet ﷺ. Today we have little or no sense of this. No one is using their senses for the hereafter. We are not even smelling the reality of that love. If we did, we might go to the ends of the earth, trying to reach the reality of the Prophet ﷺ. We would settle for nothing else.

> *The man said, "Pray for me."*
> *So he said, "Go to the ablution area and do your ablution very thoroughly, and pray two* rakaʿats *and then make this prayer, 'O Allah I am asking you for my sight. While I direct my face towards You, I seek the intermediation of the Prophet ﷺ, the Messenger of mercy. I am sending his endorsement.'"*

The Prophet ﷺ was teaching the blind man to not try to go directly to the Creator but, instead, go through the proper door. Today people want to go jump through the window. And Allah said:

وَأْتُوا الْبُيُوتَ مِنْ أَبْوَابِهَا

Enter houses by their doors.[139]

You cannot go to Allah directly and jump over Sayyidina Muhammad ﷺ. There must be *adab*—discipline, and respect. If you don't respect the role of Sayyidina Muhammad ﷺ then God, the Exalted, will reject your *duʿa*.

That is why today so often *duʿa*s are rejected. There are millions of people offering millions of prayers, but they are like foam.

---

[139] Sūratu 'l-Baqara (the Heifer), 2:189.

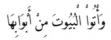

عن ثوبان قال قال رسول الله صلى الله عليه وسلم... بل أنتم يومئذ كثير ولكنكم غثاء كغثاء السيل...

Thawban narrated that the Prophet ﷺ said:
"No, you will be numerous at that time: but you will be like foam that is carried down by a torrent..."[140]

The Prophet ﷺ said that this would be like the foam at the foot of a waterfall, like Niagara Falls; so many prayers carrying so little power. This is because they are leaving out the love of Sayyidina Muhammad ﷺ. They are only calling for the love of this world—for things not related to the hereafter. They are asking for the things of this world. No one is thinking anymore.

Demonstrate to God

There are demonstrations in every country of the world. What worldly power can help you? It would be better to make demonstrations before of the Presence of Allah and sit in a group saying, "O my Lord! Please take this problem from us!" What good is it to march in the streets, demanding that government officials give you relief? If Allah doesn't send support, no support will come.

Go to Allah through the Prophet ﷺ. He taught the blind man this *du'a*:

اللهم اني اسالك واتوجه اليك بنبيك محمد نبي الرحمة يا محمد اني اتوجه بك الى الله في حاجتي هذه لتقضى لي، اللهم فشفعه في.

I am directing my face to You through Muhammad ﷺ.

That is a real hadith. Some people wrongly claim, "Don't call on Muhammad ﷺ; call only Allah." They forget:

---

[140] *Sunan Abū Dāwūd*, Book 37, Number 4284; a similar narration is found in Āḥmad's *Musnad* and mentioned by Haythamī in *Majma' al-zawā'id (7:287).*

إِنْ هُوَ إِلا وَحْيٌ يُوحَى

It is naught but revelation that is revealed to him. [141]

When he taught the *du'a* to the blind man, that was a revelation:

(The blind man said,) "O Muhammad! I am directing myself to my Lord through you, so that my problems can be solved."

Then he asked God, the Exalted, to give him his sight for the sake of the Prophet ﷺ. The next day God, the Exalted, restored his sight because of His love of Sayyidina Muhammad ﷺ.[142]

We can all learn from the example of the blind man. "For the Love of you, O Muhammad ﷺ." Praise him, mention his blessed name, recite *ṣalawāt* on him day and night. All your problems will be solved. This practice is particularly important in this month, Sha'bān.

The Prophet ﷺ said:

عن النبي صلى الله عليه وسلم ألا إنَّ رجب شهر الله، وشعبان شهري، ورمضان شهر امّتي.

Rajab is the month of Allah, Sha'bān is my month, and Ramadan is the month of the entire Community.[143]

We are in Sha'bān today.

لم أر رسول الله صلى الله عليه وسلم يصوم في شهر أكثر من صيامه لله في شعبان، كان يصوم شعبان إلا قليلا، بل كان يصومه كله

---

[141] Sūratu 'n-Najm (the Star), 53:4.
[142] Al-Ḥākim, Ibn Mājah, Tirmidhī.
[143] ad-Daylamī and Abī Shaykh.

When Sayyida 'A'ishā ﷺ was asked, "In what month did the Prophet ﷺ fast the most after Ramadan?" she said it was Sha'bān.[144]

Sha'bān is the month during which the doors of Paradise are opened. This is the time when God, the Exalted, for the love of Sayyidina Muhammad ﷺ, will accept anything from His servants. Anything they ask God, the Exalted, will be accepted for sake of the Prophet ﷺ.

The Prophet ﷺ said:
Sha'bān can gives protection from the fire. Try to fast three days of Sha'bān.

It means, even if there is a big fire then it cannot get to you.

People are granted innocence from the Hellfire on *Laylat al-bara'h.*[145]

جاءني جبريل ليلة النصف من شعبان فقال يا محمد ارفع راسك الى السماء فقلت ماهذه الليلة ، قال هذه ليلة يفتح الله فيها ثلاثمائة من ابواب الرحمة يغفر الله لجميع من لا يشرك به شيئاً

Sayyidina Abū Hurayra ﷺ[146] *said:*
The Prophet ﷺ said, "Gabriel came to me in the night of 15th Sha'bān and said, 'Yā Muhammad, ﷺ look up!' And I looked up and said, 'What is this night; it is something extraordinary!'"[147]

And in another hadith, the Prophet said:

---

[144] Bukhārī and Muslim.
[145] Arabic: *Laylat al-bara'h*—the Night of Mid-Sha'bān.
[146] A Sahabi among the foremost narrators of ahadith.
[147] *Al-Ghunyā li-ṭālib tarīq al-ḥaqq.*

معاذ بن جبل رضي الله عنه عن النبي صلى الله عليه وسلم قال : " يطلع الله إلى جميع خلقه ليلة النصف من شعبان فيغفر لجميع خلقه إلا لمشرك أو مشاحن "

On the night of 15th Shaʿbān, Allah looks at all His servants and He will forgive all of those except an idolater or a person of malice.[148]

There are two exceptions to who will be forgiven: those who make *shirk*[149] and say that Allah is not one and that Muhammad ﷺ is not His messenger; and, second, *mushāhin*, the one who provokes people to mischief and sin, to be bad citizens, to come against their governments, to come against their shaykhs, to come against their elders, to make *fitna*[150] among people. That is why Prophet ﷺ said:

الفتنة نائمة لعن الله من أيقظها

Confusion and troubles are sleeping; whoever stirred them up, Allah will curse![151]

O Muslims, to succeed, let us bring *fitna* to an end. Let us not provoke each other to go out onto the streets for nothing. No one is going to listen to you. What is planned is planned. What Allah has written is written. Look at yourself! Try to polish yourself, and when you clean yourself you will be in the Divine Presence—that is better than the entire this world.

Wa min Allāhi 't-tawfiq, bi ḥurmati 'l-Fātiḥah.

---

[148] Ibn Mājah and Ibn Manṣūr in his *Sunan*.
[149] Arabic: *shirk*—To associate partners with Allah.
[150] Arabic: *fitna*—confusion; to cause dissension.
[151] Ar-Rāfiʿī in his *Amalīyyah* from Anas ؓ.

8: ACCOUNT WITH THE PROPHET

Drinks of Forgefulness

The lesson of the three trees, "Obey God, obey the Prophet, and those in authority among you," and the story of Sultan ʿAbdul Ḥamīd show us that God, the Exalted, wants to benefit His servants.

Allah's guidance seeks out all of us. One of His Attributes is ar-Raḥmān, ar-Raḥīm. Because of His mercy, He wants everyone to believe. That is why He sent messengers: He doesn't want to keep anyone outside that divine mercy.

The story of Sultan ʿAbdul Ḥamīd showed him observing and then guiding the three gamblers. He dealt with each one according to his intention. One said he wanted to be son-in-law of Sultan ʿAbdul Ḥamīd, the other wanted the wealth of Sultan ʿAbdul Ḥamīd, and the third wanted to be Sultan ʿAbdul Ḥamīd himself.

Although Satan had entered each of the gamblers' hearts and spoiled them to some extent, there were still traces of true intentions left. The gamblers found guidance through these traces. The rooms we are sitting in now are very bright because of all the lights. However, sometimes you have no light, you may have only a candle. Even with such a faint light, you can find your way. So these traces of light persist in the heart and never go away. Allah will pull these lights towards Him just as magnets are drawn to metal.

Because of his pure heart, the first gambler became son-in-law to the Sultan. He granted the second man great wealth. Finally, Sultan Hameed showed the third gambler the true nature of kingship and how to safeguard a kingdom. This story illustrates why these three trees are important.

Once you accept Allah and his Messenger, nothing can take that away. Satan can drop veils to confuse you, but he cannot actually remove Divine Guidance. That is why Satan comes to deceive us using small and large sins. He approaches you when you are unhappy with your life, your family and your circumstances. He finds your weak points and enters from them. Even Sayyidina Adam ﷺ was tempted in this way. We must keep our hearts as clean as we can, and open them to the help that Allah offers. Adam ﷺ listened to Satan and fell. However, after his fall, the remnants of light that remained in his heart enabled Allah to lead him back from this world.

Satan's Advice: "Forget!"

When you become depressed and dissatisfied with your life, you are lost in the wilderness. Satan leads you to this unhappy place, then whispers in your ear, "Go to the bar, that will make you happy. There you will forget all your troubles. Have a drink or two, and maybe a special pill, too." He won't tell you to go to a mosque or a spiritual gathering, but rather to a place of forgetfulness.

The key is forgetfulness. There are thousands of ways to forget! Diversions are everywhere. It's a big industry. People want to forget. Look at the market for anti-depressants today! Satan says "you can drink some wine and you will forget more." You take one sip, then two, then three. This is the larger sin. After that, you will see this world change. The seductive world of illusion will become all the more attractive.

Just as heroine addicts see a different world of flickering images and phantoms, so the forgetful believer drifts into the misty world of Satan's many veils. You become very happy with what is going on. "Oh, *alḥamdūlillāh*, I found what I must do." The next day more, the next day more. This is one way that Satan can control his domain.

If you have more faith, more *imān,* he cannot pull you to the graver sins, so he will begin by presenting you with small sins. If you have a problem with your family or your wife, you might decide to go out for an evening on the town. Maybe you will go to a coffee shop and see a pretty woman. It may seem innocent enough to begin with: first a smile, then flirting, then a dinner, and finally Satan tightens his web and draws you to *kabā'ir,* the grave sin of adultery.

Even after all this, God, the Exalted, will not say, "Don't come back to me!" He will say, "My door is always open, so come back. Welcome."

The City and Its Gate

Grandshaykh ق taught his followers that when you do any good deed, be sure and immediately deposit it in your "account of deeds". Everyone from *Ummat an-Nabī,* the Community fo the Prophet ﷺ, has an account with the Prophet ﷺ. That is why the hadith tells us to wrap our *ʿamal* with *ṣalawāt*. We should say, "*Yā Sayyidī, Yā Rasūlullāh,* I am putting this *ʿamal*, deeds, in your trust. It is safe there—Satan cannot steal it." Once deposited, it is as safe as valuables locked in a safety deposit box.

Similarly, this is also how to safeguard your *shahāda*[152], prayers, *duʿa* and recitation of Qur'an. "*Wadʿatahu ʿindak yā sayyidī, Yā Rasūlullāh*—I have put these two *shahādas* in your trust so that Satan cannot take them." Mawlana said this is very important.

---

[152] Testification of faith by means of which one enters Islam. Arabic: *ashhadu an la ilāha illa 'Llāh wa ashhadu anna Muḥammadan Rasūlullāh*—I bear witness that there is no god except Allah, and I bear witness that Muhammad is the Prophet of God.

This way Satan and the four enemies cannot take the credit of your good actions away because you have kept it in a safe place.

Always remember—we are in need of Allah and his Prophet ﷺ; they are not in need of us.

"Prepare your power," God, the Exalted, said in the Qur'an. If you want to overcome a bad situation, gather whatever power you can. When you see the four enemies coming to take you away, you may draw on this source of stored power. You prepare yourself by raising your level of *imān,* faith. When you commit a sin, your level of faith drops. When the level of *imān* is not balanced and drops to nearly nothing, you begin to listen to the whispers of Satan. When the whispering starts, you know the balance is tilting in his favor and your *imān* is dropping. When the whispering is absent, your faith is the dominating factor.

This balance is critical. If you put half a spoon of salt in a gallon of water, you can't taste the change. If you increase the amount of salt it becomes noticeable and overpowers the pure taste of the water. When the whispering of Satan increases, the purity of the water decreases and faith is diluted. From very early times, this is why Friends of God wore woolen cloaks. They wore "*ṣūf*", which means "wool" in Arabic. That is where the term *taṣawwuf* came from—wool. Why wool? They could have worn cotton, as it was widely available at that time. Why would they insist on wearing wool?

In those days, religious scholars didn't understand why the mystics wore wool. They said it was an innovation, because you could get the same fabric thickness by wearing three layers of cotton clothing. Actually, mystics adopted the distinguishing practice of wearing wool to help remind them of the wild side to their nature. It was an effective way to tell their egos they were carrying wool, a fabric made from animal hair. In this manner, the animal, or base side of their nature, was constantly in view, a symbol of the wild animalism within.

If we forget the bad characteristics lurking inside, they can operate unobserved, move about freely, and gain strength. When they break free and take over, we become like animals, kicking and killing. Then, even the most basic norms of human behavior fall aside. Your actions become unrestricted and madness ensues.

We all have restrictions, *taklīf*. Allah has asked us to turn away from forbidden things and do only good things. Such rules were not created for animals. The wool acts as a daily reminder to not behave like animals.

Be Innocent as Children

Mawlana said we should observe how children are always busy doing something. While awake, they are almost never still. They take a special delight in any activity: running, writing, playing, reading. We should learn to be like these children. Instead, as we grow older, we slip into idleness, sitting and doing nothing for long periods of time.

Mawlana said we should be like children in this regard. All that enthusiasm and energy, which some choose to call "hyper", is a quality we might well cultivate as adults. Why not be hyper in the way of God, the Exalted? Don't be self-calming and self-satisfied on this path. Success lies in continuous striving towards servanthood. What Mawlana is telling us applies for each association you attend, and that effort will go on until Judgment Day. Even if you die in the meeting, an angel will replace you and carry on from that point as your representative. You cannot be removed from the meeting, nor can your reward be taken away. If an angel replaces you, you will be rewarded by the level of purity of that angel.

Angels are *m'aṣūm*—innocent and sinless.[153] They are not like

[153] Arabic: *m'aṣūm*: blameless; pure; protected from error.

us. We still have whispering in our ears and *m'asīyya*, disobedience[154] still comes. But if an angel stands in on your behalf, then your part in the gathering will be more pure.

For any association convened under the names of Grandshaykh ق and Mawlana Shaykh Nazim ق, the rewards will carry through to Judgment Day. This is true for any association held anywhere in the world under the auspices of Grandshaykh ق and Mawlana Shaykh ق. Furthermore, if you appear here in America and there are other associations taking place in China or Africa on the same day, you will benefit because angels will represent you at those gatherings as well. Think of all the associations being held daily. The *baraka* of Friends of God is constantly spreading and circling the globe.

An example of this is what happened to Sayyidina 'Alī ؤ when he stayed in the Prophet's ﷺ bed during his migration from Mecca to Madinah. Why did they resort to this risky subterfuge when bedding stuffed with pillows would have sufficed? The reason is: it was this bed where Gabriel came to the Prophet ﷺ. During that night, Sayyidina 'Alī ؤ, in the place of the Prophet ﷺ, was able to receive knowledge directly from Gabriel ؏. The Prophet ﷺ deliberately placed 'Alī ؤ in his bed niche so this would happen.

أنا مدينة العلم و علي بابها

I am the city of knowledge and 'Alī is its gate.[155]

So Sayyidina 'Alī ؤ received knowledge in this manner just as Sayyidina Abū Bakr ؤ received special knowledge in the cave.

---

[154] Arabic: *m'asīyya*: Disobedience, sin.
[155] Related by Suwaid ibn Ghafalah aṣ-Ṣanābaḥī; as-Suyūṭī and Ibn Ḥajar graded it *ḥasan*.

In the cave, Ghari Thawr, the Prophet ﷺ ordered that all prophets and Friends of God should receive knowledge flowing from this stream. In this way ʿAbdul Khāliq al-Ghujdawānī ق received the Khatm al-Khwajagan.[156] Sayyidina Abdul Khaliq ق called all the *dharrāt*, the essences, of everyone in *ṭarīqah*.[157]

This Sufi Order is now called Naqshbandiyya, but before, in his time it was called Ghujdawaniyya, and before that it was called Tayfuriyya. And so, the *ṭarīqah* is named after the Friend of God heading the order in that time.

This *ṭarīqah* is under the *talqīn*[158] of Sayyidina Muhammad ﷺ and Sayyidina Abū Bakr ؓ. The recitation, "*Allahu Allahu Allahu ḥaqq,*" was put on our tongues for doing *dhikr*. This is the reason why you will be rewarded for every association you attend under the wings of the Naqshbandi Sufi Order. It is called Naqshbandi, but after Grandshaykh ق it is called Naqshbandi-Ḥaqqaniyya, reflecting the lineage from Grandshaykh ق back to Abū Bakr aṣ-Ṣiddīq ؓ and ultimately to the Prophet ﷺ. This lineage sweeps through all the grandshaykhs including Sayyidina ʿAbdul Khāliq al-Ghujdawānī ق as he leads the Khatm al-Khwājagan.

Therefore, we are all under that *tajallī,* manifestation, and under that reward. From that time we were under that *talqīn*, and our tongues will carry the blessings of that *dhikr*. If they say "*Allāhu*", that is transmitted to our tongues. At first, is may only be an imitation of their prayers, but eventually, with much repetition, our chants will become more genuine and carry more power. The blessings of these great shaykhs bridge time and can

---

[156] Circle of the Masters—prescribed congregational ritual recitation of the Naqshbandi Sufi Order, held at least once weekly.

[157] *Dharrāt*: the essences, or spiritual "atoms" of human beings.

[158] Instruction and direction in recitation, lit. "to put on the tongue."

carry each and every one of the Naqshbandis through to Judgment Day.

God, the Exalted, never rejects anyone who is asking for His blessings and forgiveness. The Prophet ﷺ was asking God, the Exalted, on behalf of all the Friends of God, that his teachings would pass on to this chain of transmission. ʿAbdul Khāliq al-Ghujdawānī ق was a crucial link in the chain, and his blessings are still with us today. Even though we cannot see or touch it, the blessings, *baraka,*[159]of the Friends of God is all around us. The traces of light they leave on their path shows us the way forward on a path we also wish to travel.

Sin Eraser

In short, when our level of *imān* diminishes, Satan's influence increases and many of our actions become unacceptable. Conversely, when our level of *imān* increases, we may repent, which helps restore both our *imān* and our good *ʿamal*. As the Prophet ﷺ said

الصلاة المكتوبة الى الصلاة التي قبلها كفارة لما بينهما ...

Between one obligatory prayer and the one that precedes it is forgiveness of sins...[160]

For example, if I pray Ẓuhr, the noontime prayer,[161] then commit sins and then go pray ʿAsr, God, the Exalted, will take the sins away. However, I am still on the same level, as though treading water between prayers. If I pray Ẓuhr and don't commit

[159] Arabic: *baraka*—blessings.

[160] Āḥmad's *Musnad*, al-Ḥākim and al-Bayhaqī in *Shuʿb al-Imān*. The stipulation is that the one observing prayers avoids three grave sins: *shirk* (idolatry), killing a Muslim, and leaving the path of the majority (*jamaʿah*).

[161] The five daily prayers are *Fajr* (predawn), *Ẓuhr* (Midday), *ʿAsr* (afternoon), *Maghrib* (sunset), and *ʿIshā*(night).

any sins, then my level is increasing, continuing on through the day. If I reach Maghrib without committing any more sins, then the level of *imān* has increased. I will get rewarded according to my level of *imān*.

We don't want to bring the level of our *imān* down: the time between prayers is *kaffārat adh-dhunūb.*[162] If you are not making sins, then your daily cycle of prayers will help you acquire *kashf,*[163] *ilhām,*[164] and all kinds of good energy will come to your heart. Prayers performed at intervals, without sins in between, have a way of building on one another, multiplying your blessings, as though your account with the Prophet ﷺ were accumulating dividends.

Consider, O Muslims, you do have such a heavenly account! It is real. It is your most important asset. Protect it and watch its balance grow, just as you would manage your bank account!

Wa min Allāhi 't-tawfiq, bi ḥurmati 'l-Fātiḥah.

---

[162] Arabic: *kaffārat adh-dhunūb*—atonement for sins.

[163] When spiritual veils are lifted; to experience illumination of the Unseen world.

[164] Arabic: *ilhām*—Divine inspiration sent to *awlīyāullah* while *wahīy* is divine revelation sent only to prophets and messengers.

9: Divine Focus

Skies of Fire

Allah ﷻ transmits wisdom though all aspects of his creation. Each thing in creation is arranged in the best way and carries its own wisdom. For example, a photographer will carefully focus his camera to get a sharp picture. Though life may often seem chaotic and confusing, everything really does have a point. If you can find the focal point, you can begin to see the meaning behind what God, the Exalted, has sent you.

This can be a powerful tool to sort through the blurry images we have stored in our memories by the end of a hectic day. The picture of our lives, the rushed minutes, the jumbled intentions and mixed reactions all need clarification. As the pictures come into focus, you will find yourself in a better position to cope with your personal circumstances and life's challenges.

God, the Exalted, wants us to find the point of balance within our lives and His creation, just as a cameraman has to aim his lens properly to get the picture. He doesn't aim at the floor or the ceiling: he needs to frame his subject and adjust the focus. God, the Exalted, constructed the human heart in such a way that each of our deeds has a special focus. Properly used, these points in our hearts can change any situation for the better. In this world there is something called the "center of gravity". If a thing becomes unbalanced and violates its center of gravity, it will tip over. If balance is maintained, nothing will fall down, and everything will be in order. God, the Exalted, established a focal point within the universe; without it, creation would disintegrate.

Examples of balanced centers of gravity are all around us. God, the Exalted, arranged the earth within a matrix of delicately balanced forces. Orbiting through space, the globe has a thin shell of stone enclosing a set of nested spheres of magma and molten iron. When volcanoes push their way through to the earth's surface, elements of fire lurking within the depths of the planet suddenly make themselves known. Some layers contain oil and drilling rigs across the planet extract this for fuel. Who put that oil there?

Below these layers of rock and oil lies melted stone that emerges during volcanic eruptions as lava. When this happens, the lava spreads and there is *hilam*, a huge fire that destroys everything in its path.

God, the Exalted, controls the balance of forces that holds the layers of earth intact. An erupting volcano shows what happens when one layer intrudes on another. If He wished, He could unleash all these forces and blow up the entire planet. The potential energy for such an event is clearly already there, held in check by a combination of gravity and fluid dynamics. God, the Exalted, could alter the focal point of the planet, rupture the surface layer, and send fire to the skies.

يَوْمَ تُبَدَّلُ الأَرْضُ غَيْرَ الأَرْضِ وَالسَّمَاوَاتُ وَبَرَزُواْ للّهِ الْوَاحِدِ الْقَهَّارِ

One day the earth will be changed to a different earth, and so will be the heavens, and (men) will be marshalled forth, before Allah, the One, the Irresistible; [165]

Is there another earth to where we will go? We must hope so, because this earth is going to blow up into pieces.

[165] Sūrah Ibrāhīm (Abraham), 14:48.

إِذَا زُلْزِلَتِ الْأَرْضُ زِلْزَالَهَا

When Earth is shaken with her (final) earthquakes[166]

Scientists and politicians are worried about nuclear war because it could destroy everything. Astronomers say that an asteroid could hit the earth and kill all living things. Consider then, that God, the Exalted, has the power to do this and He has said that one day it will happen. At any time He could unbalance the universe and bring it to an end. We must be aware of this possibility—it could happen at any time. Even if it doesn't happen in our time, it will happen eventually. When God, the Exalted, says something will happen, it will happen. If you are a believer, then do not sit on the side with the disbelievers. If you believe in Allah's ﷻ message, then you must believe that day is coming.

إِذَا السَّمَاء انفَطَرَتْ وَإِذَا الْكَوَاكِبُ انتَثَرَتْ وَإِذَا الْبِحَارُ فُجِّرَتْ وَإِذَا الْقُبُورُ بُعْثِرَتْ
عَلِمَتْ نَفْسٌ مَّا قَدَّمَتْ وَأَخَّرَتْ

When the Sky is cleft asunder; When the Stars are scattered; When the Oceans are suffered to burst forth; And when the Graves are turned upside down;- (Then) shall each soul know what it hath sent forward and (what it hath) kept back.[167]

If the skies explode or implode, what is going to happen to the earth? When the oceans are vaporized and the mountains are ground to dust, what will be left of the planet? Nothing! To be sure, that day is coming. In many ways, our physical, human systems are like the earth, always burning from within. That is why people are not at peace: there are things inside us that make

---

[166] Sūratu 'l-Zalzalah (the Earthquake), 99:1.
[167] Sūratu 'l-Infiṭār (the Cleaving Asunder), 82:1-5.

us burn as though we might explode at any moment. When tempers flare and rage erupts, we lose control. Failing to contain the turmoil within, our egos simply blow up.

While earth's final explosion will occur at some point, the explosion of our selves is happening at every moment. That is why people are not happy with what God, the Exalted, gave them. If they were happy they would be at peace.[168]

The Flock of Prophet Abraham

Consider Prophet Abraham عليه السلام and his flock. Grandshaykh ق relates:

> God, the Exalted, decided to make a caliph on earth. The angels wondered aloud why God, the Exalted, would establish a caliph for a race that would engage in bloodshed and corruption. "Humans," they said, "are not good."
>
> وَإِذْ قَالَ رَبُّكَ لِلْمَلاَئِكَةِ إِنِّي جَاعِلٌ فِي الأَرْضِ خَلِيفَةً قَالُواْ أَتَجْعَلُ فِيهَا مَن يُفْسِدُ
> فِيهَا وَيَسْفِكُ الدِّمَاء وَنَحْنُ نُسَبِّحُ بِحَمْدِكَ وَنُقَدِّسُ لَكَ قَالَ إِنِّي أَعْلَمُ مَا لاَ تَعْلَمُونَ
>
> *Behold, thy Lord said to the angels: "I will create a vicegerent on earth." They said: "Will You place therein one who will make mischief therein and shed blood?- whilst we do celebrate Your praises and glorify Your holy (Name)?" He said: "I know what you know not."*[169]
>
> God, the Exalted, asked, "Who told you that? I will show you one of My servants."

---

[168] This is the station of *an-nafs al-mutma'inna*, the contented, tranquil self.
[169] Sūratu 'l-Baqara (the Heifer), 2:30.

Here, God, the Exalted, is teaching us through the Holy Qur'an, and through his messengers. So He sent Gabriel 🖎 while all angels looked on.

Grandshaykh ق said:

God, the Exalted, sent Gabriel 🖎 in the form of a human being. He appeared before Prophet Abraham 🖎 and his son Ishmaell 🖎 while they tended their flocks of sheep, goats, camels, cows and all kinds of domestic animals. God, the Exalted, ordered the angels to listen in on the conversation between Prophet Abraham 🖎 and Archangel Gabriel 🖎. So Gabriel 🖎, in his disguised form, said, "O my brother, I see that you are very rich."

Even in those times, there was a distinction between the rich and the poor, and people—then as now—had to accept what God, the Exalted, had given them. If He gave you great wealth, *Alhamdūlillāh*, thanks be to God. If He didn't, *Alhamdūlillāh*, thanks be to God. That is the character of a Friend of God. We must try as much as we can to accept our circumstances.

So, *mā qussim ilayk hāsil ilayk*—what has been allocated to you, you will receive—no one will receive it other than you, so no one can take what is allocated specifically to you. Whatever is written about how many bites you will eat from this dish, you will eat exactly that amount, no more and no less. If it is written you will have this amount of wealth, you will get precisely that amount, no more and no less. When we reach *qana'a* satisfaction, we reach a state of peace within ourselves.

God, the Exalted, also sent Archangel Gabriel 🖎 to question Prophet Abraham's 🖎 right to such wealth, and to take it from him.

The angel said, "What is this; is this all for you?"

Prophet Abraham 🖎 replied, "Yes, Allah gave it to me."

The angel said, "It is too much!"

Prophet Abraham ﷺ answered, "Do you want some of this flock?" The angel said, "Yes." Prophet Abraham ﷺ "then say:

سُبوحٌ قُدوسٌ رَبُّ المَلائِكَةِ وَ الرُوح

"Subūḥun quddūs, rabbu 'l-malā'ikati wa 'r-rūḥ."

The angel said, *"Subūḥun quddūs, rabbu 'l-malā'ikati wa 'r-rūḥ.* Glory to Allah, the Most Pure, creator of the angels and the Holy Spirit! How many animals from your flock will you give me?"

Prophet Abraham ﷺ answered, "Don't ask; say it and I will give whatever you request. Oh my brother, I will give you one-third."

"Why do you want to give me one-third? Did you count them?" the angel asked, complaining and bargaining even though he had been promised a third of the flock. "I need exactly one-third."

Prophet Abraham ﷺ replied, "Yes I will count and give you one-third, or if you want more, I will give more."

"Yes, I want more," the angel said.

Then Prophet Abraham ﷺ said, *"Subūḥun quddūs, rabbu 'l-malā'ikati wa 'r-rūḥ*— Glory to Allah, the Most Pure, creator of the angels and the Holy Spirit!"

The angels witnessed and Allah was pleased, because before that they were complaining.

Praising Allah, Prophet Abraham ﷺ said, "O my brother, now I am giving you the second third."

"But still you have a lot," the angel answered.

"Do you want them all?" asked Prophet Abraham ﷺ.

"Why not?" the angel answered, "Say: *Subūḥun quddūs, rabbu 'l-malā'ikati wa 'r-rūḥ*." He motioned towards the flock saying, "Look, all of this is yours. Come my son, we will leave now."

Gabriel عليه السلام is an angel and doesn't need a flock of sheep. What would he do with it?

He said, "O Prophet Abraham عليه السلام, come here. What will I do with all these animals?"

"What you do with them is up to you," Prophet Abraham عليه السلام said. "Are you playing games? These three verses are enough for me. You think I don't know you are Gabriel? Before you came I knew you were coming."

How did he know? Because the eyes of his heart were open. Prophet Abraham عليه السلام had a balanced system. There was no fire within, no eruption of the volcano of the self. He had reached the place of peace within himself.

God, the Exalted, said: "*Yā* Gabriel عليه السلام, leave them, My saints will take care of them."

Then Grandshaykh ق said that these animals have all been sent to a place behind Mount Qāf[170] and will remain there until the time of Imam Mahdi عليه السلام. They are still reproducing and thus you cannot imagine how large the flock has become.

Prophet Abraham عليه السلام said, "Don't worry about this flock; I have put them in trust for Mecca, Madinah, and Shām."

Grandshaykh ق said:

Whenever there is a shortage of domestic animals on earth, God, the Exalted, orders jinns to take some of these animals from behind Qāf Mountain and feed humanity.

---

[170] Jabal Qāf—a vast mountain existing outside the realm of this worldly life.

Imagine then, how great is the *baraka* of the Prophet ﷺ! He is not just giving us meat for our tables, he is giving us spiritual meat that will give us sustenance that can help our bodies and souls live forever.

Love of Wealth Binds our Hands

In this story, God, the Exalted, is showing us an example of someone who doesn't have any problem with what God, the Exalted, has given him, whether of wealth or of poverty. He gave it *fī sabīlillāh*—for Allah's sake. He said, "Whatever you are, I took my rights, these three verses."

Who gives his wealth today for that phrase: *Subūḥun quddūs, rabbu 'l-malā'ikati wa 'r-rūḥ*?

You see how far we are from reality. We cannot give except when our faith is strong. At that level you would give everything you owned, because at that point you realize whatever you own God, the Exalted, has given it you. You don't control your possessions, He does. Why not give it all away in His Name if the situation arises? We generally don't rise to the occasion, because at any time, Satan can whisper in your ear, "You have this and you have that, so why are you giving everything away?"

You begin to hold your hand back. When this happens, know that your faith is dropping. This is happening everywhere. Doubts press in all around us like the instruments of body piercing. Today, you see men everywhere with earrings, nose rings and tongues pierced. These pieces of metal are like the stabbing doubts that Satan put in our hearts concerning the actions of our shaykhs.

Shaykhhood is not a title you give yourself, or that someone can give you. That title can only be given by order of the Prophet ﷺ. Only the authorized Grandshaykh ق or shaykh knows when that title has been granted. When that title has been given, no one can take it away. Whether it is the title of shaykh, caliph, Friend of God—it is all the same. Only the Prophet ﷺ gives such titles. The full embodiment of these titles has meaning only when it comes from the line of the Prophet ﷺ.

So when that person is given the title of shaykh, don't object when he does things you don't understand. You are not balanced, and he is. You have fire seething within you, ready to erupt at moment when your normal equilibrium is disturbed. Satan will whisper doubts in your ear. Resist him and say, "I don't know. I must not harbor any doubts concerning my shaykh." When you begin to doubt your teacher, you invite a world of problems.

Mawlana Shaykh's Photographic Memory

Mawlana Shaykh spoke only two lines and from this the whole *suhbat* emerged, which he wrote from memory. One time Grandshaykh ق made *du'a,* invocation, for Shaykh Nazim, that God, the Exalted, would grant him an unfailing memory. So after *Ṣalāt al-'Isha,* when Mawlana Shaykh Nazim went home, he used to sit and write from memory the entire teachings of the day, and he would not miss one word.

Grandshaykh related that in the Diwān al-Awlīyā:[171]

> I asked the Prophet, *"Yā Rasūlullāh,* my son Nazim Effendi yesterday asked me, since he is writing down every *suhbat* and he is sometimes missing something, he is requesting your *du'a* that he be able to write everything."
>
> So from that time, Shaykh Nazim never needed to bring a notebook to write in. He would only listen to the *suhbat* that I am giving.

I never saw someone like Grandshaykh. When he speaks, it is not half an hour and not one hour but it is two or three hours.

---

[171] Arabic: *Diwān al-Awlīyā*—the gathering of saints with the Prophet in the spiritual dimension. This takes place every night.

And if a new guest comes he continues talking for that new guest another two or thee hours. From morning to ‘Isha, his words were coming like a fountain.

And from that time, after sitting with Grandshaykh all the day, Shaykh Nazim never needed a notebook. Instead, he would go home at night and then sit and write in his notebook. He was able to transfer everything that Grandshaykh had said to paper, not missing one dot and not missing one comma.

And Shaykh Jibrīl[172] has noticed I am sure, the small notebooks in Mawlana Shaykh's house in Damascus, in Turkish and Arabic. These are the ones that Mawlana Shaykh wrote after he went back home at night, not missing one point, one period or one comma.

Wa min Allāhi 't-tawfīq, bi ḥurmati 'l-Fātiḥah.

[172] Shaykh Hisham is addressing Dr. Gibril Fouad Haddad, a scholar of hadith, who lived for many years in Shaykh Nazim's home in Damascus.

10: THIS WORLD IS A TOY

The Earthly Comedy

This *suhbat* was given on Friday, 17 Safar 1392 Hijri. May Allah bless his soul, Grandshaykh ق said, "This world in which we find ourselves is merely a toy."

In and of itself, this world has no meaning. Watch how children play with their toys! You can learn much about yourself from just watching them play. As much as you love this world, so you are fascinated with that toy. Girls play with dolls, and boys play with cars.

Mawlana is telling us that our relationship to this world resembles that of a child to his playthings. You play and play until the toy is broken, then you throw it away.

He said:

> this world is a *maskhara*—a joke. To Friends of God, this world is a joke. What is important to them is the Divine Presence: this world has no meaning. The Friends of God define themselves based on their orientation to the Prophet ﷺ and the Divine Presence.
>
> This poses an interesting question: why did Allah create this world? *Mā annahu la aṣla lahā.* Although it has a lesser reality, like a toy—nevertheless, He created it and gave it to us. This gift, is from *Ata'ullāh,* Allah's Divine Grants,[173] and cannot be understood in ordinary, earthly terms. *Ata'ullāh* has no limits. What Allah grants you is not directly related to what you

---

[173] Arabic: *Ata'ullāh,* Allah's Divine Grants.

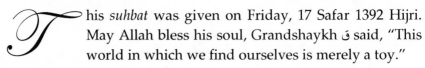

achieve in this world, because this world is like a toy, a joke. You don't take a toy from a child and give him diamonds in exchange. However, God, the Exalted, gives us diamonds, regardless of our apparent situation in *dunyā*, this world, this land of toys. His favors are endless. He gives us things so high that we cannot even imagine them. Despite that, we remain like children, playing with this world's toys.

Grandshaykh ق said:

The special prayers of the Friends of God, the *munājāt*, are never rejected, especially those performed in Ṣalāt an-Najat before Fajr. Because of their *du'a*s—Friends of God in general and especially those of the nine chief Friends of God of the Naqshbandi Sufi Order—special benefits are granted to us. By virtue of their prayers, all of us who follow the shaykhs of the Golden Chain will be brought directly to Paradise in the line behind the prophets. Followers from the time of the Prophet ﷺ to Grandshaykh ق and Shaykh Nazim, will be resurrected and brought into Paradise in Jannat al-Firdaus.[174]

وَمَن يُطِعِ اللّهَ وَالرَّسُولَ فَأُوْلَـئِكَ مَعَ الَّذِينَ أَنْعَمَ اللّهُ عَلَيْهِم مِّنَ النَّبِيِّينَ وَالصِّدِّيقِينَ

وَالشُّهَدَاء وَالصَّالِحِينَ وَحَسُنَ أُولَـئِكَ رَفِيقًا

All who obey Allah and the apostle are in the company of those on whom is the Grace of Allah,- of the prophets (who teach), the sincere (lovers of Truth), the witnesses (who testify), and the Righteous (who do good): Ah! what a beautiful fellowship![175]

---

[174] Jannat al-Firdaus: the highest heaven in Paradise.
[175] Sūratu 'n-Nisā (Women), 4:69.

Followers of the Naqshbandi Golden Chain[176] will find themselves in the line of the Prophet ﷺ, who will represent them to the Divine Presence. Grandshaykh ق said that has been given to us because of their *du'as*, not because of our achievements. We have been granted this gift, even though we continue to be fascinated with the toys of this world. We hold the toys tightly in our hands, and become upset when they are taken from us.

مِنَ الْمُؤْمِنِينَ رِجَالٌ صَدَقُوا مَا عَاهَدُوا اللَّهَ عَلَيْهِ فَمِنْهُم مَّن قَضَى نَحْبَهُ وَمِنْهُم مَّن يَنتَظِرُ وَمَا بَدَّلُوا تَبْدِيلًا

Among the Believers are men who have been true to their covenant with Allah. of them some have completed their vow (to the extreme), and some (still) wait: but they have never changed (their determination) in the least: [177]

God, the Exalted, sends some Friends of God honor and wealth, because they endured suffering and great difficulties in their lives and will always keep their covenant with their Lord. They never changed. God, the Exalted, looks beyond our outward behavior through to our hearts. He gives according to what He sees there. A Friend of God or a even a prophet might appear to others as a normal person, but he is simply hiding himself.

Grandshaykh ق often said he had to treat his family in an ordinary manner, because they would not understand *wilāyah.*[178] He sat with them, played with them, ate with them, because that is the way of Islam. The Prophet ﷺ spent much time with his family, and in particular, with his blessed daughter Fāṭima az-

---

[176] Going back to Sayyidina Abū Bakr ؓ, the chain of succession from one saint to the next, reaching the current leader of the Order.

[177] Sūratu 'l-Aḥzāb (the Confederates), 33:23.

[178] Arabic: *wilāyah*—sainthood.

Zahrā ﷺ, taking her to the Ka'bah. His lifelong relationship with her emphasizes the connection and relationship between father and daughter. No one questioned this; the Companions didn't complain that the Prophet ﷺ took Fāṭima az-Zahrā ﷺ with him everywhere.

That is why Grandshaykh ق warned us, don't question the behavior of a Friend of God and complain if he gives more attention to his wife and family than to you, for you are merely the student. A false sense of familiarity with a Friend of God can burn you, diminish your faith, and raise too many counter-productive questions in your mind.

Awlīyāullāh operate on an entirely different level than the rest of us. The range of their experiences and perceptions are not ours: their beings, while human, are considerably more developed than ours. Though we all live in the same ocean of air, they take in different nourishment with each breath. Through the grace of God, the Exalted, they absorb and refine impressions and experiences in an utterly different way from ordinary people. Therefore, beware, and do not equate your motives and intentions with theirs; do not presume to understand them all the time. In short, they are not your peers.

The Companions understood this, and never questioned the actions of the Prophet ﷺ. They accepted the fact that his family took up a great deal of his time. Sometimes when he would pray, his grandsons, Sayyidina al-Hasan and Sayyidina al-Husayn ﷺ would jump on his back and he would lengthen his *sajda*, prostration until they got off to avoid disturbing their play. Other times they would jump on his lap while he was talking to the Companions. In this, he demonstrated the *hikmah*, or wisdom, of maintaining family ties: a prime element in Islam and a test for all of us.

Be careful when approaching Friends of God! Check your intentions first! You may not understand all that you observe.

Approach the Sultan cautiously, as you would approach a roaring fire. That is why the Prophet ﷺ said that a prayer in Mecca carries one hundred thousands times the weight of prayers offered elsewhere, and sins weigh down even more. There, even bad inspirations will be written against you. Outside Mecca and Madinah, bad inspirations are not written as sins, but in these two sanctuaries they are. This is because in the two holy cities intentions and motives are amplified. Friends of God have that *karamah,* specialty, as well: a certain aura surrounds them. As God's servants they are, in a sense, extensions of His Divine Will. As such, our conduct in their presence, both internal and external, takes on a special significance. In this intense light, we become temporarily transparent. In a strange way, the presence of a Friend of God tests us in the very moments when our spiritual potential is being measured—all the more reason to guard our tongues and hearts during such an encounter.

The Divine Oath

On an even larger scale, God, the Exalted, brings Adam عليه السلام and all his offspring into His Divine Presence and asks them if He is their Lord. Given the impact of His glory and radiance, everyone agrees in that moment that He is, indeed, their Lord. But when we leave the Divine Presence and enter this world, we forget. This is our great tragedy—the very signature of the mortal dilemma. In that moment we are pure, washed clean, bathed in an ocean of Divine Light and Mercy. In such a magnificent court, who would not eagerly agree that the King, seated in all his glory, was their ruler? And yet, with exile to this world comes forgetfulness. Close on the heels of forgetfulness comes heedlessness. Something deep within our natures longs for the sleep of the world. We become hypnotized by the sights and sounds of the earth. Like children in a toy shop, we run after the toys of this world.

The Friends of God remind us of our true natures. They carry the secret of the audience we once had in the Divine Presence.

They know that Allah's ﷻ Mercy encompassed us and dressed us in that moment. If we acknowledge the authority of the Friends of God, we can begin to reconnect to that all-important moment when we stood before God, the Exalted. This is a mercy in and of itself. When a guide offers his help, our heedlessness can be reversed—the ladder back to heaven stands before us.

وَمَا كَانَ عَطَاءُ رَبِّكَ مَحْظُورًا

The bounties of thy Lord are not closed (to anyone).[179]

What God, the Exalted, gives is limitless, without bounds and unending. He is always giving. We were dressed in His Divine Presence with certain attributes which may, in some way, provide the key to our fulfillment, our journey, our fate—our very connection to Him.

His servants carry this knowledge and stand as sentinels on the path of return.

The Three Idolatries

إِنَّ اللَّهَ لاَ يَغْفِرُ أَن يُشْرَكَ بِهِ وَيَغْفِرُ مَا دُونَ ذَلِكَ لِمَن يَشَاءُ وَمَن يُشْرِكْ بِاللَّهِ فَقَدِ افْتَرَى إِثْمًا عَظِيمًا

Allah forgives not that partners should be set up with Him; but He forgives anything else, to whom He pleases; to set up partners with Allah is to devise a sin most heinous indeed.[180]

While God, the Exalted, is merciful and forgives many things, He does not like anyone to make *shirk* with Him. Other than that,

[179] Sūratu 'l-Isrā (the Night Journey), 17:20.
[180] Sūratu 'n-Nisā (Women), 4:48.

God, the Exalted, grants you everything. He dressed us with that unlimited mercy.

There are three different kinds of *shirk*: *akbar*—greater, *awsaṭ* intermediate, and *khafī*—hidden.[181] Consider the least, which is the hidden *shirk*. An example of this is when someone begins with every intention of praying to God, the Exalted, but changes slightly when he sees someone approaching. His intention shifts ever so slightly and he perfects his prayer more for show than for God, the Exalted. Perhaps he begins moving his head up and down like a chicken, exaggerating his display of piety. This change in focus transfers the object of the prayers away from God, the Exalted. That is hidden *shirk*. Satan comes quickly. He is clever and can trick you into making your prayers a performance for others to see. Does this mean your audience is more important than God, the Exalted? This is hidden *shirk*, but it is forgivable.

There is a second type of *shirk*, the intermediate *shirk*, which is also forgivable. An example is when you go to the mosque in order to show people you are praying, but when there is no one there, you don't pray. That is intentional *rīyā*, a more serious kind of showing off.

The third *shirk*, the greater one, which is not forgivable, is of itself of three classes. The first is the case in which you believe there is a Creator, but you don't care. You say to God, the Exalted, "I know You are there, but I am not going to pray to You."

This is the first level of *shirk*. The second level of *shikr* is to associate someone with God, the Exalted. The third level of *shirk* is to hold someone as a son of God. This goes beyond merely associating someone with God, but virtually equates that person with Allah.

---

[181] Arabic: *shirk akbar* the greater idolatry, *shirk awsaṭ*, the middle and *shirk khafī*, the hidden idolatry.

Allah forgives *awsaṭ* and *khafī*. However the three kinds of *shirk* go with you to the grave. You die with them, and there is no forgiveness.

The *rīyā* and intentional *rīyā*, whereby you prayed for affect or began to show off, can be easily forgiven according to the verse:

قُلْ يَا عِبَادِيَ الَّذِينَ أَسْرَفُوا عَلَى أَنفُسِهِمْ لَا تَقْنَطُوا مِن رَّحْمَةِ اللَّهِ إِنَّ اللَّهَ يَغْفِرُ
الذُّنُوبَ جَمِيعًا إِنَّهُ هُوَ الْغَفُورُ الرَّحِيمُ

Say: "O my Servants who have transgressed against their souls! Despair not of the Mercy of Allah. For Allah forgives all sins: for He is Oft-Forgiving, Most Merciful.[182]

But the third is far more serious. If you insist on committing *shirk*, God, the Exalted, will throw you away. This error can manifest in many different ways, particularly when a theme emerges in someone's life that, perhaps unnoticed, gradually supplants the love of God, the Exalted, for something else.

Consider the miser who loves gold, the intellectual who treasures his learning, the artist who is fascinated by his over-refined sensibilities, the model who is obsessed with her own beauty, or the ruler who worships only his power. Over the course of a lifetime, all these are passions spent at great spiritual and emotional cost.

Furthermore, if any of us ordinary people were to examine what occupies our thoughts from moment to moment on any given day, it would probably not reveal any sort of coherent spiritual awareness. Our minds flit from one thing to the next, unsteadily drifting about, more or less depending on the outside scenery and whether lunch agreed with us or not. Compare that to

---

[182] Sūratu 'z-Zumar (the Groups), 39:53.

the saints, who reportedly feel guilty when they forget God, the Exalted, even for an instant! Observe carefully, and you will see that this *shirk* hits close to home. It can come in many forms and degrees, and divert you at any moment.

God, the Exalted, sent messengers and prophets to this world. In turn, the Friends of God inherited the knowledge of the prophets. Because of their prayers, we are granted many blessings in spite of our attachment to the toys of this world. Though we are exiled to this world, we must accept God, the Exalted, and not leave our prayers. Don't be like the people who say they like "diet Islam" or "Islam lite." They say, "Don't ask me to pray or to fast!" That is not Islam, it is only a name without a form.

Grandshaykh ق said that God, the Exalted, will grant the students of the Friends of God endless mercy and Divine manifestations, *tajallīyāt.*[183] That is why it is important to have a guide who will show you how to cross the desert, not on a camel, but on a rocket. He knows the way around the jagged peaks and blowing sandstorms.

When the Prophet ﷺ migrated from Mecca to Madinah with Sayyidina Abū Bakr ؓ, he took a guide. Of course, considering he was the Messenger of God ﷺ, the Exalted, he needed no guide. But, as an object lesson for all of us, the story of his journey emphasizes that we all need a guide in the desert. The guide knows where the sandstorms scour the landscape and the scorpions lie in wait. Friends of God can guide us safely across the desert.

May Allah bless you.

Wa min Allāhi 't-tawfiq, bi ḥurmati 'l-Fātiḥah.

---

[183] Arabic: *Tajallīyāt*—Plural of *tajallī*; Divine manifestations.

11: Reflections

Vital Signs

Each day God, the Exalted, reveals different manifestations of His Attributes to the Prophet ﷺ. Mawlana has posed the question: what is the importance of *rizq*—sustenance?[184]

Sustenance is important; it can maintain your energy level and give you the power to move forward to the next stage. There are two kinds of sustenance: *ẓāhirī,* physical, and *maʿnawī,* spiritual. The spiritual energy is part of what God, the Exalted, is sending to His Prophet ﷺ which, in turn, flows from the Prophet ﷺ out to everyone. This spiritual provision is the more important of the two. It will last forever, while the physical kind has a limited number of days. God, the Exalted, measures out physical lifetimes not in years, but in breaths.

فَلَا تَعْجَلْ عَلَيْهِمْ إِنَّمَا نَعُدُّ لَهُمْ عَدًّا

So make no haste against them, for We but count out to them a (limited) number.[185]

Everything connected with our lives is counted in breaths, coming in and going out. Our last breath will go out, but not back in.

On the other hand, spiritual respiration continues after our physical deaths, because God, the Exalted, doesn't want us to stop

---

[184] Our sustenance, ordained by Allah.

[185] Sūrah Maryam, (the Virgin Mary), 19:84.

breathing in the life-giving nourishment of spiritual "oxygen". When it goes out, it means that you are losing the energy of that breath; that is the time Satan is playing with you. At that time your *imān*, faith, will drop.

Picture a special barometer that could graph your spiritual state as measured in breaths. You would see a line wandering up and down across the chart. It goes up when you inhale, then drops sharply when you exhale. Indeed, measured in spiritual terms, the very breath of life is a good index of our spiritual states. Up and down, in and out: we gain and lose energy, remembering and forgetting God, the Exalted, with the rapid cycle of our breathing. In some regard, we gain a reflection of the Divine Names and Attributes when we inhale, and lose it when we exhale. This limiting cycle is a perfect example of our inconstant natures.

In contrast to our varying natures and states, if you could look at a chart of a Friend of God's spiritual state, the line would always be going up. They do not lose energy each time they exhale. They retain the light of the reflection of the Divine Names they have inhaled, and grow in a special way that ordinary people do not experience and science has yet to discover. Their metabolisms operate on a completely different level from ours. In a word, nothing is lost on them. Their lives' moments and breaths do not slip away from them in a blur of confusion and forgetfulness. The moments of our lives drift in and out of focus because we lack the unifying constant of the remembrance of God, the Exalted. Friends of God, to varying degrees, can hold the light of the Divine Names within themselves and, over a lifetime, they become transformed beings.

Classes of Saints

There are five special classes of saints: Budalā, Nujabā, Nuqabā, Awtād, and Akhyār.[186] Among these, the Budala are those that God, the Exalted, created as Substitutes, and the Prophet ﷺ mentioned them in a hadith:

عن عتبة بن غزوان عن النبي صلى الله عليه وسلم قال :إذا أضل احدكم شيئا أو أراد عونا و هو بأرض ليس بها أنيس فليقل يا عباد الله أعينوني

The Prophet (s) said: "If one of you loses something or needs help and he is in a deserted land with not companion, let him say: "O servants of Allah, help me! (Yā ʿibādullāh aʿīnunī)."[187]

These are the Budala. He said that they were given a need for food, because God, the Exalted, wants to show them *ʿajz*—helplessness and dependency.[188] He wants them to remember that they are human beings who possess human weaknesses. Only prophets have no weakness: they are *mʿaṣūm*, protected from sin. The Friends of God are *mahfūẓ*[189]—preserved from sin. They are in need of food only two times a year, they don't need food every day. God, the Exalted, sends the Friends of God food two times a year and it is enough for them. And what is the nature of this food? It is heavenly food. For example, when Prophet Jesus عليه السلام asked:

إِذْ قَالَ الْحَوَارِيُّونَ يَا عِيسَى ابْنَ مَرْيَمَ هَلْ يَسْتَطِيعُ رَبُّكَ أَن يُنَزِّلَ عَلَيْنَا مَآئِدَةً مِّنَ السَّمَاء قَالَ اتَّقُواْ اللّهَ إِن كُنتُم مُّؤْمِنِينَ قَالُواْ نُرِيدُ أَن نَّأْكُلَ مِنْهَا وَتَطْمَئِنَّ قُلُوبُنَا وَنَعْلَمَ

---

[186] Different groups of saints.

[187] Ṭabarānī, and similar narrations are related by Ibn as-Sanī, Abū Yaʿla, and Nawawī.

[188] Inability to obtain what is sought.

[189] Preserved.

أَن قَدْ صَدَقْتَنَا وَنَكُونَ عَلَيْهَا مِنَ قَالَ عِيسَى ابْنُ مَرْيَمَ اللَّهُمَّ رَبَّنَا أَنزِلْ عَلَيْنَا مَآئِدَةً
مِّنَ السَّمَاء تَكُونُ لَنَا عِيداً لِّأَوَّلِنَا وَآخِرِنَا وَآيَةً مِّنكَ وَارْزُقْنَا وَأَنتَ خَيْرُ الرَّازِقِينَ
قَالَ اللّهُ إِنِّي مُنَزِّلُهَا عَلَيْكُمْ فَمَن يَكْفُرْ بَعْدُ مِنكُمْ فَإِنِّي أُعَذِّبُهُ عَذَابًا لاَّ أُعَذِّبُهُ
أَحَدًا مِّنَ الْعَالَمِينَ

Behold! The disciples, said: "O Jesus, the son of Mary! Can your Lord send down to us a table set (with viands) from heaven?" Said Jesus: "Fear Allah, if you have faith." They said: "We only wish to eat thereof and satisfy our hearts, and to know that you have indeed told us the truth; and that we ourselves may be witnesses to the miracle." Said Jesus, the son of Mary: "O Allah, our Lord! Send us from heaven a table set (with viands), that there may be for us—for the first and the last of us—a solemn festival and a sign from You; and provide for our sustenance, for You are the best Sustainer (of our needs)." Allah said: "I will send it down unto you, but if any of you after that resists faith, I will punish him with a penalty such as I have not inflicted on anyone among all the peoples." [190]

His students said to Prophet Jesus عليه السلام, "Can Allah send us a table of food?"

He replied, "*Ittaqullāh*—Fear God! Don't ask that! Don't you think that Allah can send that?"

They said, "We want it to be an Eid for our first and our last."

---

[190] Sūratu 'l-Mā'idah (the Table Spread), 5:112-115.

> He said, "O my Lord! Send us down a table from heavens."
>
> Allah said, "On one condition. I will send that table, but anyone disobeys Me after that should be in fear of his destruction."

This is because, when God, the Exalted, sends the proof of His message by such a miracle, you can no longer disobey. You must follow.

When God, the Exalted, sends Friends of God a heavenly table, they know where it came from, and value its contents. And what is that food? It is fish. He didn't say meat. He said "fish" because fish lives in the ocean.

This means, "I am sending you the secret of the oceans of the Beautiful Names and Attributes. Each Beautiful Name is an ocean, and I am sending to you things from that ocean of knowledge." This is the inner interpretation of the meaning of what Mawlana is saying. Fish do not make the heart hard. Meat makes the heart hard.

That is why the Prophet ﷺ was not eating meat every day, as they do now. That makes for a certain hardness of the heart, and causes harshness and difficulties between people today. Even among brothers and sisters, husbands and wives, it seems there are always problems.

God, the Exalted, sent them fish, an indication that He wanted them to have a soft food. He sends them this nourishment twice a year and it is enough to keep them the entire year. This is the nature of the spiritual knowledge that Allah gives to the Friends of God.

The Dance of Light

Friends of God receive these spiritual manifestations from the Prophet ﷺ. How does it reach them and what is the manner of this transmission? There are two factors to consider in this process: the *ʿaqis* and *al-maʿqūs*: the reflector and the one upon whom the light is reflected.

When light circulates, it flows from one object to the next. From the source it flows onto the reflector initially, glances off that object and flies off in another direction. It has to go somewhere. It cannot be traveling endlessly in space. There must be a target for the light or there would have been no purpose for the reflector to reflect. So it is within the solar system. The sun originates the flow of light, and the moon reflects some of that light back towards earth.

This is an example of the workings of *ḍīyā*—the source of illumination. The sun is a huge nuclear furnace that generates light and heat both within and above its surface. In a complex dance of magnetic loops of superheated plasma, temperatures are generated that far exceed the surface of the star. Here the Beautiful Names and Attributes react with one another combining all these different kinds of energy to produce and radiate light across the orbiting planets. The moon catches some of this light, and brightens the night skies on earth.

Just as the physical engines of the sun supply all light and warmth for our lives, so the Beautiful Names and Attributes stream forth from the door of creation and blend in harmony to sustain and raise creation. It is here that the Prophet ﷺ serves as the primary reflector for all of creation. As He holds this all-important position in the flow of Divine Light, He directs the flow out to those who are waiting for it, reaching the different Friends of God, each according to his level.

That is why he said in a very important *hadith:*

عن أبي هريرة،عن رسول اللّه صلى اللّه عليه وسلم قال: "المؤمن مرآة المؤمن

"The mu'min, believer, is the mirror of the believer."[191]

The believer always reflects what is shining on him to his brother, and when it is reflected, that believer becomes a mirror to the other. Friends of God use that system to reach their followers through a dynamic network of reflections. This explains how a Friend of God has the power to reach his followers everywhere even though they don't meet physically.

Clearly, this sort of transmission and reflection is of a higher order than the simpler optical physics of mirrors and light rays. This kind light literally moves from heart to heart in the form of dreams and visions. It is consciously directed—it informs—it is alive—it transcends time and space. Many people feel that someone is reaching out to them, often appearing as a guide who can lead them on the right path. Such messages can vary from the subtlest of impressions to the most direct and vivid contacts. But they all share a common origin: the light sent to humanity from the Prophet ﷺ as he reflects the original stream of light.

Friends of God become the secondary mirrors for the light that the Prophet ﷺ sends. That is why we say in *tasawwuf*, Sufism, it is said that when God, the Exalted, wants to see Himself, He looks to the Prophet ﷺ. God, the Exalted, sees the reflection of His Beautiful Names and Attributes in His perfect mirror. He looks to the mirror he created and it is nothing less than the Seal of the Messengers ﷺ, whose job is to transmit the essence of reflection out into Allah's creation.

If you align two mirrors directly opposite one another and stand between them, you will see yourself hundreds of times. Your image is multiplied to infinity.

---

[191] Abū Dāwūd, 4918.

Friends of God reflect this knowledge to humanity and everyone becomes *ʿaqis* and *maʿqūs*, reflectors and receivers of reflections.

We are now in a state of heedlessness. God, the Exalted, gives us the hours, minutes and seconds of our lives; we must not waste them. We should learn to be highly polished mirrors so that we can properly receive and reflect the light that is sent our way. This special kind of light needs to circulate. It does not want to stop at a dead-end. If you receive light and fail to properly reflect it on your brothers and sisters, then you have wasted it by blocking its continued movement. This energy is meant to propagate in a chain reaction, rippling throughout humanity, building in strength and enlightening those who can accept it.

Clean Your Mirror

Friends of God are given mirrors for each of their followers. Each one is polished differently. It all depends on how much the student is able to receive. If the surface of the heart is marred, the reflection will be blurry, milky and opaque. Smooth off the rough edges of your heart. Be kind and gentle with people, even when you are under stress. When you stand before your shaykh, the reflections connect all the way up to the Prophet ﷺ. Polish your mirror in order to hold these reflections. Keep good manners and make *wuḍū*, ablution! Make more and more ablution! When you lose ablution immediately make new ablution! Even if you have *wuḍū*, make a new *wuḍū* before praying. It is "*Nūrun ʿalā nūr—Divine Light upon Divine Light*" as Allah said:

وَالْأَرْضِ مَثَلُ نُورِهِ كَمِشْكَاةٍ فِيهَا مِصْبَاحٌ الْمِصْبَاحُ فِي زُجَاجَةٍ الزُّجَاجَةُ كَأَنَّهَا

كَوْكَبٌ دُرِّيٌّ يُوقَدُ مِن شَجَرَةٍ مُّبَارَكَةٍ زَيْتُونَةٍ لَّا شَرْقِيَّةٍ وَلَا غَرْبِيَّةٍ يَكَادُ زَيْتُهَا يُضِيءُ

وَلَوْ لَمْ تَمْسَسْهُ نَارٌ نُورٌ عَلَى نُورٍ يَهْدِي اللَّهُ لِنُورِهِ مَنْ يَشَاءُ وَيَضْرِبُ اللَّهُ الْأَمْثَالَ

لِلنَّاسِ وَاللَّهُ بِكُلِّ شَيْءٍ عَلِيمٌ

Allah is the Light of the heavens and the earth. The Parable of His Light is as if there were a Niche and within it a Lamp: the Lamp enclosed in Glass: the glass as it were a brilliant star: Lit from a blessed Tree, an Olive, neither of the east nor of the west, whose oil is well-nigh luminous, though fire scarce touched it: Light upon Light! Allah doth guide whom He will to His Light: Allah doth set forth Parables for men: and Allah doth know all things.[192]

Here God, the Exalted, states that He is the light of heavens and earth. His light is like an array of lamps. He wants us to understand that when you reflect light, it becomes light upon light. This is why the Prophet ﷺ said,

قَالَ رَسُولُ اللَّهِ صلى الله عليه وسلم " أَنْتُمُ الْغُرُّ الْمُحَجَّلُونَ يَوْمَ الْقِيَامَةِ مِنْ اِسْبَاغِ الْوُضُوءِ فَمَنِ اسْتَطَاعَ مِنْكُمْ فَلْيُطِلْ غُرَّتَهُ وَتَحْجِيلَهُ "

"On Judgment Day there will be people, muraqaṭīn, *who will have two-colored skin,"*

Muraqaṭīn[193] means just like the camouflage fatigues that soldiers wear with green and brown patterns.

On Judgment Day there will be a group of people who will display different colors. People will wonder, who are these special ones with the spots of different colors? God, the Exalted, will grant this group high respect. These are the ones who kept their ablution, and performed ablution over

[192] Sūratu 'n-Nūr (the Light), 24:35.
[193] Arabic: *muraqaṭūn*—spotted, speckled.

ablution. And wherever the water reaches, it will become like light: light from hands; from face; from ears; from feet. He calls these people the *muraqaṭūn*, the spotted ones. So ablution is "*nūrun ʿalā nūr*—Light upon light."

This is a very direct way to clean your mirror, and achieve a high level of reflectivity. Friends of God can send light to such an individual and know it will not be wasted.

Keep your ablution and when you lose it, rush to make it fresh again. If you can do this, God, the Exalted, will count you among the *muraqaṭūn* and make your heart a mirror that can receive the light and reflect it across great distances. Try to keep your mirror clean! May God, the Exalted, let us benefit from this kind of knowledge. May we follow in the footsteps and of the Prophet ﷺ and the Friends of God.

Wa min Allāhi 't-tawfīq, bi ḥurmati 'l-Fātiḥah.

12: Characteristics of the Friends of God

First Characteristic

The first quality of Friends of God is, they know how to judge people based on their inner condition rather than merely on their outer appearance. Think how often we ordinary people dismiss someone as unworthy of our attention or friendship based on how he or she looks.

God, the Exalted, has sent Prophet Muhammad ﷺ as a mercy for all of humanity. As such, every person on earth has a share of that mercy. We must all respect one another, both for the drops of mercy within ourselves and within others, because these drops are reflections of the light of Sayyidina Muhammad ﷺ and he directly reflects the light of the Beautiful Names and Attributes of God, the Exalted.

Anyone can make mistakes. No one is *mʿaṣūm*, perfect, except the prophets. Friends of God have this understanding, but since they are not *mʿaṣūm*, occasionally they may look into something that is of no concern to them.

Friends of God can have many different levels of development. Some manifest al-Wakīl, the Trustee[194] the one who is al-Walee, the Friend, like a trusted lawyer who can represent your best interest. In certain cases, you may even grant a power of attorney to someone who you particularly trust. Depending on which country you are in, and what the circumstances may be,

---

[194] Al-Wakīl is one of Allah's Beautiful Names and Attributes.

you can give someone a restricted, private or general power of attorney.

The private kind is granted when you want a specific issue resolved. If you are granting a general power of attorney, the authorities will ask you if you are certain. They do not question you when it is merely for the private kind. For a general power of attorney, the judge might say, "No, go home and think on it overnight!" If you give such a power of attorney, it means you have given someone signing authority for all your papers and legal matters. Islamically, in Muslim countries, someone granted such power can decide your affairs, even in your absence. He could even divorce you from your wife, marry you to someone else, or arrange an engagement for your daughter.

This is why you might be questioned closely when granting a general power of attorney. A person with such powers might one day become angry with you and dispose of all your property. You would need to love and trust someone a great to deal to give them such power over you. As a rule, the father of a family seldom gives this kind of power to his children. Nor does a sister grant this to a brother. This would not occur unless there was a high level of trust between them.

Consider then, what it means when God, the Exalted, says His name is al-Wakīl, the Trustee. What is He telling us? In the most important and complete sense imaginable, He is our protector. Wakīl means He represents you. If you put your trust in Him, He will support you. He is saying, "Sign this contract with Me!"

The Divine Contract

And whether we remember it or not, indeed, we all signed that contract on the Day of Promises[195]. We signed the contract that says, "Oh Allah, You are our *wakīl*." This is why when He brought the contract to the descendants of Adam ﷺ He said:

وَإِذْ أَخَذَ رَبُّكَ مِن بَنِي آدَمَ مِن ظُهُورِهِمْ ذُرِّيَّتَهُمْ وَأَشْهَدَهُمْ عَلَى أَنفُسِهِمْ أَلَسْتُ بِرَبِّكُمْ قَالُوا بَلَى شَهِدْنَا أَن تَقُولُوا يَوْمَ الْقِيَامَةِ إِنَّا كُنَّا عَنْ هَذَا غَافِلِينَ

When thy Lord drew forth from the Children of Adam - from their loins - their descendants, and made them testify concerning themselves, (saying): "Am I not your Lord (who cherishes and sustains you)?"- They said: "Yea! We do testify!" (This), lest ye should say on the Day of Judgment: "Of this we were never mindful"[196]

They said "*balā*!", and they signed the contract.

He is best of trustees! Why are you trying to run away from that contract, which you signed and thereby appointed God, the Exalted, as your *wakīl*?

When you raise your hand and make *du'a* you say, "You are my *wakīl*, You are my guardian, *ḥasbunAllāh wa ni'am al-Wakīl—sufficient is God and Most generous of protectors.*"

We are surrendering all our problems to God, the Exalted; only He can solve our difficulties. We depend on Him, because He is the best One to represent us. Represent us to whom? Represent us to Himself. When you appoint the head of the court himself as your *wakīl*, of course the decision will go in your favor. In this

---

[195] Arabic: *Yawm al-'ahdi wa 'l-mīthāq*—The Day of Promises and Pacts.

[196] Sūratu 'l-'Arāf (the Heights), 7:172.

country the Supreme Court is your legal *wakīl*: imagine then, the authority of a *wakīl* who is also the Creator of the universe!

You have signed this contract, so don't look to humanity seeking approval or acceptance. Don't put your *irāda*, will, there. If you begin to think of yourself as a Friend of God, you may fall, because Friends of God can also fall. God, the Exalted, did not give everything to the Friends of God; He hid much from them. And Friends of God, according to their level, might do things which are not accepted, one Friend of God might not accept what another is doing, and one may know more than the other. So, it is best to keep a low profile.

Grandshaykh ق delivered this *suhbat* on the subject of Friends of God forty years ago. He also told this story to illustrate why we should all be humble and not view ourselves as better than others.

Judge Not

A Friend of God saw a Bedouin in the desert. The shepherd's clothes were dirty and he smelled from tending sheep. As he entered the village, the Friend of God looked at him with distaste. Clearly, this was not the right attitude, for we are all smelly in one way or another.

> One day, Prophet Jesus ﷺ was with his Apostles, the Ḥawāriyyūn, when they saw a dead animal in the forest. The carcass was a week old and in a state of advanced decay. The worms were doing their work and the smell was very strong. The disciples of Prophet Jesus ﷺ put their hands over their noses.
>
> Prophet Jesus ﷺ looked at them and said, "Observe!"
>
> He walked up to the carcass and pushed back its lips to show the creature's teeth. Despite the state of the rest of the body, the teeth were intact. Then he ordered them to take their hands away from over their mouths and said, "Look at the beauty of his teeth; see how God, the Exalted, has made the

teeth and the bones so perfectly. Consider the greatness of the Creator and not the smell! One day, you will smell worse."

That animal had no ego, but you do. Remember then, that you will smell even worse in the grave, because you do not respect people. Don't look at the bad things that people around you are doing. Don't say you like some people more than others. Avoid backbiting, either openly or in secret. We must be very careful in our dealings with others.

Now, back to the story of the Friend of God and the shepherd. When the Friend of God saw the Bedouin coming to join the prayers with his dusty, smelly clothes he said, "Oh my brother, God, the Exalted, did not order us to pray with dirty clothes. We must have clean clothes."

That shepherd he said, "Oh my brother. You are right."

But God, the Exalted, said in a *qudsī* hadith[197]:

عَنْ اَبي هُرَيْرَةَ، قَالَ قَالَ رَسُولُ اللَّهِ صَلَّى اللَّهُ عَلَيْهِ وَسَلَّمَ: إن اللّه لا ينظر الى أجسامكم ولا إلى صوركم ولكن ينظر إلى قلوبكم

God, the Exalted, does not look at your forms, but He looks at your heart.[198]

And the Prophet ﷺ said:

رواه أنس في حديثه ، عن النبي صلى اللّه عليه وسلم" :رُبَّ أشعث أغبر ذي طمرين لا يُؤبه له ، لو أقسم على اللّه لأبرَّه"

It might be that an unkempt, greasy-haired person can Allah (set) for something and get an immediate response...[199]

---

[197] Revelation from Allah ﷻ to the Prophet ﷺ that is not part of the Holy Qur'an.
[198] Āḥmad's Musnad, Saḥīḥ Muslim.
[199] Tirmidhī, *Musnad Āḥmad* and Muslim.

The shepherd said, "Look at my heart, not my clothes!"

When the Friend of God looked into the Bedouin's heart, he saw the light of Sayyidina Muhammad ﷺ, which is the manifestation of the light of God, the Exalted, shining through his heart. This made the Friend of God ashamed of himself. He started saying "*astaghfirullāh*" over and over. Even a Friend of God is compelled to say *astaghfirullāh*.

He said, "O My Lord! I will never again judge people at face value and assume they are not worthy. I cannot know such things. I will not look to the shortcomings of people. I must look at my own faults."

Today people are busy looking at each others flaws. They are not looking at their own shortcomings. They are not keeping that in their hearts. They forget immediately.

When you ask, "O my Lord! please be my *wakīl*," God, the Exalted, will build you up, because He wants to give you the best. When you acknowledge Him as your *wakīl*, He will represent you in the best way possible.

Where will He represent you? He will present you in a favorable light in His own presence. He won't look at your clothes or anything else about your external appearance. The *wakīl* will hide the faults and failures of the person he represents. We always try to hide our own flaws. Imagine then, how well God, the Exalted, might be able to do this! He will try to keep you at the highest level of respect in His Presence.

That is why a hadith of Prophet ﷺ says:

...إِنْ ذَكَرَنِي فِي مَلَإٍ ذَكَرْتُهُ فِي مَلَإٍ هُمْ خَيْرٌ مِنْهُمْ...

"Whoever remembers me in an association, I will remember him in a better association."[200]

This means, "In His Presence."

It means, "If he remembers that I am his *Wakīl*, I will send angels to guide him."

When people sit in a gathering of remembrance, God, the Exalted, sends angels that assemble around them and form a connection to Paradise. So we must not look at the shortcomings of others. We don't know what is in their heart. The Bedouin looked like a simple shepherd, but he was higher than the Friend of God.

Second Characteristic

The second quality of Friends of God is their ability to control their own actions by first asking permission. They check with a higher authority before taking action. In so doing, they harmonize their actions with the line of causation passing through the Prophet ﷺ. In effect, they are consulting a divine map before setting foot out the door.

For example, Friends of God must ask permission for their travel from the Prophet ﷺ. That is why students of a Friend of God must ask permission when they want to travel from their shaykh, because he will ask permission on their behalf from the Prophet ﷺ. If we don't ask permission from our shaykh to travel, anything might happen to us because they are not protecting us.

Today if you want to travel, they tell you buy insurance. But they don't guarantee your safety—they will pay your survivors if you die on your journey. However, when you request permission from the Prophet ﷺ, your safety is guaranteed. Asking permission

---

[200] Bukhārī, Muslim, *Musnad Āḥmad*, Tirmidhī's *Sunan*.

from a Friend of God amounts to the same thing, because he asks permission from his shaykh, who in turn asks permission from the Prophet ﷺ. Even if a ship is sinking, things will be arranged to save the ship.

يَمْحُو اللّهُ مَا يَشَاء وَيُثْبِتُ وَعِندَهُ أُمُّ الْكِتَابِ

Allah doth blot out or confirm what He pleaseth: with Him is the Mother of the Book.[201]

Friends of God will immediately intervene on your behalf and ask the Prophet ﷺ to save you, just as He will intercede for His entire community, the Ummah. Whether it's on a sinking ship or a dangerous jungle path, if you had permission for that trip, they can save you. Friends of God have this ability because they always strive to be in the presence of the Prophet ﷺ.

God, the Exalted, described them in the Holy Qur'an:

أَلا إِنَّ أَوْلِيَاء اللّهِ لاَ خَوْفٌ عَلَيْهِمْ وَلاَ هُمْ يَحْزَنُونَ

Behold! Verily on the Friends of God, there is no fear nor shall they grieve.[202]

They have reached a level of good tidings and safety. For them, Paradise is guaranteed.

They are mentioned in the hadith as:

إنَّ أَوْلِيَائِي تَحْتَ قِبَابِي لاَ يَعْرِفُهُمْ غَيْرِي

My saints are under My domes; no one knows them except Me.[203]

---

[201] Sūratu 'r-Ra'd (Thunder), 13:39.

[202] Sūratu 'l-Anbīyā (the Prophets), 10:62.

[203] Imām Ghazālī, *Ihyā 'ulūm ad-dīn.*

This is why the Friends of God are responsible for everything they do. They are not like children who, because of their immaturity, cannot be held accountable for their behavior. Many adults are also immature and make mistakes. Then, when they repent and ask for Allah's forgiveness, He grants it.

In contrast, Friends of God are held to a higher standard. If they fall into error, they must take the consequences. They must be in *istighfār*, repentance and seeking forgiveness. That is why Rabiʿa al-ʿAdawīyya spent all her life in *istighfār*.

She said, "My *istighfār* needs *istighfār*."

This is why the Friend of God always needs to ask permission from the Prophet ﷺ for whatever action he considers. If he doesn't ask for this permission, he will face consequences. Similarly, the disciple of the shaykh has to ask permission of his shaykh or he will also face the consequences.

The Incessant Innovator

Allah is al-Badiʿ, the Innovator. He posesses the quality of *ibdaʿ*: He does what no one can do. In some measure, the Friends of God can take from Allah's *ibdaʿ*, from the name al-Badiʿ, the One who fashions things in an appealing manner with supreme artistry and variation.

For example, you might grow a vast garden of only red roses. It might produce a striking impression at first, but the novelty would soon wear off, and the single color would become boring, if not oppressive. A master gardener will mix the colors and shapes of his flowers to produce a lasting, more natural beauty. Friends of God are also fashioned and woven together in such a way that they harmonize with one another. You are happy when you see them together and sense the work of the Ultimate Fashioner behind the scenes.

The 124,000 Friends of God across the planet operate on different levels. The Divine Name, al-Badiʿ, generates these variations for everything in the universe. If everything and everyone were the same, the richness and beauty of creation would vanish. Picture how our world would look if it had no color. If the trees, sky, flowers and gemstones were all black and white, there would be no *ibdaʿ* in it. God, the Exalted, the Fashioner, weaves beauty and magnificence into His creation. He is not showing us a black and white movie, as though we were color blind. Since we can differentiate colors, we far prefer color films to black and white.

When you make your wardrobe choices, you consider the colors and patterns carefully before walking out the door. If you choose mismatched pieces against all advice and taste, people will think you are a donkey and say, "If he doesn't know what he is wearing, how can he see into the hearts of people?"

God, the Exalted, the Creator made everything in nature with supreme artistry. This is part of His greatness that we can witness directly. The pageantry of the alternating seasons shows us the rhythm of life, death, and resurrection. In winter, the trees lose their leaves and snow lies on the ground. The trunks and branches appear black against the snow. The entire composition is painted in black, white, and grey. Much of the beauty vanishes with the onset of the colorless winter. Yet, when spring comes, life and beauty return.

يُخْرِجُ الْحَيَّ مِنَ الْمَيِّتِ وَيُخْرِجُ الْمَيِّتَ مِنَ الْحَيِّ وَيُحْيِي الْأَرْضَ بَعْدَ مَوْتِهَا وَكَذَلِكَ
تُخْرَجُونَ

It is He Who brings out the living from the dead, and brings out the dead from the living, and Who gives life to the earth after it is dead: and thus shall ye be brought out (from the dead). [204]

How could anyone deny that there will be a Resurrection Day when every year there is a rebirth of nature? The trees, grass, and flowers come back to life on a grand scale across each hemisphere: life returns after death. In the winter it is difficult to distinguish between a dead or dormant tree, but in spring you can distinguish if it is living or not.

God, the Exalted, has arranged the universe in layers, and each layer is governed by different time scales. On earth, the cycles of life, death, and rebirth run on a yearly basis, but the solar system's life cycle is set at billions of years. Scientists now say that stars eventually run out of nuclear fuel, flare out in a death throe, and engulf their planets in a wall of flame before shrinking into a dormant dwarf.

They say our very own sun will do this one day, billions of years in the future.

يَوْمَ تُبَدَّلُ الأَرْضُ غَيْرَ الأَرْضِ وَالسَّمَاوَاتُ وَبَرَزُوا لله الْوَاحِدِ الْقَهَّارِ

One day the earth will be changed to a different earth, and so will be the heavens, and (men) will be marshalled forth, before Allah, the One, the Irresistible;[205]

It means the earth and moon and sun will clash when the sun expands into a red giant just before it dies. Everything in the solar system will be annihilated. But ﷻ Allah will bring a new earth on Resurrection Day, just as He brings new forests and gardens in spring.

---

[204] Sūratu 'r-Rūm (Rome), 30:19.

[205] Sūrat Ibrāhīm (Abraham), 14:48).

The evidence is in the Holy Qur'an

وَجُمِعَ الشَّمْسُ وَالْقَمَرُ

and the sun and the moon are brought together[206]

The sun and moon will one day collide. Only in modern times has science arrived at the same conclusion. This means that 1400 years ago, God, the Exalted, gave us evidence of the demise of the solar system in the Holy Qur'an. He told His beloved Prophet ﷺ that the earth, sun, and moon would fuse and come to an end.

God, the Exalted, has planned out the universe at different scales. In the sub-atomic world events are timed in milliseconds, on earth in annual cycles, and the solar system proceeds in unimaginable lengths of time, in billions of years. The precision of these interlocking cycles is exact; nothing is out of place.

This is why the Friends of God must ask permission for anything they do. God, the Exalted, has planned everything very carefully at all points of the universe.

أَأَنتُمْ تَزْرَعُونَهُ أَمْ نَحْنُ الزَّارِعُونَ

Are you the one who is planting these and perfecting things, or is God, the Exalted?[207]

Of course Allah is doing it! So it means that everything is set in its place to perfection. A seed by itself doesn't look like a living thing. When planted, however, it comes to life, grows a trunk, branches, leaves and fruit.

يُخْرِجُ الْحَيَّ مِنَ الْمَيِّتِ

---

[206] Sūratu 'l-Qiyāmah (The Resurrection), 75:9.

[207] Sūratu 'l-Waqiʿa (The Overwhelming Event), 56:64.

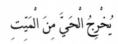

He causeth the living to issue from the dead;[208]

There are four different categories of existence: *jamādāt* (inanimate, like minerals), *nabatāt* (plants and trees), *ḥaywanāt* (animals), and *ins* (human beings). God, the Exalted, created the inanimate objects without minds or mobility. He created the plants to grow and photosynthesize, but they do not walk about; they stand still in Allah's Presence, always in submission. Animals though move about and seek their sustenance. Finally, humans were given minds and some degree of self-awareness.

وَلَقَدْ كَرَّمْنَا بَنِي آدَمَ

We have honored the sons of Adam;[209]

The Friends of God understand that this honor entails certain responsibilities and rules. They do nothing without permission. When a Friend of God wants to move about, he must ask permission from his shaykh. If he is a shaykh, he must ask for permission from the Prophet ﷺ. That is why students must ask for permission to travel and to make major decisions.

Mandatory Petitions

Three things fall into the category of seeking permission from the shaykh: marriage, divorce, and travel. These are big things in anyone's life. If you travel, you don't know if you will return. When you leave there is no guarantee that you come back safely. So you must ask for permission, especially when you go for hajj. The shaykh can look and see if there is a problem or not. He can see if the manifestation of the Divine Name ar-Raḥmān[210] is there or whether forgiveness, *ghufrān,* will come or not.

---

[208] Sūratu 'l-An'am (Cattle), 6:95.

[209] Sūratu 'l-Isrā (the Night Journey), 17:70.

[210] Allah's Name, the Most Compassionate.

A Saint's Moment of Heedlessness

Once there was a Friend of God who, in the heat of the moment, heedlessly set out on a trip without first asking permission. He decided to travel by boat across the Mediterranean Sea from North Africa to Egypt, then on to hajj. In those days pilgrims were protected on caravans to hajj by the Ottoman army. The Friend of God didn't remember to ask permission until he was already in the middle of the sea. He spent his time on the voyage practicing his private litanies and teaching his students. They were far out to sea when a huge storm rose. Its waves towered about the boat and threatened to smash it to pieces. Everyone on board went into submission, asking for Allah's forgiveness, because they knew they were going to die.

Before you decide to go on a trip you must ask permission from a living shaykh, and then you must recite:

بِسْمِ اللهِ الرَّحْمنِ الرَّحِيمِ ذَلِكَ تَقْدِيرُ الْعَزِيزِ الْعَلِيمِ

In the name of Allah, the Merciful, the Compassionate, that is the decree of (Him), the Exalted in Might, the All-Knowing.[211]

Bismi'l-Lāhi 'r-Raḥmāni 'r-Raḥīm dhālika taqdīru 'l-ʿazīzu 'l-ʿalīm one hundred times. You must ask the Creator if it is in His plan for you to go. If you recite that, it can save you. In this act, you acknowledge that everything is in Allah's Hands.

Everyone on that boat began to recite that verse, but in reality it should have been recited before they embarked on the journey. So it did not match the code of manifestation of safety. So what happened? We shall leave that for another time.

---

[211] Sūrah Yāsīn, 36:38.

Friends of God ask permission before taking action in case anything goes wrong. With these precautions in place, they are able to move in special ways in space and time. In this, they manifest one of the six realities of the heart: *Ḥaqīqatu'l-jadhbah, Ḥaqīqatu 'l-fayḍ, Ḥaqīqatu 't-tawajjuh, Ḥaqīqatu 't-tawassul, Ḥaqīqatu 'ṭ-Ṭayy, Ḥaqīqatu 'l-irshād.*

Ḥaqīqatu'l-jadhbah is the Power of Attraction of either objects or people to the Shaykh. *Ḥaqīqatu 'l-fayḍ* is the Power of Emanation or Outpouring of experience from the Prophet ﷺ through the Chain of transmission to the heart of the disciple. *Ḥaqīqatu 't-tawajjuh* is the Power of Alignment of the Shaykh's heart towards the disciple's, and of the disciple's towards his spiritual goal. *Ḥaqīqatu 't-tawassul* is the Power of Connection to Divine power and favors through the Golden Chain. *Ḥaqīqatu 'l-irshād* is the Power of Guidance onto the destination embarked upon through the Power of Connection. *Ḥaqīqatu 'ṭ-Ṭayy* is the Power of Folding Time and Space.

أبو هريرة قال: قال رسول الله صلى الله عليه وسلم يتقارب الزمان..

Abū Hurayra ؓ related that the Prophet ﷺ said:
[Among the Signs of the Last Days] are that time will contract...

As the Prophet ﷺ mentioned in hadith, time will contract. I explained this hadith in *Approach of Armageddon*:

> The means of travel and communication would be developed to make time contract, so that differences in time would be reduced or eliminated. In the past travel was measured in units of time: days, months or years. Now, a journey is measured by distance: miles or kilometers.[212]

---

[212] Shaykh Muhammad Hisham Kabbani, *The Approach of Armageddon: An Islamic Perspective*, Islamic Supreme Council of America, Washington DC, 2001, p. 105.

This means distances are shortened. The Friends of God are more powerful than airplanes; they can shorten physical distances. If God, the Exalted, gave human beings the minds to invent airplanes, did He not give the Friends of God the power to create modes of travel that transcend our ordinary notions of space and time? Of He course did! A Friend of God would not be a Friend of God if he could not do such things. However, the Friends of God, and in particular, the Naqshbandi shaykhs, do not openly show these abilities. They also take great care to not talk about such things.

This is a key point. This Order does not emphasize supernatural or miraculous capacities, either as a teaching method or as an ongoing aim of practice. Today I see so many students telling everyone they meet about their special insights and visions. You would think that they were being interviewed by Oprah Winfrey before a national television audience. The ego can thrive in what might pass for a group therapy session of shared "mystical" experiences.

If you have been granted an extraordinary moment, it is best to keep it to yourself. It is yours and yours alone. Presenting it for "Show and Tell", like an elementary school child, will only spoil it and cut you off from the very source that granted you the insight in the first place. Imitate your shaykhs and hold these experiences within. We are all designed in different styles: other people will not necessarily understand or accept your particular spiritual flights. Don't try to dress others with your clothes—they won't fit. If you are very slim and the other person is big, it simply won't work. People forced into ill-fitting clothes are uncomfortable and look foolish.

I am always surprised when people come to me in an open setting and begin describing such experiences. It is alright to tell Mawlana Shaykh or his representatives in a private session, but don't talk about it in public! Hide it! If you don't hide such things, you devalue the spiritual nourishment you were given. These special moments are like individual diamonds: rare, protected, and unique. Don't toss them about in a crowd like pieces of candy!

Third Characteristic

The Friends of God love and protect their disciples. Friends of God monitor you for what is good in you, and if you are following your better instincts they move you forward on your spiritual path. Every action we take, every thought we have, is known to God, the Exalted, and to the Prophet ﷺ. We must realize that the *ūli 'l-amr,* those in authority, are monitoring our physical and spiritual actions.

Although they want everyone to avoid heedlessness, sometimes God, the Exalted, will send something even to a Friend of God to test him. For example, in the case of the Friend of God who set out on hajj without first asking permission, as a result the storm arose during his voyage. When you travel, marry, or divorce, you must ask permission and guidance from those who have authority over you. This is because they may foresee otherwise invisible difficulties. Unless the Friends of God first obtain permission from the Prophet ﷺ when they travel, there may be no safety on the road.

Because Friends of God love the Prophet ﷺ they want you to ask permission. Accordingly, out of his love for you, your shaykh wants you to ask for permission. Friends of God understand the importance of love in everything we do. They see in the life of the Prophet ﷺ an example of pure love in everything he did. In turn, the Friends of God love the Prophet ﷺ and wish to obey him.

قُلْ إِن كُنتُمْ تُحِبُّونَ اللَّهَ فَاتَّبِعُونِي يُحْبِبْكُمُ اللَّهُ وَيَغْفِرْ لَكُمْ ذُنُوبَكُمْ وَاللَّهُ غَفُورٌ رَّحِيمٌ

Say: "If ye do love Allah, Follow me: Allah will love you and forgive you your sins: For Allah is Oft-Forgiving, Most Merciful."[213]

Love leads to obedience. The Prophet ﷺ wants the Friends of God to obey him and always be aware that they are ruled by a higher authority. If you are heedless in your love, even for one second, it diminishes. In that instant of forgetfulness, your being is reduced and your path is made longer.

Love of the Prophet Makes Miracles

The Prophet's ﷺ love extends to all creation. Even animals knew to go to his door with their grievances.

أخرج ابن شاهين في دلائل النبوة عن عبد الله ابن جعفر قال : أردفني رسول الله صلى الله عليه وسلم ذات يوم خلفه ، فدخل حائط رجل من الأنصار فإذا جمل فلما رأى النبي صلى الله عليه وسلم حن فذرفت عيناه فأتاه النبي صلى الله عليه وسلم فمسح ذرفتاه فسكن ثم قال : من رب هذا الجمل ، فجاء فتى من الأنصارفقال : هذا لي .فقال ألا تتقي الله في هذه البهيمة التي ملّكك الله إياها فإنه شكا إليّ أنك تُجيعه وتُدئبه . وهوحديث حسن .

One day, the Prophet ﷺ was going to ziyāra[214] *with one of the Companions. A camel was standing near the house where they were gathering. The camel looked at the Prophet ﷺ and he returned the creature's gaze. Tears came to the eyes of the camel.*
The Prophet ﷺ asked, "Who owns that camel?"
Someone replied, "Such-an-such Sahabi owns this camel."

---

[213] Sūrat Āli-ʿImrān (the Family of ʿImrān), 3:31.
[214] Arabic: *ziyāra*—visitation of a holy place.

Prophet ﷺ said to the owner, "That camel is complaining about you." [215]
The camel was overloaded, so it complained to the Prophet ﷺ.

See how the Prophet's ﷺ love extends to everything. He wants everything to be in order, to work in harmony. He even wants animals and humans to be in harmony. Even more importantly, he wants the relationships among humans to be in harmony.

The Prophet ﷺ even cares about inanimate objects. When someone creates a work of art, he loves it. The Prophet ﷺ wants a relationship with everyone. Know that Sayyidina Muhammad ﷺ is in you! He was sent as *raḥmatan li 'l-ʿalamīn*, a mercy to all the worlds. You must realize that is very important. When you feel mercy for someone, it is from love. The Prophet ﷺ loves his Community. He wants you to be safe; he wants you to be careful in every step you take and to follow the principles, whether you are a Friend of God or not. Don't jump from windows, but enter the house through the door.

رواه الترمذي و غيره عن أنس رضي الله عنه قال: قال رجل: يا رسول الله!
أعقلها و أتوكل أو أطلقها و أتوكل؟ قال: "اعقلها و توكل".

Don't be like those who said, "Yā Rasūlullāh, do we leave the camel or tie it? Should we just leave it and trust in God, the Exalted?"
He answered, "No, aʿaqilhā wa tawakkal. *Tie it and then trust [in God]."*[216]

Of course if you leave it, it will wander out into the desert and be lost. Each relationship dictates its own appropriate conduct.

---

[215] Ibn Shāhīn in Dalā'il an-Nubūwwah.
[216] Tirmidhī.

لما كان يخطب بالقوم كان يستند إلى جذع نخلة يبيس فلما صنع له الصحابة منبر ثلاثة درجات ، حنّ جذع النخلة على فراق النبي صلى الله عليه وسلم فسمع أنينه من كان في المسجد فنزل إليه الرسول فالتزمه فسكت.

When the Prophet ﷺ delivered his Friday khutbah[217], *he would lean upon a wooden post set upright in the ground. Over time, some of the Companions noticed that, as the crowds grew larger, it was growing more difficult for everyone to see him. They decided to build a* minbar, *a platform with several steps, so that the Prophet ﷺ would be visible to everyone during his sermons. When they delivered this* minbar *and the Prophet ﷺ ascended it, immediately, everyone heard the sound of crying from the direction of the wooden post.*
The post missed the touch of the Prophet ﷺ and, even though it was only an inanimate object, long since cut from its living tree, it so loved the Prophet ﷺ, it began to weep. So the Prophet stepped down from the minbar and put his hand on the wooden post and it stopped weeping.[218]

When you love your children you put your hand on them, you hug them, and that energy goes from them to you. That flow of energy is important. Imagine then the intensity of the energy that flows from the hand of Prophet ﷺ.

The wood was moaning and crying for all to hear, so Prophet ﷺ stepped down from the minbar.

Anyone else might have kept the *minbar* and tossed the log on the trash heap. Consider the difference!

It is love and love alone that creates energy and sets it in motion. Remember how the Bur'aq was crying out of love of the

[217] Arabic: *khutbah*—sermon to the congregation.
[218] This is mentioned in *Saḥīḥ ibn Khuzaymah, Sunan ad-Dārimī, Sunan at-Tirmidhī.*

Prophet ﷺ. As its tears fell, they became gems. Pearls, sapphires, and diamonds dropped from its eyes, each one larger than the earth. These jewels will be fashioned into palaces for the believers on the Day of Judgment. This is the manifestation of a love so immense that it cannot be described. Grandshaykh ق relates:

> When the Prophet ﷺ stepped down from the *minbar* and looked at the post he said, "Do you love me?"
>
> The post replied, "Yes, *Yā Rasūlullāh*. I love you and that is why I don't want you to use the *minbar*. I want the blessings of your hand resting on me. I cannot remain standing without it."
>
> Prophet ﷺ said, "Would you like me to be with me in this world, or in the hereafter? The choice is yours. If you wish to be with me in this world, I will keep putting my hand on you, but if you wish to be with me in the hereafter, I will guarantee you that in Paradise."
>
> The post said, "*Yā Rasūlullāh*! I wish to be with you in this life and in the next, but as you like."
>
> See how the Prophet ﷺ made a piece of wood come to life.
>
> Finally, it said, "I prefer to be with you in the hereafter." With that, the Prophet ﷺ ordered the wood be buried as though it were a dead person.

The wood was not heedless—it wanted to be with the Prophet ﷺ always and God, the Exalted, granted it that honor. Because of its love of Asḥāb al-Kahf,[219] the Prophet ﷺ even intervened for their dog to be given permission to reside in Paradise.

---

[219] Asḥāb al-Kahf—the Companions of the Cave; a narration in the Qurʿan.

In the matter of the ship, the Friend of God, and the storm, usually a Friend of God could use the power of *ṭayy*[220] in such an emergency. However, because he had failed to ask permission prior to embarking on his trip, he could not summon this power.

That is why it is recommended to recite *Bismi'l-Lāhi 'r-Raḥmāni 'r-Raḥīm dhālika taqdīr al-'azīz ar-Raḥīm* 100 times before you travel. God, the Exalted, has created angels that under that name, *dhālika taqdīr al-'azīz ar-Raḥīm*. God, the Exalted, created rescuing angels that assist anyone who recites this phrase at the right time. The angels will come, whether he is on a boat, train, or plane, lift him out of danger, and fly him to a safe place.

Luckily for the forgetful Friend of God, there was another Friend of God on the boat who had remembered to ask permission before taking his journey. When the storm came and the ship began to break apart, he found safety on a wooden plank torn from the deck of the boat. He floated on it as though it were a lifeboat, while the others struggled in the rising waves.

This is similar to what happened when Nimrod tried to destroy Prophet Abraham ﷺ.

Prophet Abraham's Absolute Dependence on God

The king Nimrod built a huge fire and threw Prophet Abraham ﷺ into it with a catapult. They used a hurling device because no one could go close to the raging fire.

The archangel Gabriel immediately came to his aid and said, "O Abraham ﷺ, do you want any help?"

---

220 Arabic: *ṭayy*—the power to fold spaces to compact them.

Prophet Abraham ﵇ looked at him, "Why must I ask you for help? When I need help I ask for it from the One who sent you. God, the Exalted, knows my situation. He will determine if He wants me to be burned or not. I am submitting to His Will. I will not change anything."

The angel said, "O Abraham, I can stop the fire."

Prophet Abraham ﵇ replied, "I don't want it from you, I want it from Him. If He wished to act, He knows my situation better."

Gabriel ﵇ said, "O Prophet Abraham ﵇, "Give me the authority, and I will help you."

The reply came, "O Gabriel ﵇, your words are like the words of children. When they threw me in the fire, did not God, the Exalted, see me? If He wants to save me, He will save me. I don't like to listen to children's words."

With that, God, the Exalted, cooled the flames and sent peace on Prophet Abraham ﵇. Immediately it became a Paradise.

قُلْنَا يَا نَارُ كُونِي بَرْدًا وَسَلَامًا عَلَى إِبْرَاهِيمَ

[But] We said: "O fire! Be thou cool, and (a source of) inner peace for Abraham!"[221]

Returning to Grandshaykh's story:

When the second Friend of God asked permission from the Prophet ﷺ, in effect, he rendered everything to God, the Exalted. This is why asking permission is very important. Even though the second Friend of God was of a lower status than the first, he was able to float safely on his makeshift raft

---

[221] Sūratu 'l-Anbīyā (the Prophets), 21:69.

while the first one was suffering. So, he called out to the Friend of God in the water, just as Gabriel ﷺ had to Prophet Abraham ﷺ, "Let me help you, my brother."

The first one said, "Oh my brother, until now I never did something against Allah's Will. I never before was disobedient to God, the Exalted. So now, in my current difficulty, I am surrendering to God, the Exalted. I must remain patient. I can't accept your help."

The second Friend of God began to laugh and said, "Well, we will see how long you will last until you beg me to save you."

The first Friend of God began swallowing sea water. He knew he was going to die, and panic seized him.

The second Friend of God said, "Now is it time to help you or are you still on arrogance?"

The reply came back, "No, I am not asking for your help, I am surrendering to Allah's Will."

The first Friend of God continued to flounder in the raging mountains and valleys of the stormy sea. He began to sink.

The second one persisted, "Will you give me permission now?"

They continued back and forth for some time as the sinking Friend of God's situation became more desperate.

Finally, from the safety of his raft the second Friend of God called out, "O my brother, why are you floundering and splashing around, as if you don't have patience with the Divine Will?"

The first Friend of God said, "Oh my brother, it is the right of the body, to flounder and splash, but God, the Exalted, doesn't look at the body, he looks at the heart. Look into my heart. Is it panicking or not?"

The second Friend of God looked into the heart of the man in the water. As though a door had suddenly been opened, he saw the Divine Light flooding out from the Friend of God's heart. His submission and patience was so complete that the Prophet ﷺ himself was sending him mercy. When the second Friend of God saw this, he was so overcome with the light that he fell off his plank and began to drown. The first Friend of God then used the power of his vision to save his drowning companion and transported him to the safety of a distant shore.

This power came from the *tajallīyāt,* manifestations, of Allah's Name aṣ-Ṣabūr, the Patient. The second Friend of God was not able to control himself. Nevertheless, under the *tajallīyāt* of that name, the first Friend of God was obliged to save him and for that God, the Exalted, saved the first Friend of God, for his help to the second one.

You Cannot Understand the Friends of God

The Friends of God operate from different levels of spiritual development. Although you might see them physically struggling or apparently quarrelling, you might not necessarily understand what is going on between them. Some might object, "Why are they quarreling with each other? Why do they speak like that?" However, they are looking at the outside of the relationship and not the inside. Similarly, it is often difficult to see how much the shaykh cares for his disciple or representative from the outward signs.

God, the Exalted, himself does not judge based on our external circumstances. Try to avoid falling into the trap of judging people and situations by superficial appearances. Matters of the heart often elude first impressions. In the case of the two Friend of Gods, the higher one always takes precedence over the lower one. The lower one cannot understand the higher one. The higher Friend of God is always more patient and merciful. His judgment and actions are tempered with a higher degree of love and mercy.

So don't judge what is going on between Friends of God. You may end up burning your fingers. Don't say, "I am like that. My name is this or my name is that. I must be respected." Instead, simply be yourself. Remember God, the Exalted, said in the Holy Qur'an, "فَلَا تُزَكُّوا أَنفُسَكُمْ —*Don't praise yourselves.*" Don't listen to a fuzzy signal and say, "I am this and I am that." May Allah forgive us.

Wa min Allāhi 't-tawfīq, bi ḥurmati 'l-Fātiḥah.

13: The Gatherers and the Gathered

Straight or Zigzag Paths

Grandshaykh taught us that humility is the key to progress on this spiritual path. Degrees of sainthood are directly determined by degrees of humility, submission and sincerity. Pride and arrogance block the road to (*ḥaqīqah*), truth and gnosticism (*ma'rifah*). The more a heart is filled with arrogance and its offspring, hypocrisy and disbelief, the farther away it is from the Divine Presence. Arrogance generates the negative energies of evil, misunderstanding and *'ubūdīyya*.

Arrogance manifests itself in many different ways. One common symptom is that you fail to accept advice gracefully, if at all. You are stubborn and hold to your opinion longer and more adamantly than you should. If someone points out a better way, you grow angry and argumentative. Eventually, even if you accept the advice of another, you are still resentful and your heart continues to boil. If you outwardly accept what a guide is telling you, you still manage to voice complaints. If your shaykh is working on your negative characteristics and gives you some difficult advice and you can't control your tongue, at least try to say one word to ask to be excused by God, the Exalted. God, the Exalted, said:

فَلَا تُزَكُّوا أَنفُسَكُمْ

Therefore justify not yourselves;[222]

---

[222] Sūratu 'n-Najm (the Star), 53:32.

As it is said in the Holy Qur'an:

لَّا يُحِبُّ اللَّهُ الْجَهْرَ بِالسُّوءِ مِنَ الْقَوْلِ إِلَّا مَن ظُلِمَ وَكَانَ اللَّهُ سَمِيعًا عَلِيمًا

Allah loves not that evil should be noised abroad in public speech, except where injustice has been done; for Allah is He who hears and knows all things.[223]

Unless we are genuinely being oppressed, God, the Exalted, doesn't like us to complain and habitually grumble about our situation. For example, it is not a form of oppression when your shaykh is cleaning and testing you. This is mentioned in the verse above—God, the Exalted, doesn't love complaining, whether it is from the tongue or the heart.

In any event, the tongue doesn't move without the heart's consent. It is well understood that the moods and passions of the heart drive the nervous system which, in turn, signal the body's muscles to smile, frown, tense, relax or, in short, reflect any combination of psychological reactions in what is commonly referred to as body language. Our reactions, whether emotional or physical, form a closely knit system of human response mechanisms.

A great deal of our interaction with other people is driven automatically, based on deep-seated instincts of self-preservation. Under the onslaught of criticism, very few people can control themselves and arrest the automatic flow of built-in defensive mechanisms. Grace under stress is widely recognized as a rare quality. The brain and the heart generally mobilize their defenses and take over the body before we even know what is happening to us. This is good in cases where quick reflexes are required, such as dodging bullets and oncoming cars, but it can be counter-

[223] Sūratu 'n-Nisā (Women), 4:148.

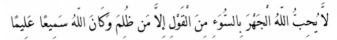

productive in a social context. Swallowing your pride in pivotal circumstances amounts to absorbing a shock to smooth the way, like the rubber tires and suspension system on a car. An experienced courtier or diplomat knows that good manners and self-effacement are his most valuable tools.

Again, this is seldom our reaction to unpleasant people, accusations or attacks. Consider the case of Sayyidina ʿAlī ☙.

في معركة الخندق ، وعندما أراد المشركون غزو المدينة ، حفر المسلمون بأمر النبي خندقاً

لحماية المدينة من العدوان ، وكانت الأوضاع في غاية الخطورة ، خاصة عندما تمكن بعض

فرسان المشركين ، وفي طليعتهم " عمْر بن عبد ود " من اقتحام الخندق وتحدّي المسلمين.

ولم يكن "عمْر بن عبد ود" شخصاً عادياً بل كان بطلاً شجاعاً أحجم كثير من المسلمين عن

مواجهته ، وهنا نهض علي بطل الإسلام لمنازلته وتقدم إليه بشجاعة وكان الرسول ينظر إليه

ويقول : "برز الإيمان كلّه إلى الشرك كلّه."

حاول "عمرو" أن يتفادى القتال مع علي ، فقال -: ارجع فأنا لا أحب أن أقتلك.

فأجابه علي بإيمان عظيم: ولكني أحب أن أقتلك.

وهنا غضب " عمرو بن عبد ود " و سدّد ضربة قوية إلى علي تفاداها علي ، وردّ على ضربته

بضربة قاضية سقط فيها "ابن ودّ" صريعاً على الأرض.

وكان لهذا المشهد المثير أثره في بث الذعر في نفوس رفاقه من المشركين الذين لاذوا بالفرار.

وعندما اعتلى علي صدر خصمه بصق "ابن ودّ" في وجه علي ، وشعر علي

بالغضب ولكنه توقف فلم يقدم على قتله إلى أن سكن غضبه حتى لا يكون قتله

انتقاماً ، بل خالصاً لوجه الله.

During a battle, an enemy soldier he had pinned to the ground spit in his face and commanded him to go ahead and kill him. Sayyidina ʿAlī ☙, a perfect warrior, instantly overcame the ordinary reactionary processes of anger, and told the defeated warrior he would be spared, explaining that because he had become angered for an instant, he could not kill the defeated soldier. His opponent was so impressed that he converted to Islam on the spot.

Consider carefully what happened here: ʿAlī ﷺ, a noble and spiritually advanced soldier, in the heat of battle, with adrenalin coursing full force through his veins and someone's spit dripping from his face, arrested the natural impulses of anger and revenge in an instant, pulled back his sword arm, mastered his tongue, and calmly told his opponent that he was spared.

This is certainly not just anyone's first reaction to such an insult. The key difference between us and Sayyidina ʿAlī ﷺ is that he, a mighty warrior and companion of the Prophet ﷺ, had conquered his arrogance. This suggests, among other things that, once the common precedence of self has been supplanted with another, higher value, the more primitive circuitry of the nervous system, which governs fight and flight, can be rewired. Sayyidina Ali's ﷺ refined reaction transformed what could have been just another soon forgotten sword fight into an enduring example of self-control, forgiveness and Islamic chivalry.

The supreme self-mastery of a Companion such as Sayyidina ʿAlī ﷺ is far beyond us, but the example is telling. If we could occasionally get out of our own way, step aside from the ordinary sense of self, the binding web of image and automatic reaction, maybe new things could happen. Certainly Sayyidina ʿAlī ﷺ, who managed this miracle of self control in a difficult moment, enjoyed the benefits of direct exposure to his father-in-law, the perfect Messenger ﷺ, but all of us must wonder—what would it be like to get out of ourselves on occasion and really move directly forward on the Path of Surrender?

اهدنَــا الصِّرَاطَ المُستَقِيمَ

Guide us to the straight path.[224]

This is the straight path: no zigzags, no wandering, no side trips and no distractions. Any school child knows that the shortest distance between two points is a straight line. Just as a zigzag pattern of travel creates a longer physical trip, so a meandering spiritual journey stretches out the distance to the goal. If you have embarked on the Path of Surrender, Satan's primary power over you is to misdirect you and lead you off the path, at least temporarily. You will still reach the goal, but the journey is extended.

If you are under the *baya*ʿ of a shaykh, he has the duty to bring you there, but it takes longer. As you waver on the path it creates vibrations that are detectable by your shaykh. That is why it's best not to ask, "Why I am not receiving my *amānat*?" The reason is that your journey is becoming longer because, strictly speaking, you are not taking *ṣirāṭ al-mustaqīm*—the straight path. That is the mode of travel for people who kept their covenant with God, the Exalted. They are always straightforward.

Even when a child entered the room, Sayyidina Shaykh Sharafuddīn ق would stand as though a king had arrived. For him, the king and child were equal, because both were servants of God, the Exalted, and both were accompanied by angels. By this example, we should know to avoid showing disrespect to anyone, *tuḥaqqir maʿrufah.* If someone appears to be at a lower station, spiritually or otherwise, it is no reason to show contempt. If someone is not performing the *ʿibādah* at a certain level, or not part of your group, you have no reason to criticize or imagine yourself in a superior position. The Prophet ﷺ came:

---

[224] Sūratu 'l-Fatiha (the Opening), 1:6.

وَمَا أَرْسَلْنَاكَ إِلَّا كَافَّةً لِّلنَّاسِ بَشِيرًا وَنَذِيرًا وَلَكِنَّ أَكْثَرَ النَّاسِ لَا يَعْلَمُونَ

We have not sent you (O Muhammad) otherwise than to mankind at large, giving them glad tidings, and warning them, but most men understand not.[225]

وَمَا أَرْسَلْنَاكَ إِلَّا رَحْمَةً لِّلْعَالَمِينَ

We sent thee not, but as a Mercy for all creatures. [226]

You cannot say he came only for the Companions and not for others.

وددت أني لقيت إخواني! قالوا: يا رسول الله! ألسنا إخوانك؟ قال: أنتم أصحابي، وإخواني قوم يجيئون من بعدي يؤمنون بي ولم يروني، ثم قال: يا أبا بكر! ألا تحب قوما بلغهم أنك تحبني فأحبوك بحبك إياي؟ فأحبهم أحبهم الله."

*The Prophet ﷺ said, "I would love that we could meet our brothers (*ikhwāninā*)." The Companions said, "Are we not your brothers O Messenger of Allah?" He said, "You are my companions, but my brothers are people who come after me, they will believe in me without seeing." The he said, "O Aba Bakr! Do you not love a people who heard that you love me and for that they loved you for your love to me? I loved them and Allah loves them."*[227]

See how much importance he attached to us, though coming with all kinds of sins and corruption the importance is not the sins and corruption, but that we believed without seeing.

---

[225] Sūrah Ṣaba (Sheba), 34:28.

[226] Sūratu 'l-Anbīyā (the Prophets), 21:107.

[227] Ibn 'Asākir. In some versions of this hadith, the Prophet ﷺ came to the graveyard and said, "*as-salām 'alaykum*, abode of believing folk, and we are insha-Allah joining you... and the rest of the hadith is similar.

The importance thing to remember is that we are in association with a guide, Mawlana Shaykh Nazim, may Allah give him long life. He said that in the time of Shaykh Sharafuddīn, Grandshaykh's daughter was receiving special training from Shaykh Sharafuddīn. Her name was Rabiʿa. Her uncle, Shaykh Sharafuddīn, carefully supervised her upbringing. She began fasting at a very young age and was encouraged to follow the full cycle of prayers. He said Rabiʿa was always awake before him at *sahūr* time.

One day, Rabiʿa told her father, Grandshaykh ق, of an extraordinary sight she had seen. She said that when her uncle went to wash before his prayers, the flies around the bathroom area would approach him and be burned to a cinder. She said, "When at night I see him going for ablution, I set a light out for him and as soon as a fly approaches him, it immediately burns. The flies can't get anywhere near him." She was amazed and he told her, "Don't be like these black flies who are like those who look after people's faults and dirt. Better to be like the butterfly that goes from flower to flower and is very beautiful or like a bee. But don't go to the low level of the fly."

Mawlana Shaykh explained:

This is the reality of *ʿishq*, the fire of love, a special energy that Shaykh Sharafuddīn ق had built in himself through the love of God, the Exalted, and love of the Prophet ﷺ. In effect, this created a force field around him that blocked any bad things from approaching him. The flies represented bad characteristics and influences sent by Satan. Shaykh Sharafuddīn ق could shield himself from these flies with his light and burn them even as they flew in his direction.

Friends of God as Exemplars

A major role for the Friends of God is to serve as exemplars for the rest of us. We are supposed to look carefully at how they conduct themselves and follow their ways. To follow their example, we must try not look to look at the bad behavior of people and criticize them. God, the Exalted, knows best, it's best to leave them to God, the Exalted.

I'm going to relate something that Mawlana Shaykh said forty years ago. Anyone who can read Arabic can see it here in the notes. In a talk of the highest order, he explains where we should direct our love. Without such direction, we might fall into a deep abyss from which no one but the shaykh could rescue us.

> It is surprising that in this talk he said, "*Mubārakayn*, I have two blessed students: Shaykh Nazim and Shaykh Hussayn." Usually he says, "I have two apprentices: Shaykh Nazim and Shaykh Hussayn. *yajtamiʿu ʿalayhim kullu 'n-nās*, all the people gathered around them." This means when he was not there then the disciples gathered around these two pillars, Shaykh Nazim and Shaykh Hussayn (forty years ago). He said, "*yadhunūna annahum awlīyāullāh,* People thought them Friends of God, they think they are saints."
>
> He is directing us, "Be careful! When I am present, living, your focus must be on me; you cannot focus on someone else. Even when Shaykh Nazim and Shaykh Hussayn are with you, remember that each and every second they are under my authority."

This means that you cannot make people gather around you. You must be very careful to never loose the reality of the shaykh, and to direct the love of people to the shaykh.

Grandshaykh ق went on to say:

> There is a sickness that appears when people gather around my representatives. Without great care, they can lose their

love for me, to the point where there is no way to bring them back.

During one his of seclusions, Grandshaykh ق received visions from Shaykh Sharafuddīn concerning things that Shah Naqshband said about Judgment Day,when Prophet Muhammad ﷺ will fill many paradises by interceding on behalf of the Naqshbandi disciples.

This is recounted in book *The Naqshbandi Sufi Way*. He spoke about Sayyidina Shah Naqshband ق and the secrets he is receiving from the Prophet ﷺ. When Grandshaykh ق heard this, love for Shah Naqshband ق began to grow in his heart, to the intensity of a laser beam. This is a special kind of light that grows with concentration and has the power to heal. However, if such a beam of light is divided, it begins to lose power. One beam of light began to borrow from the other. The love that was in his heart, though increasing, was divided into two lines as it grew.

Each day during his seclusion, Grandshaykh ق would knock on his door for his wife to bring him food. One day he didn't knock. This went on for three days. His wife became worried so she went to Shaykh Sharafuddīn ق and said, "I think he might have died."

Shaykh Sharafuddīn ق said, "No he is fine, don't bother him. He is in a trance." When the love for Shah Naqshband ق grew in Grandshaykh's heart, the greatness of Shah Naqshband was revealed to him. He told him, "*Yā waladī*, be careful. You cannot water two fields with one windmill. You love must be focused to your shaykh."

This was a lesson to me. Grandshaykh ق said, "People are gathered around Shaykh Nazim and Shaykh Husayn and though these shaykhs direct the people to me, because of the way they handle them there is a problem. The disciples grow confused and divide their love between my representatives and me. This division of focus can create a sickness in the disciples which is reflected back on me when they come to visit."

This is *marad,* illness. Forty years ago Grandshaykh ق privately told this to me and Shaykh Adnan: "You must be very careful when you call the people." That is the major problem that people face when they begin to direct their focus in a way that takes them away from love of the shaykh. If you don't fix it, it will develop to the point where you can no longer control it.

He said:

> This is an illness that makes the people to come to the representatives and not to the shaykh. Take the four enemies and put them in a can and abandon yourselves and make yourself absent. These words are the spirit of hadith, *ṭarīqah,* and Qur'an.

Call Them by the Names of Their Fathers

What all this means is that when you begin to feel that a certain love is being created in the heart of the student for you, a representative, rather than for the shaykh, you must destroy it. This can lead to an illness that will lead you to the jungle of the ego. The ego will be thinking "I am something, I am something," and in the end it will grow. This problem can make even more problems for you later in your development when it will be very difficult to root it out. Make sure you don't fall into that sickness. It means:

ادْعُوهُمْ لِآبَائِهِمْ هُوَ أَقْسَطُ عِندَ اللَّهِ فَإِن لَّمْ تَعْلَمُوا آبَاءَهُمْ فَإِخْوَانُكُمْ فِي الدِّينِ
وَمَوَالِيكُمْ وَلَيْسَ عَلَيْكُمْ جُنَاحٌ فِيمَا أَخْطَأْتُم بِهِ وَلَكِن مَّا تَعَمَّدَتْ قُلُوبُكُمْ وَكَانَ اللَّهُ
غَفُورًا رَّحِيمًا

Call them by (the names of) their fathers: that is more just in the sight of Allah. But if ye know not their fathers (names, call them) your brothers in faith, or your maulas. But there is no blame on you if ye make a mistake therein: (what counts is) the intention of your hearts, and Allah is Oft-Returning, Most Merciful.[228]

"*Call them to their fathers.*" You must know who your spiritual father is and call the people to that spiritual father. Don't call them to yourself. You will create confusion in the followers and be blamed for it later.

Two years ago I was in the presence of Mawlana Shaykh, may Allah bless him, when he pulled out a paper from beneath a table. Imagine how many papers Mawlana receives each day. If you go upstairs to see where he sits, you will see thousands of envelopes. But this particular paper had caught his attention. He showed it to me. It contained only four lines.

It was in Arabic, thanking Shaykh Nazim for sending Shaykh Hisham to America. The note opened with, *alḥamdūlillāh wa 's-ṣalāt wa 's-salām 'ala Rasūlillāh*. Then it praised Grandshaykh ق as well as Mawlana Shaykh Nazim ق, but the latter not by name. Then it praised me by name and also by a special spiritual name given to me.

Mawlana Shaykh Nazim ق pointed to the note and said, "Look, he made my name absent, as if I don't exist."

That is the sign of the illness I have been describing. People must be called to their spiritual father, and to him alone. At that point, I had to defend the author of the note as well as myself, but Mawlana didn't want to hear this. I realized this is a teaching to make sure we are following the right way. It is very

---

[228] Sūratu 'l-Aḥzāb (the Confederates), 33:5.

important to understand it came through the *suhbat* that Grandshaykh ق gave forty years ago.

The point is this: Mawlana does not care who comes and who doesn't come. What he cares about is that those who are very near to his heart do not lose their love, and lose their way in *ṭarīqah*. When you lose your way, something grows between you and the straight path. It blocks your return like a huge tree with rapidly spreading branches and roots. Then you must kill it from the roots up. If it is large, you will need a chainsaw. When it is still a small stick, you can crack it and break with your hands. Don't let it become a huge trunk. May Allah forgive us and bless this meeting.

In a special blend of manners and clarity, all disciples must keep the pre-eminence of our living shaykh, Shaykh Nazim, in the forefront. It can become a big problem if you lose sight of this. We don't want to fall into hands of Satan. My duty is to tell people that our shaykh is Mawlana Shaykh Nazim and Allah says:

وَذَكِّرْ فَإِنَّ الذِّكْرَى تَنفَعُ الْمُؤْمِنِينَ

Remind!: for, verily, such a reminder will profit the believers.[229]

If you can keep reminding yourself of this, you will be on the right track. Consider yourself as nothing, and Shaykh Nazim as everything. Don't say, "I want to be something," because then you will get nothing. This is how it works. We struggle, we want to be known and respected; it is our nature, but we need to get rid of that nature.

If we insist we are building the way to bring people toward the shaykh and we see this sickness growing, then it's time to cut it off. That will be the only way to keep us from the fire. It may

[229] Sūratu 'dh-Dhārīyāt (the Winds that Scatter), 51:55.

only seem like good manners to put Shaykh Nazim first, but it is much more than that. The realization of its significance can be a powerful way to orient yourself in *ṭarīqah,* and connect to reality itself.

When I travel to Cyprus and meet people who want to sit with me, I avoid it altogether. I do not go there to speak or to be seen. I go only to see Mawlana Shaykh Nazim. The followers are his followers in his *ṭarīqah.* The people belong to him. We are only as Grandshaykh ق said, "The hunter needs a dog with him." So we are the dogs of the hunter—nothing more.

The hunter loves his dog and the dog is loyal to the hunter, but the dog doesn't eat the prey. Does he eat the prey? I must be very careful. So we must not touch the prey. Our duty is to fetch the prey for the hunter, but not to eat it. Even though the trained dogs carry the prey with their mouths, they don't eat what would otherwise be their natural food. If the shaykh wants to give a share to the dog to eat, he will do so. If he wants to give him a particular spiritual station and raise him up, he will. That is *ṭarīqah.* He wants to see how far you go.

If he gives you something, *alḥamdūlillāh*—all praise is for Allah. If he doesn't, *alḥamdūlillāh.* If he doesn't give you something physically, he will give you a spiritual gift for your hard work. And remember, you are doing hard work. This kind of effort and its rewards cannot be equated with money or with any physical contribution from the shaykh to you. He will give you a spiritual quality that you never imagined you would achieve with your *ʿamal,* actions. If the shaykh is pleased with you, he will give and give. You might later find that on a difficult stretch of your path, the jungle will suddenly turn to Paradise. At the beginning you will find obstacle after obstacle... and then suddenly the way will open.

كُلاًّ نُمِدُّ هَـؤُلاء وَهَـؤُلاء مِنْ عَطَاء رَبِّكَ وَمَا كَانَ عَطَاء رَبِّكَ مَحْظُورًا

Of the bounties of your Lord, We bestow freely on all, these as well as those. The bounties of your Lord are not closed (to anyone).[230]

Your Lord's favors are never limited. When He gives, it is with abundance. It may not be clear what is taking place. You might be running, but appear to be getting nowhere. They don't show you. Your duty is to keep running and not turn back. You are on a racetrack and they chase you until you reach the finish line. That is the place of heavenly Paradise. So don't stop!

Wa min Allāhi 't-tawfiq, bi ḥurmati 'l-Fātiḥah.

[230] Sūratu 'l-Isrā (the Night Journey), 17:20.

14: Humility Foremost

وَمَا أَرْسَلْنَاكَ إِلَّا كَافَّةً لِّلنَّاسِ بَشِيرًا وَنَذِيرًا وَلَكِنَّ أَكْثَرَ النَّاسِ لَا يَعْلَمُونَ

We have not sent thee but as a universal (Messenger) to men, giving them glad tidings, and warning them (against sin), but most men understand not. [231]

وَمَا أَرْسَلْنَاكَ إِلَّا رَحْمَةً لِّلْعَالَمِينَ

We sent you not (O Muhammad!) except as a mercy for all creatures. [232]

Firm Foundations

We spoke of *tawāḍaʿ*, humility, in the previous session and that everything is achieved through humility. Nothing can be achieved by arrogance and pride. Grandshaykh ق, may Allah bless his soul, said:

> The Lebanese students, Hisham and Adnan, were filled with arrogance. *Lā yatanazalūna an yataqabalu rā'īs jumhūrīyya*—They thought they were above presidents.

> But he added:

> Through my teaching, I had also taught them how to be humble. I showed them how to treat kings and everyday people with equal degrees of courtesy.

---

[231] Sūrah Ṣaba (Sheba), 34:28.

[232] Sūratu 'l-Anbīyā (the Prophets), 21:107.

If you can cultivate humility, your character will be altered. Humility will draw you nearer to God, the Exalted. For humans, humility is the cornerstone: the entire structure of your spiritual life rests on it. Grandshaykh ق was most insistent on this point. People today are arrogant. They are proud of their knowledge and believe they can teach everyone everything.

To learn *tawāda*ʿ, humility, you must understand you cannot interpret the words of your shaykh. This is a crucial point.

While some things can be interpreted, when your shaykh says something you must not say, "he meant this or that." Take what is said literally. Avoid interpretations as they can take you in many wrong directions. "I don't want to hear any more interpretations,"

Grandshaykh ق said:

> You must take my words as I speak them. Only when you reach a certain level can you make interpretations. When you humble yourself, don't say that you are doing so. Keep it to yourself, it is your corner stone. Build on your humility and you will be on a firm foundation.

We interpret what we hear more or less continuously; it's an ingrained habit. We tend to filter everything through the lens of our experience and sensibilities. These filters protect us in some ways and harm us in others. It is as though we admit some colors of light, and block others. These colored filters define who we are in many respects and highlight our strengths, our possibilities, our links to the Divine Attributes and our weaknesses where Satan maintains his heavy hold.

In this light, the exercise of not interpreting your shaykh's words takes on a special importance. The willing suspension of disbelief—or in this case, the suspension of interpretation—may temporarily open us to new ideas and influences by arresting the usual mental editing we do following each new experience. Inside our heads, this internal chatter would precede the outward act of hazarding an ill-advised guess at what the shaykh might have meant. Without humility, the foundation of your relationship to your shaykh will be built on shifting sand. The reason is simple: the failure to question your own notions about things before opening your mouth implies that what you are being taught is going in one ear and out the other, or worse still, right out through your mouth even before the new material has been carefully examined and digested.

For shaykhs do, in fact, bring you genuinely new material: using your old filters to block out or distort their teaching must be resisted, and the attitude of humility is the key. The light that a shaykh can shine on you is not ordinary light, not everyday information. Normal or diffused light is weak and bounces off various surfaces, appearing as what's left over after the subtraction of color based on the absorption properties of whatever it first touches. This is what we see all the time: indirect, diffused light. On the other hand, the light of a shaykh is like the coherent light of a laser beam: it carries greater power, transmits with more bandwidth, and is piercing. It is also rare, and therefore valuable, and should not be muted, modified, twisted, or diffused, like ordinary daily impressions.

In short, when your shaykh is speaking, (especially in this Sufi order), assume you do not fully grasp what is being said in all it dimensions and levels, observe your reactions, and avoid any thoughtless comments which can deflect the meaning altogether. Some shaykhs have a singular way of speaking. Their words address the precise circumstances of the moment, the collective nature of the audience present at that moment and, most remarkably, the urgent and separate needs of each listener, even though all present are apparently hearing the same words. The experience of such a public, albeit private, communication from a shaykh is potentially humbling in itself.

In this light, humility is not merely an attribute of the downtrodden, the meek, or the mild, nor necessarily a state following an unhappy humiliation, but rather a powerful tool to open the way to new levels of spiritual understanding and perception. A secret that protects itself, humility is a complete mystery to those who lack it. At the simplest level, it amounts to the ability to accept a gift graciously and marvel at its beauty. For the disciple, such a great gift has a price: open ears, open heart, and closed mouth.

Sayyida ʿA'isha and the Mirror

أَفَمَنْ أَسَّسَ بُنْيَانَهُ عَلَى تَقْوَى مِنَ اللّهِ وَرِضْوَانٍ خَيْرٌ أَم مَّنْ أَسَّسَ بُنْيَانَهُ عَلَىَ شَفَا
جُرُفٍ هَارٍ فَانْهَارَ بِهِ فِي نَارِ جَهَنَّمَ وَاللّهُ لاَ يَهْدِي الْقَوْمَ الظَّالِمِينَ

Which then is best, he that lays his foundation on piety to Allah and His good pleasure, or he that lays his foundation on an undermined sand-cliff ready to crumble to pieces? And it does crumble to pieces with him, into the fire of Hell. And Allah guideth not people that do wrong.[233]

Build your spiritual life on a firm foundation! Anything else will result in a collapse as surely as a poorly built house will fall in an earthquake. Everything will be destroyed, drop off a cliff into Hell, taking the structure and all its occupants along with it. Building on interpretation is not a strong foundation. The underlying foundation must be built on literal meanings.

There is an example of this in the life of Sayyida ʿA'ishā ﵂, may God, the Exalted, reward her, the wife of the Prophet ﷺ. She was a notable teacher of the Companions, who often went to her

---

[233] at-Tawbah (Repentance), 9:109.

seeking knowledge. Yet even she ran into difficulty in the matter of interpretations.

Grandshaykh ق said:

One day when the Prophet ﷺ was going to the mosque, and Allah said:

يَا بَنِي آدَمَ خُذُواْ زِينَتَكُمْ عِندَ كُلِّ مَسْجِدٍ وكُلُواْ وَاشْرَبُواْ وَلاَ تُسْرِفُواْ إِنَّهُ لاَ يُحِبُّ الْمُسْرِفِينَ

O human beings, take all your medallions and ornaments when you go the masjid...[234]

So the Prophet ﷺ did not filter this command by way of interpretation. The properly interpreted meaning of this command is to maintain your best manners when going to the mosque. At this point, the Prophet ﷺ gave us a good example of how not to interpret a command, and acted on it, quite literally, by grooming and dressing himself very carefully before setting out.

Sayyida 'A'ishā ؓ noticed that he looked particularly nice and stopped him at the door asking, "Where are you going?"

Prophet ﷺ replied, "I am going to the mosque."

She asked, "Why are you dressing so well and combing your hair and putting on perfume?"

This exchange might seem perfectly normal between an ordinary husband and wife, but Sayyida 'A'ishā ؓ was the teacher of the Companions. Her knowledge of the Prophet ﷺ was unparalleled. As the noble wife of Sayyidina Muhammad ﷺ, she is

---

[234] Sūratu ' l-'Arāf (the Heights), 7:31.

Umm al-mu'minīn, Mother of the Believers,[235] and not only a Companion herself, but a teacher of Companions.

This is a problem in all of us. No matter what your level, you must maintain a firm foundation. ʿA'ishā ﵂ asked, "Where are you going?" With the best manners, *adab,* the Prophet ﷺ responded, "I am going to the mosque." She persisted, "Why are you dressing so nicely and putting on perfume? Do you still love other women… are you going to see a woman?"

No doubt, countless similar conversations occur everyday across the planet when a wife confronts an especially well-groomed husband as he leaves to go out on the town, but Sayyida ʿA'ishā ﵂ was to be held to a higher standard.

The Prophet ﷺ replied, "O my beloved ʿA'ishā, take the mirror and see who is in the mirror!"

She looked in the mirror and said, "I see myself, ʿA'ishā, in the mirror."

And Prophet ﷺ said, "*Yā* ʿA'ishā, the mirror reflects exactly what it sees. We are all mirrors. I am a mirror. So when you look at me suspiciously because I am dressed nicely and looking well, you see what is in you. The believer is the mirror of his brother. You are seeing yourself, your own bad character; you are not seeing me. You still have the sickness of jealousy."[236]

Even though she was at a high enough level to teach the Companions, nevertheless, from the level of the Prophet ﷺ, she learned of an imperfection in her spiritual foundation.

---

[235] Arabic: *Umm al-mu'minīn*—title for the wife of the Prophet ﷺ; literally meaning, "Mother of the Believers."

[236] This is the origin of the hadith, "*al-mu'min mirrata ākhi,* the believer is the mirror of his brother."

So the Prophet ﷺ left and he was not happy. Sayyidina Abū Bakr ﵁, ʿA'ishā's father, found out that she had somehow upset the Prophet ﷺ. He went to her house and asked what had happened. She told him what had transpired, and her father sternly reprimanded her in a way that the Prophet ﷺ would not. The shock of her father's scolding brought her back to herself. This woke her up and reminded her that spiritual understanding required a solid base.

The Prophet ﷺ said, "Whoever humbles himself for his Lord, God, the Exalted, will raise him up."

We can only see in others what already exists in ourselves. The supremely polished heart of the Prophet ﷺ reflected a very clear image back upon those who were lucky enough to lay eyes on him. When we are not clean, these imperfections are reflected by those who are, in effect, psychological mirrors. Your brother will reflect your bad character. In other words, the detection of flaws in other people constitutes, more often than not, the recognition of our own flaws, if only we could recognize it. The acceptance of such a possibility is all the more difficult when you habitually see a great deal wrong with other people. The louder you complain about people, in or beyond their earshot, the less you have accepted the light from this special mirror.

These magical mirrors work both ways: some things are rendered altogether too visible, while other images are masked. For example, an especially unhappy, exacting person might remain in a constant state of agitation, always overwhelmed by the perceived foibles of his fellow humans. At the same time, he might attribute a saintly act of charity to an ulterior motive, and reject a well-meaning gesture from a friend. One the one side, the mirror presented him with only ugly, but unexamined things locked up within himself, and on the other side of the mirror, he could not see the goodness of a well-intended act, because there was nothing in himself that corresponded to such an image.

How often have you heard it said that mirrors and cameras can be so unkind? The mirror alternately shines and obscures. This unhappy, sharp-tongued person is in all of us.

As Sherlock Holmes often said to Mr. Watson, "You look, but you do not observe." When we complain about other people, we must first subconsciously recognize the flaw to even hang a name on it, summon the name to our lips to assign blame, and in so doing, reject the deep meaning of the mirror: that the reflection is our own.

Most social interactions are eventually poisoned by this very process. Learn to quietly accept the message of the mirror. Internalize these things you apparently see in others instead of immediately chattering on about them to anyone who will listen. You are the one who has to straighten yourself up. Always blame yourself, blame yourself, blame yourself!

What better exercise could there be for the month of Ramadan when backbiting is discouraged! Fast from food and also fast from negative comments; the pattern is clear. If you succeed, even to a small degree, it is a beginning that might carry over into the balance of the year.

Shaykh Nazim ق tells us:

> Consider the steady stream of people who come our way each day as messengers who, as part of Allah's design, are telling us something about ourselves that we need to know. Don't shoot the messenger! Say rather, "I am wrong." Don't let Satan trick you! Don't say, "I am a Friend of God, I am a sincere person." No! Leave such things to your shaykh. The correct internal posture is to tell yourself, "I am nothing… I am trying to learn to be nothing… I am not a Friend of God, nor a caliph, I'm just nothing."

Start with a clean slate. Then you will be able to reach a higher level. It is our duty to respect our brothers and sisters, to reach the higher levels that God, the Exalted, intends for us. The Prophet ﷺ said:

ادبني ربي فاحسن تاديبي

My Lord taught me good manners and He perfected my manners.[237]

From that secret you will be able to learn and inherit.

Even though he holds a position at the pinnacle of creation, he holds that position in *sajda,* prostration, and accordingly is humble before his Lord, his Lord's creation, and even us, who are part of that creation. This central paradox rests on the Prophet's ﷺ abiding humility. While God, the Exalted, created everyone from the light of the Prophet ﷺ, he does not regard himself as above mankind, but rather as part of humanity. Such is the nature of complete, transcendent, humility. For our part, we must regard Him as the highest in creation, even though He does not.

قُلْ إِنَّمَا أَنَا بَشَرٌ مِّثْلُكُمْ يُوحَى إِلَيَّ أَنَّمَا إِلَهُكُمْ إِلَهٌ وَاحِدٌ

Say: "I am but a man like yourselves, (but) the inspiration has come to me, that your Allah is one Allah.[238]

No one can reach the level of understanding of the Prophet, whose knowledge began before the beginning of time. Quite naturally, Sayyida 'A'ishā's knowledge was not of this level, and she made a mistake. After she confronted her husband she subsequently learned a valuable lesson, and so must we all. The occasional correction along the path keeps us on the Straight Way. This is why God, the Exalted, sent us here; otherwise, we would have remained in Paradise. We would not have understood the key

[237] Ibn Samaʿnī in *Adab al-malā*.

[238] Sūratu 'l-Kahf (the Cave), 18:110.

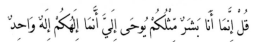

to our trust had we only received praise. God, the Exalted, sent us to this world so we may understand the importance of the key.

Our *ʿamal* alone cannot take us anywhere, but obedience to Allah, to His prophet ﷺ, and to our teachers, will take us to our goals.

The Best-Spent Wealth

Grandshaykh ق, may God, the Exalted, bless Him, said:

> If a human being spent all the wealth God gave him in the way of his Creator, he would never regret it, even if all the wealth of the world had fallen into his lap.

We all look for the trust, the inheritance God, the Exalted, has in store for us. When you find yourself thinking, "I want my trust, I want my trust," you will not get it. But when you lose hope of getting your trust, then slowly the shaykh will give it to you. So you must decide whether you want something or not. If you want something, you will never get it. This is the way of God, the Exalted.

Ordinarily, people worship for rewards. If you reach a higher level, you will worship Allah solely because He is your lord, you love Him, and seek His love. The higher level is worship for the love of the Community.

Like Shaykh Bayāzīd al-Bistāmī ق, who asked, "O God, the Exalted, they are Your creation! Make me the scapegoat for all of them. Let no one enter the fire; take me instead."

To whom do you make *sajda*? Are you making that prostration to God, the Exalted, or you are making it to wealth and to this world? You must think about this. You must ask yourself, "Am I really doing this for God, the Exalted?" That prostration is the key to the place which lies beyond this world, beyond the senses, beyond the bounds of your everyday perceptions and desires. Without this key, your trust will not open. What we know as our life in this world is only the tip of the iceberg. There is a much larger part of our existence of which we know nothing.

No one should imagine that his trust has opened in this world. This world cannot begin to contain the dimensions of the spirit. Our way is a path that leads in that direction and, *insha-Allah,* one day God, the Exalted, will open these things to us. He is generous. The gifts He has in store for us are too big for this world. Our exile here in this world ends in the grave, and it is there He will open these things for us.

But we only pray: "O my Lord! we are not asking You to open our trust in this world, like an ordinary reward. You are the Most Generous of the generous. You make Your servants happy."

Grandshaykh ق relates:

In the time of Sayyidina ʿAbdul Khāliq al-Ghujdawānī, there was an epidemic, and thousands were going to die. He looked at all his students' hearts to find someone able to lift that affliction. He looked right and left (and in Grandshaykh's words), "He looked and looked, and he didn't find except two between all his students, like Adnan and Hisham, and they owned two big oxen."

In that time, people owned one plow ox that they used in their daily tasks. He said, "O my children, I didn't find except you." He called them and said, "O my children there is a big plague coming and I am asking God, the Exalted, to take away that plague, and in order that I will be able to take away that plague, Allah showed me (through a vision) Sayyidina Muhammad ﷺ saying to me, '*Yā* Abdul Khaliq, let someone slaughter his ox, bring that to me, and I will write on the skin of the ox some verses of Holy Qur'an,' and I didn't find anyone except you two capable of doing that. So I am asking you to bring your oxen, each one of you, and *lā aqdir an ukaliffu ghayrakum*—I cannot ask anyone to carry that task except you both. So go get your oxen and come."

These two were *fanā fī 'sh-shaykh*[239]. If the shaykh tells them "slaughter yourself" they will do so for his sake.

Wa min Allāhi 't-tawfīq, bi ḥurmati 'l-Fātiḥah.

[239] Totally annihilated in their shaykh.

15: HAJJ: THE JOURNEY OF LIFE

Pilgrimage Must be Purely for God

Grandshaykh asked, "Why do human beings go for hajj?" People go to hajj to obey Allah's Orders, and the people going this year will be fulfilling their intention, *niyyah*. Some people go early, some go late, but all will stand on 'Arafat,[240] which is a central rite of the hajj. To go on hajj constitutes an acceptance of Allah's Orders.

In that spirit, you must avoid anger throughout the pilgrimage and not show even one *mithqāla dharattin,* atom's weight, of anger. Such anger is part of the material world and can negate an entire hajj. Allah does not want us to grow angry as we swim away from this world towards the ocean of His mercy.

A successful completion of the hajj rituals requires a certain purity of intention, which extends over a number of days. On any journey, you must leave behind one place to arrive at another. On hajj, the trip involves the escape from the distractions of everyday concerns to reach another state of being. If you become upset when you lose your luggage and worry about your money during the trip, you have not really moved or transcended. Your body has made the journey: you took a plane or a boat to travel to Mecca, but your internal state has not moved.

In one second, an angry outburst will block the spiritual gifts waiting to shower you at the hajj. You will be considered as *muṣrifūn*—those who always waste their time and money. You had good intentions to go there, but that intention changed when

---

[240] A mountain outside Mecca.

you got angry over some worldly issue. If in the midst of the hajj you get upset, then that *'amal*, action, is canceled, because you have put something in it other than Allah. You went only for Allah, so when you put a material thing in between you and Allah, you have committed *shirk*—idolatry.

Why is it hajj? Because it is in obedience to Allah, as if you are going on a pilgrimage to the Divine Presence. This means any *'amal* with the proper intention (to do something in the way of Allah) is a continuation of hajj.

وَقَالَ الَّذِينَ لَا يَرْجُونَ لِقَاءَنَا لَوْلَا أُنزِلَ عَلَيْنَا الْمَلَائِكَةُ

أَوْ نَرَى رَبَّنَا لَقَدِ اسْتَكْبَرُوا فِي أَنفُسِهِمْ وَعَتَوْا عُتُوًّا كَبِيرًا

But those who do not believe that they are destined to meet Us are want to say, "Why have no angels been sent down to us?" Or, "Why do we not see our Sustainer?" Indeed, they are far too proud of themselves, having rebelled (against God's truth) with utter disdain![241]

وَقَدِمْنَا إِلَى مَا عَمِلُوا مِنْ عَمَلٍ فَجَعَلْنَاهُ هَبَاءً مَّنثُورًا

And We will turn to whatever deeds they did (in this life), and We will make such deeds as floating dust scattered about.[242]

God, the Exalted, knows their intentions. He knows they traded many things with Satan during that journey, they did not perform the hajj for Allah, and He throws their deeds in their faces. God, the Exalted, does not accept anything from mixed intentions; He does not like that. Our deeds and intentions must be very pure, for Allah. Sometimes we start with a good intention,

---

[241] Sūratu 'l-Furqān (the Criterion), 25:21.
[242] Sūratu 'l-Furqān (the Criterion), 25:23.

and something happens in the midst of it; if you avoided that distraction and followed your original good intention, you kept on the way of a good actions. But if you strayed from that good intention and followed that which led you to anger, then you join those called *al-mubadhirīn*, the squanderers, in the Holy Qur'an:

إِنَّ الْمُبَذِّرِينَ كَانُوا إِخْوَانَ الشَّيَاطِينِ وَكَانَ الشَّيْطَانُ لِرَبِّهِ كَفُورًا

Lo! the squanderers were ever brothers of the devils, and the devil was ever an ingrate to his Lord.[243]

You will be responsible and *maḥkūm*, under the control of Satan. All the effort and expense you invested is dissolved, finished!

Grandshaykh ق said, "If you go for hajj and a poor man comes to you and extends his hand, and you didn't give him anything, your entire hajj is not accepted."

It means any deed you do is a form of pilgrimage, and if someone comes seeking your advice, that person was sent to raise your level, to give you more reward on the hajj.

This *ṭarīqah* is a pilgrimage—you are following the way of Friends of God and *zuhād,* ascetics and *ittiba*ʿ *an-Nabī,* following the Prophet ﷺ. If someone comes to give you advice and you throw him out, it means you are lost. Allah sent that person to you to give you advice. Listen to that advice and check it. If that advice coincides with Shariah, go with it.

People will begin to argue, especially on the Internet. Don't argue with anyone. If it is a matter of Shariʿah, it's alright: if not, then don't reply or else it will create *fitna*—strife and confusion. That is if we want the hereafter.

---

[243] Sūratu 'l-Isrā (the Night Journey), 17:27.

Give Freely in Hajj

Poor people in hajj, it is their land, they are living there. The time of hajj is their crop, like in spring you plant and later in summer you harvest. So they wait to harvest in hajj time. You will see thousands of people there coming to harvest. Help them in the harvest and Allah will help you in your harvest on Judgment Day.

Allah is checking on Judgment Day, whatever you planted in this world you will reap in the hereafter. So Judgment Day is the harvest. And hajj is a harvest. If you didn't put fertilizer, you will not find any harvest. So on the way to hajj give, give, give. Accept advice if it is in accordance with Shariah, don't create problems, and then you will reach what Allah wants you to reach.

Grandshaykh ق said if anything takes you for hajj, or any *'amal* which we consider to be a pilgrimage, don't let anything disrupt it.

قُلْ إِنَّمَا أَنَا بَشَرٌ مِّثْلُكُمْ يُوحَى إِلَيَّ أَنَّمَا إِلَهُكُمْ إِلَهٌ وَاحِدٌ فَمَن كَانَ يَرْجُو لِقَاء رَبِّهِ فَلْيَعْمَلْ عَمَلًا صَالِحًا وَلَا يُشْرِكْ بِعِبَادَةِ رَبِّهِ أَحَدًا

Say: I am only a mortal like you. My Lord inspireth in me that your God is only One God. And whoever hopeth for the meeting with his Lord, let him do righteous work, and make none sharer of the worship due unto his Lord. [244]

Anyone who wants to go on pilgrimage to Allah, who wants to devote his actions in Allah's way, must not associate anyone with Allah. Don't give way to your ego by rejecting any poor person, or rejecting anyone on the way. He is teaching us etiquette.

---

[244] Sūratu 'l-Kahf (The Cave) 18:110.

When the Ka'bah Returns Your Greeting

Grandshaykh ق said

The real hajj, that you know is accepted, is when you give
salām to Ka'bah and it answers you back. I went ten times for
hajj and ten times gave *salām* to Ka'bah, and once Ka'bah
returned the *salām*."

When you say, "*As-salāmu 'alayka yā Baytullāh*—and peace be
upon you O House of God," when the Ka'bah replies, "*wa
'alayka as-salām yā 'abdallāh*—and peace be upon you O servant
of God" at that time you know what *tarīqah* means, you know
what shaykhs mean, you know what guides mean, you know
the meaning of Companions ﴾, and you understand what is
the meaning of the Prophet ﷺ. So until that time, if we don't
hear that *salām*, we are like:

$$ وَمَن كَانَ فِي هَذِهِ أَعْمَى فَهُوَ فِي الآخِرَةِ أَعْمَى وَأَضَلُّ سَبِيلاً $$

*those who were blind in this world, will be blind in the
hereafter;*[245]

it means we do not understand the meaning. When Ka'bah
returns the *salām*, it means your name is written in that house,
you are welcome into that house, and you have achieved the
station to enter that house.

Not like those who enter it today to clean it, they are only
seeing four walls. When you reach the level of "hearing the
Ka'bah" you will not see four walls; it will be a Paradise, like the
hereafter. Everything you cannot imagine in Paradise, you will
find there. Though Paradise is described in the Holy Qur'an, its
reality cannot be accurately described by words. Those who

---

[245] Sūratu 'l-Isrā (the Night Journey), 17:72.

receive the *salām* of Ka'bah will understand the reality of gnosis, *ma'rifatullāh.*[246]

How many of us went for hajj, did we hear *salām*? All of these people who go two, three million every year, did they hear *salām*. And he said:

> If you didn't hear the *salām*, your hajj is rejected. But rejected from the view of *ma'rifatullāh*, not rejected from the point of view of your obligation you will be written as one who completed the fifth pillar of Islam.

> Grandshaykh ق said:

> When you are engulfed in anger, in material life, and in Satan's whispers, how are you going to hear the heavenly voice that Ka'bah brings to you? It is impossible, for it is blocked.

فَمَن يَعْمَلْ مِثْقَالَ ذَرَّةٍ خَيْرًا يَرَهُ

Whoever does one atom of goodness will see it.[247]

One atom of good deeds in the way of Allah is a pilgrimage, and will open the *salām* of Ka'bah. That means the less than one atom of good we are doing is blended with hidden *shirk*, idolatry, that danger which the Prophet ﷺ feared most for his Community. That is disrupting our journey. Allah said:

فَمَن يَعْمَلْ مِثْقَالَ ذَرَّةٍ خَيْرًا يَرَهُ

And so, he who shall have done an atom's weight of good, shall behold it;[248]

---

[246] Arabic: *ma'rifatullāh*—knowledge of God.
[247] Sūratu 'l-Zalzalah (the Earthquake), 99:7.

Why are we not seeing good? Because we are not able to achieve even one atom. How then do you want to become a Friend of God? People consider themselves a Friend of God or a great shaykh, and yet one atom of goodness we cannot achieve.

Allah said that *'alā mithqāla dharratin*—for an atom of goodness—He will reward you. Grandshaykh ق said angels are under a big responsibility to be sure that you will be rewarded for that atom. Angels do not err, so as they are responsible, if we are doing an atom of goodness, it will be acknowledged and rewarded. When we do an atom's weight of good, it will open and we will feel and see. It is for those the Friends of God are reaching. We are not seeing or feeling that. So what is the result when our deeds are combined with hidden idolatry?

إِلَّا مَن تَابَ وَآمَنَ وَعَمِلَ عَمَلًا صَالِحًا فَأُوْلَٰئِكَ يُبَدِّلُ اللَّهُ سَيِّئَاتِهِمْ حَسَنَاتٍ وَكَانَ اللَّهُ غَفُورًا رَّحِيمًا

Unless he repents, believes, and works righteous deeds, for Allah will change the evil of such persons into good, and Allah is Oft-Forgiving, Most Merciful;[249]

Every atom of every good *'amal* has its nearness to the Divine Presence. Every good action has engraved on it proximity to the Creator, according to that atom of goodness it contains. According to that atom there is a light, although it might be a very small one, but there must be a Divine Presence that opens from that action. Slowly, one by one they increase and that will open to the Friends of God.

---

[248] Sūratu 'l-Zalzalah (the Earthquake), 99:7.

[249] Sūratu 'l-Furqān (the Criterion), 25:70.

The Stingy One has No Acceptable Worship

Grandshaykh ق said:

> *Al-bakhīl lā ḥajj wa la zīyārat maqbūl wa lā ṣalāt wa lā sadaqah*—the stingy one has no hajj, and no visitation of the Prophet, and no prayers and no charity.

This means all his worship is unacceptable in the Divine Presence.

We go back to the first verse we mentioned regarding deeds that are tainted with hidden *shirk*, so they are thrown back in their faces.

Grandshaykh ق said, "What is the best offering accepted by God, the Exalted? It is to be generous."

Even if you are poor, be generous! In Allah's Sight, we are all impoverished, and yet, generosity opens the door for everything. Some people were generous, then Allah opened the spiritual path for them and they made progress, but their ego prevented them from going further. You must be very careful. If something opened because of your generosity and love, don't let your ego play tricks, or despite your generosity and love you may be blocked in the Way to Allah.

Even if you give everything in charity for Allah's sake, and He opens the spiritual path to you, don't block the way by being stingy. Don't refuse to teach others, or look for compensation. Knowledge cannot be stopped. We must not follow the tricks of Satan, looking for payment, expecting something in return. You cannot sell Allah's knowledge. Sayyidina Muhammad ﷺ, the pinnacle of knowledge, took nothing; he gave

Look how Sayyidina Salmān ☙ sold himself into slavery to reach the Prophet ﷺ.[250] The last monk whom he served told him the signs of the Last Prophet, one being that he doesn't take charity, and he only accepts gift. When Sayyidina Salmān ☙ presented the Prophet ﷺ with charity he didn't take it, but rather gave it to the Companions, but when Sayyidina Salmān ☙ gave the Prophet ﷺ a gift, he accepted it.

That is why according to Shari'ah, it is not acceptable to sell Allah's Word, or Islamic teachings, or even reciting the *adhān*. If payment is offered for these services you may accept it, but if not then don't ask. This is the safe course.

Wa min Allāhi 't-tawfīq, bi ḥurmati 'l-Fātiḥah.

---

[250] Salmān al-Fārsī ☙ is a famous Sahabi who traveled from Persia in search of the Prophet ﷺ.

16: A SERVANT'S GIFT

Rote Learning or Comprehension?

When God, the Exalted, gives to His servants, it is according to His greatness and His generosity. Allah gave to Sayyidina Muhammad ﷺ *ʿulūm al-awalīn wa 'l-ākhirīn*—knowledge of the beginnings and the endings, from which the Friends of God inherit.

God, the Exalted, taught His Prophet ﷺ 70,000 years before He created anyone. No one knows when Allah created the light of Sayyidina Muhammad ﷺ. Allah taught him knowledges that no one knew. That is when the Prophet ﷺ said, *ashhadu an lā ilāha illa 'Llāh*—I bear witness that there is no god but Allah (The Creator).

Grandshaykh ق said:

> From every side, Allah has given me knowledge in order to advise Ummat an-Nabī—the Community of the Prophet ﷺ, and Allah gave me a guarantee from every side, to enable me to bring my students to the presence of the Prophet ﷺ clean.

ʿAlauddīn al-Bukhārī ق was the student and caliph of Shah Bahauddin Naqshband ق, as well as his scribe. He memorized every word Shah Naqshband ق spoke to him, and had the power to memorize every word he heard.

Shah Naqshband ق said to ʿAlauddin al-Bukhari, "*Lā taḥfaẓ al-qawl bal aḥfaẓ al-ʿamal*—don't memorize the letters and the words, safeguard the actions; if you don't, you are losing all the words I have spoken."

Today we memorize the words and letters, and no one is analyzing their notes from the *suhbats* to act upon them and apply the knowledge transmitted in them.

Shah Naqshband ق said, "There are knowledges coming to me from the hereafter, from the knowledge of heavens." Allah said:

> I have created for you in Paradise beautiful pearls, which are these beautiful maidens, *ḥūr al-ʿayn,*[251] and if one such maiden will show her finger to this world the entire world will swoon.

> What is the meaning here of *ḥūr al-ʿayn*? It is not the beautiful and magnificent wives Allah will give in Paradise, for if the Friends of God think in these common terms, Allah would throw them out from His Presence. In this case, *ḥūr al-ʿayn* are the manifestation of the Beautiful Names and Attributes of Allah, Who manifests the beauty of His Essence to His Friends. To Friends of God, these manifestations are like what *ḥūr al-ʿayn* are to common people. The goal of the Friends of God is the Creator, not the creation.

> Grandshaykh ق continues:

> I am saying something that has not been heard before. I am telling you something happening in heavens from the angels. From the moment I am in now, and from moment to moment, things change, things double.

> It means events occur like a nuclear reaction: very, very fast.

The Distributor

All these manifestations and paradises Allah gives to the Prophet ﷺ to distribute to those who are following him. Whatever the

---

[251] Arabic: *ḥūr al-ʿayn* - Beautiful maidens in Paradise who are the promised companions at the service of believing men; similarly, women are promised *wildānan mukhaladūn*, eternal youths at their service (c.f. Holy Qur'an Sūratu 'l-Wāqiʿa (The Overwhelming Event), 56:17).

Prophet ﷺ receives, he divides and distributes. That is why his name is "Abū 'l-Qāsim," the continuous distributor of Allah's favors without even a moment's interruption. If he keeps it to himself then no more comes, because then the container is full. To continue to receive from God, the Exalted, Prophet must give.

In this world and in the hereafter, Abū 'l-Qāsim ﷺ will distribute these manifestations Allah is giving to him ﷺ. We say Allah is al-Khāliq, the Creator, so creation never stops, as God, the Exalted, is continuously creating without cessation.

With the name Abū 'l-Qāsim, Allah gave the Prophet ﷺ authority to continuously distribute what he receives. Also, the Prophet ﷺ knows all members of his Community by name, and he knows the capacity of each heart. Imagine such power, to be able to look at all the hearts and in one instant and give them their fill.

He is spiritual father of all prophets and they are all giving to their nations. He dispenses God's grants to them and they then give to their communities. But he gives us directly as we are his Community, the Ummah.

Sometimes when I speak, if someone is on the phone, he cannot listen to me and the phone conversation at the same time. Some people can listen to me and to another conversation simultaneously; they have that talent. Imagine three conversations at the same time. Imagine ten people are talking to you simultaneously; can you understand? Why can't we understand that, but we can understand a symphony? It is due to harmony: when it is present, you can listen to hundreds at the same time.

The Prophet ﷺ does not look to the physical speeches of the people, but he looks to their hearts, where harmony resides, full of heavenly light. The light he pours into their hearts is like a heavenly symphony; for while they play a musical tone they are simultaneously all experiencing this beautiful manifestation in a harmonious way that can never be described.

You might look at a carpet and notice the colors are discordant. Look at this one, and it is more harmonious. Bring a Persian silk carpet and you cannot stop looking at it because its colors and designs blend in such harmony.

To be in harmony is most important. When students live in harmony with each other, the shaykh gives more. If they fight one another, harmony cannot be present. We live in a time when there is little harmony, even between a husband and wife, or between parents and their children. When they reach that balance and are content with what Allah has given them, they become harmonious.

كُنتُمْ خَيْرَ أُمَّةٍ أُخْرِجَتْ لِلنَّاسِ تَأْمُرُونَ بِالْمَعْرُوفِ وَتَنْهَوْنَ عَنِ الْمُنكَرِ وَتُؤْمِنُونَ بِاللَّهِ
وَلَوْ آمَنَ أَهْلُ الْكِتَابِ لَكَانَ خَيْرًا لَّهُم مِّنْهُمُ الْمُؤْمِنُونَ وَأَكْثَرُهُمُ الْفَاسِقُونَ

You are the best of people, evolved for mankind, enjoining what is right, forbidding what is wrong, and believing in Allah.[252]

You are the best of the nations that have been sent, but not because of your deeds; rather, you are the best of nations because of Muhammad ﷺ, because of that dispensation that he is distributing to you and keeps filling you with, making you ever more harmonious with each other.

Heavenly Moments

In every moment Allah is giving the Prophet ﷺ something He didn't give him in the previous moment, and it is impossible to give him the same thing from one moment to another.

Let us define a "moment" as one-sixtieth of a second. Let us say for example this year is 365 days, times 24 hours, times 60

[252] Sūrat Āli-ʿImrān (the Family of ʿImrān), 3:110.

minutes, times 60 seconds, times 60 fractions of a second, our "moment." How much is that? (((360 x 24= 8760) x 60 = 525600) x 60 = 31536000) x 60 = 1892160000 or 1.9 billion, nearly two billion moments. In that two-billionth of a year moment, Allah is giving knowledge that is completely different from what He gave in the previous moment, and different from the next moment.

Allah is not like us; He gives an ocean in one moment. Imagine how much He is giving and how much the Prophet ﷺ is distributing, and one moment doesn't resemble another, and imagine one year, the second year, the third year. That knowledge is present in the heart, but it is veiled.

Imagine how many billions of years and how many "moments" pass from the Day of Promises[253] to Resurrection Day. It is beyond the imagination to comprehend. You cannot imagine or understand what Allah gave to the Prophet ﷺ, and no one can understand what Allah gave to one individual heart. If that veil is lifted, you will find yourself in the Divine Presence with the full power of what Allah gave you.

Grandshaykh ق said:

> What is given in every moment is different from what was given before, and is known as *rūḥ al-ḥayāt,* soul of the spiritual life. The *rūḥ al-ḥayāt* sustains the distribution of *niʿam,* provisions, and sustains our physical bodies. That is why the soul cannot go to the grave.

إِنَّا لله وَإِنَّا إِلَيه رَاجِعونَ

To Allah We belong, and to Him is our return.[254]

---

[253] When all souls were gathered to Allah and pledged to worship Him alone and uphold the Divine Law.

[254] Sūratu 'l-Baqara (the Heifer), 2:156.

The *rūḥ al-ḥayāt* must return to its origin, facing the Prophet ﷺ, where it stands, receiving its destined Divine provision from him. Then there is no physical body to cage the soul; it is free-standing, or freelancing. It is not restricted in a cubicle of an office in a company. From wherever you are, you can send reports. You are freelancing in the cave with the Prophet ﷺ, and the other prophets, along with all the other souls of the Community that have died, because they are all there in harmony.

Imām Ghazālī[255] said, "We are blind until we die, and then our eyes are opened."

Wa min Allāhi 't-tawfiq, bi ḥurmati 'l-Fātiḥah.

[255] Imām Abū Ḥāmid al-Ghazālī was a 12th century jurist, theologian, and mystic whose luminous works, including *Iḥyā al-'Ulūm al-Dīn* (The Revival of Religious Sciences) influenced the Jewish philosopher Maimonides, and Christian theologian St. Thomas Aquinas.

17: Beauty and Majesty

Drops of Light

Awliyāullāh pray, "O Allah, give us in Paradise from *ḥūr al-ʿayn*—the radiant blessed heavenly maidens of Paradise." And Grandshaykh ق explained *ḥūr al-ʿayn* is the description two of the Beautiful Names of God: *Jalāl* (Beauty) and *Jamāl* (Majesty). If a Friend of God's intention is the physical understanding of *ḥūr al-ʿayn,* the heavenly maidens, he will be thrown out from sainthood, because they are from what is *mā siwallāh*—that which is other than Allah. The intention of Friends of God is only Allah and His Prophet ﷺ; they are not interested in anything else.

Grandshaykh ق said:

I am not talking to you of something that was heard before, but I am bringing to you from the realities that manifest from one moment to another, from *ḥayāt*, something that has life in it, from realities, and from what He gives of favors, *niʿam*, and whatever He gives is from something that appears always, without end. And the distributor for all of that is Sayyidina Muhammad ﷺ and that is why he is titled Abū 'l-Qāsim ﷺ. And in every moment there are new realities appearing and they don't resemble each other, for they are completely unique.

Grandshaykh ق continued:

God, the Exalted, does not leave us, He is creating more and more, and the Prophet ﷺ is distributing more and more. If what He is sending were to manifest more than what it does, the wheel of the world would stop moving. People would no longer be looking to this world, and they would stop acting for this world completely and only look to the hereafter. In that case there would be no more generations to come, as everything would stop [i.e even relations between husbands and wives].

So if that *tajallī*, manifestation, opens to anyone who is not a Friend of God (because only Friends of God have the capacity to hold it), they will stop whatever they are doing, or run away from society to a cave or a jungle, and stop doing anything. In Muslim countries you find people in this state and they want nothing to do with this world. They were unveiled to these realities and are so attracted to the Divine that they became *majādhib*,[256] in a trance, completely disconnected from this world, and only Allah can bring them back.

They are now seeking these Beautiful Attributes, so how can you bring them back to this dirty life? To such as them this world has become something of no importance. If the rest of us see wealth, or a business opportunity that brings substantial profit, we run after it. If a man sees a beautiful lady or a lady a handsome man, they run after the other. The complete focus today is on desires of this world.

So these people who have been affected, when they see the Divine Attributes of Jalāl, Magnificence, and Jamāl, Beauty, open only slightly, the attractions of this world become insignificant.

Grandshaykh ق said:

> These are realities that a shaykh gives his student, just as a surgeon numbs his patient with anesthesia; he then does not feel what is being poured into his heart, but on Judgment Day it will appear, and these students will be like shining stars.

---

[256] Arabic: *majādhib* (sing. *majdhūb*), attracted, entranced, people "mad" in love of God.

Allah created the Prophet to carry His light and that is why He created his light first. Prophet ﷺ said:

عن جابر بن عبد الله بلفظ قال قلت: يا رسول الله، بأبي أنت وأمي، أخبرني عن أول شيء خلقه الله قبل الأشياء . قال: يا جابر، إن الله تعالى خلق قبل الأشياء نور نبيك من نوره، ...

The first thing that Allah created was the light of your Prophet, O Jābir...[257]

Allah is sending directly, and under His observance that light is constantly being focused through the manifestation of the Beautiful Divine Names and Attributes from the Hidden Essence, the Hidden Treasure that no one knows. From the Hidden Treasure that manifestation comes and falls on Prophet ﷺ and the light of Prophet ﷺ was molded with that.

We explained previously in another series of associations, that Grandshaykh ق said:

The light of the Prophet ﷺ was in a lamp and was molded with the Beautiful Divine Names and Attributes, and from the sweat of the Prophet ﷺ that is generated by his shyness over taking all these knowledges, his light begins to shine more and more, and from that a drop emerged. From that drop Allah created the remainder of the 124,000 prophets, and from the succeeding drop Allah created Sayyidina Abū Bakr aṣ-Ṣiddīq ؓ.

From the residue of the light of Sayyidina Muhammad ﷺ, Allah molded the reality of Sayyidina Abū Bakr aṣ-Ṣiddīq ؓ, and from the residue of the light of Sayyidina Abū Bakr aṣ-

[257] 'Abd al-Razzāq narrates it in his *Muṣannaf*. Bayhaqī narrates it with a different wording in *Dalā'il al-nubūwwah* and Diyārbakrī in *Tārīkh al-khāmis*.

Ṣiddīq ☙, Allah created the light of the students and apprentices of the Naqshbandi Sufi order.

From that light of Sayyidina Abū Bakr ☙ our light was created, and everyone takes his children with him, meaning his spiritual children. Sayyidina Adam ﷺ is the physical father of the human race and Sayyidina Abū Bakr ☙ is the spiritual father of all the students of the Naqshbandiyya Sufi order, and they have been granted *tawāda'*, humbleness.

A Light Beyond Prison Walls

Grandshaykh ق said:

> Although we still have arrogance, we struggle with it, but you can find humility with these students. That is why we don't hate the people of beards[258] — we love them, and we love shaykhs, and we love the elderly. We don't look at them in a bad way. Today, some look at the people of beards in a bad way. Some *ṭarīqats* have no respect at all for people of beards, and in some *ṭarīqats* they say men must be clean-shaved and completely normal [Western] dress is their *ṭarīqah*. Although dress isn't an issue to make one in or out of *ṭarīqah*, but it symbolizes the love for what you believe in.

> The father of *arwāḥ*, souls,[259] is Sayyidina Abū Bakr ☙. In the association of the Friends of God, Sayyidina Bayāzīd al-Bistāmī ق said, "Abu Bakr aṣ-Ṣiddīq is going to fill four paradises with the intercession of the Prophet ﷺ, and it is a shame that we remaining Friends of God cannot fill the rest."

Grandshaykh ق said:

---

[258] A reference to those who follow the Prophetic sunnah of growing the beard.
[259] Arabic: *arwāḥ*: spirits; plural of *rūḥ*.

Sayyidina Shah Naqshband will also fill four paradises and so
how can Sayyidina Abū Bakr ؈ fill four and Shah Naqshband
ق fill four?

He answered, "It is light upon light."

It means that Sayyidina Shah Naqshband ق will send more
from the light that Sayyidina Abū Bakr ؈ has sent and that will be
light upon light for intercession.

Grandshaykh ق said:

You must be patient with this prison. This body is a prison for
you and all people are in the prison of the world. Allah has
the Name aṣ-Ṣabūr—The Most Patient. After He put 98
Divine Names, Allah placed aṣ-Ṣabūr at the end. The Prophet
؈ said:

$$\text{لا راحة فى الدين}$$

"There is no rest in religion,"

so it is an ongoing struggle. Whoever is able to remain patient
through the course of this struggle will reach a tremendous
reward: on Judgment Day God, the Exalted, will reflect on
him the 99 Beautiful Names and Attributes, which will be
manifested on that servant.

Because 1+1=2, +1=3, +1=4. So it is accumulating. Hūwa Allah,
ar-Raḥmān, ar-Raḥīm, al-Malik, al-Quddūs, as-Salām... on and on
to the 99th Name, they are accumulating. So all of them add to 99
and that Name is aṣ-Ṣabūr. If you take one out you cannot arrive
at aṣ-Ṣabūr—you would reach the Name preceding aṣ-Ṣabūr. One
must follow another in a complete sequence in order to reach aṣ-
Ṣabūr.

So when you are patient in this world with what you have
been given, patient in this "prison" in which you have been
placed, through that patience you will reach to the Divine Name
aṣ-Ṣabūr. Only with patience can you reach the realities of all

these Divine Names, and on Judgment Day the reality of these Beautiful Names and Attributes will adorn you, causing you to appear like a shining star. There will appear shining stars under the manifestations of each of the Beautiful Names and Attributes, and such people will be sent to Paradise, clean. And they will take their children with them, saying, "These are mine."

Sayyidina Abū Bakr ﵁ is the friend of the Prophet ﷺ, and so he is with the Prophet ﷺ in the highest paradise, Jannat al-Firdaws.

مَعَ الَّذِينَ أَنْعَمَ اللهُ عَلَيْهِم مِّنَ النَّبِيِّينَ وَالصِّدِّيقِينَ وَالشُّهَدَاء وَالصَّالِحِينَ وَحَسُنَ أُولَـئِكَ رَفِيقًا

All who obey Allah and the apostle are in the company of those on whom is the Grace of Allah, of the prophets (who teach), the sincere (lovers of Truth), the witnesses (who testify), and the Righteous (who do good): Ah! what a beautiful fellowship![260]

He will take with him all the spiritual children upon whom this Divine Light has been adorned. So what we need is to be patient; with our wives, with our children, with our friends, and similarly wives need to be patient with their husbands and their children and their friends.

Inasmuch as you are patient and try to cover what wrongs those related to you have done, similarly Sayyidina Abū Bakr ﵁ will be granted from what he is given to veil whatever wrong his spiritual children have done. So we must learn to cover faults of others in this world and not expose one another. We must be very healthy by being patient with each other. Do not argue. If you see someone arguing, stop the conversation and move forward. There

---

[260] Sūratu 'n-Nisā (Women), 4:69.

is no way to convince a drunken person. When you are drunk with anger and similarly he is drunk, then you may kill each other. You cannot drive when you are drunk, you cannot fly on a plane, as now they check you. So how are you going to drive your body and your ego when you are drunk? Of course you will take the body to places that are not acceptable, and thus, the soul is forced to go to places it doesn't like.

Then Grandshaykh ق said, "*Wayy, wayy, wayy!*"[261] He was stunned by what was manifesting to him when he was giving that *suhbat*. He said:

> Don't think there is an end to the Realities and Beauty and Manifestations of Allah's Beautiful Names and Attributes that Allah will prepare for His servants. I am saying this is a drop from the ocean of the Friends of God, and all that the Friends of God have been given is but a drop from what Allah has given to Sayyidina Muhammad ﷺ from one moment to another, and no one knows all the rest of these moments except the Prophet ﷺ. All of these moments are from what Allah is preparing for Sayyidina Muhammad ﷺ, for the Friends of God, and for the whole Community. So imagine what is being stored up for the Community. It is impossible to comprehend, for it is beyond the mind.

Grandshaykh ق continues:

> Whatever Allah has granted of levels, realities, and manifestations that will be given to human beings, no one can take away. What Allah gave is what He granted in the past, the future, and the present. You cannot reduce it or eliminate it. The one controlling that is Allah, so neither Satan nor anyone else can take it. What Allah is giving, He is giving,

[261] Dagestani: *wayy*—an exclamatory word in Grandshaykh's homeland.

and what He granted, He granted, and there is no change in that.

Grandshaykh ق elaborates further:

From the time of Sayyidina Adam ﷺ, how many people have come and gone, and how many sins did they commit? If, from the time of Sayyidina Adam ﷺ until today, you add up all the sins that Children of Adam have committed, and if one person today were by himself to commit all those sins, still there is a possibility that he can receive guidance and that Allah will forgive him! How? To do so would be but a drop in an ocean of His *raḥmah*, mercy.

Allah's mercy is endless, and His guidance is endless. So if sins were committed non-stop from the time of the first man until now, one drop from the ocean of Allah's mercy would be enough to cover them! Even in this example, we cannot adequately express the meaning of ar-Raḥmān ar-Raḥīm. Allah guides and gives mercy without limit. What limits everything is not the sins, but our arrogance.

It means when you truly see yourself, you will see the idolatry in your actions. How often did you attribute your success, progress, or an achievement to yourself, as if Allah was somehow absent?

إِنَّ اللّهَ لاَ يَغْفِرُ أَن يُشْرَكَ بِهِ وَيَغْفِرُ مَا دُونَ ذَلِكَ لِمَن يَشَاء وَمَن يُشْرِكْ بِاللّهِ فَقَدِ افْتَرَى إِثْمًا عَظِيمًا

Allah forgives not that partners should be associated with Him; but He forgives anything else, to whom He pleases. To

associate partners with Allah is to devise a sin most heinous indeed.[262]

There is no way God, the Exalted, will tolerate or forgive *shirk*, idolatry. He says, "I am Ghafūr and Raḥīm, Forgiving, Merciful. I will forgive everything, except *shirk*; don't worship anything except Me."

O Ummat an-Nabī ﷺ, be happy! Allah has given us mercy forever, because the Community of the Prophet ﷺ never makes *shirk*.

قال رسول الله صلى الله عليه وسلم يقول: ان امتي امة مقدسة مباركة مرحومة، لا عذاب عليها يوم القيامة، انما عذابهم بينهم في الدنيا بالفتن.

*Verily my Community is a holy, blessed and bestowed with mercy—*marḥūma. *There is no punishment for it on the Day of Rising. Verily their punishment is from amongst themselves through tribulations and trials.*[263]

You are *ummatan marḥūma.*[264] Before Allah created you in this world, when you were souls and spirits, Allah forgave you because you didn't make *shirk*. Allah will not forgive anyone who makes *shirk*.

Anyone who makes sins, the resolution is easy: repent and He forgives. But you cannot repent from committing idolatry, *shirk*, and there is no forgiveness. So don't be arrogant: be like a fish in the water, submitting and surrendering. Be like a river going down to the ocean, entering the ocean. You are a small river entering the ocean in submission.

Wa min Allāhi 't-tawfīq, bi ḥurmati 'l-Fātiḥah.

---

[262] Sūratu 'n-Nisā (Women), 4:48.

[263] at-Ṭabarānī.

[264] Arabic: *marḥūma*—A nation bestowed with Allah's mercy.

18: The Trick of False Pride

A Sin Worse than Disbelief

In every story of Prophet ﷺ with the Companions there are jewels, and these jewels need to be extracted as they demonstrate to us what is right and what is wrong. Grandshaykh ق asked, "Is there anything worse that can be done more than the disbelief of the unbelievers?"

There is nothing greater than the disbelief of unbelievers, as we read this verse of Qur'an:

إِنَّ اللّهَ لاَ يَغْفِرُ أَن يُشْرَكَ بِهِ وَيَغْفِرُ مَا دُونَ ذَلِكَ لِمَن يَشَاء وَمَن يُشْرِكْ بِاللّهِ فَقَدِ افْتَرَى إِثْمًا عَظِيمًا

Allah forgives not that partners should be set up with Him, but He forgives anything else to whom He pleases; to set up partners with Allah is to devise a sin most heinous indeed. [265]

Allah does not forgive anyone that associates partners with Him, and whoever associates with Allah has deviated very far from the main line, *Ṣirāṭ al-mustaqīm*—the Straight Path.

And Grandshaykh ق is asking, "Is there anyone commiting greater *shirk* than a *kāfir*?" He said, "Yes, there is: the one who sees himself as something."

This is teaching *adab,* good conduct. It means we must be very careful, as Satan said:

---

[265] Sūratu 'n-Nisā (Women), 4:48.

قَالَ أَنَا خَيْرٌ مِّنْهُ

"I am better than him."[266]

Satan still believes in Allah and never claimed "there is no creator." In fact, he prostrated to Allah in every hand-span of creation. But when Allah commanded him to prostrate before Adam, he refused.

So there is one worse than an unbeliever: the one who sees himself as better than others. For example, someone may think, "I am a *qārī,*[267] reciting Qur'an in a beautiful voice." You can be a reciter of Qur'an, but don't see yourself as the best reciter, or even a great reciter. Such people don't see their pride as a mistake but more as a right or a fact, and therefore, they do not repent.[268]

Grandshaykh ق said:

> The *kāfir* may repent one day and change his mind and become Muslim and convert, but the one who sees himself as better than others never understands he must repent, and he dies without repenting.

Stop the Car!

Once I was driving Mawlana Shaykh Nazim from Damascus to Beirut during September at the time they have the Christian holy day "Festival of the Cross" and the streets are decorated with crucifixes. So we were passing from the Christian district to the Muslim district and I said, "*Alḥamdūlillāh,* Allah created us Muslim."

---

[266] Sūratu 'l-Aʿraf (the Heights), 7:12.

[267] Arabic: *qārī* —one highly trained and certified in recitation of Holy Qurʿan.

[268] This is why some people are quick to attribute their success or good fortune to Allah ﷻ, i.e. "What a beautiful baby, *māshāAllāh*!" "*Alḥamdulillāh,* I passed my exams!" "*Subḥanallāh,* our vacation was absolutely perfect!"

Mawlana said, "Stop the car! I am getting out."

I asked, "What happened?"

Mawlana said, "What you said, Allah did not like. You are seeing yourself better than them, because you are Muslim and they are Christian. What if Allah created you an unbeliever? You must see that Allah created everyone with something they are happy with. So keep that with you and say, 'O Allah, guide them.' Do not see yourself as better than them. It might be one day the unbeliever will repent and Allah will forgive him, as the Prophet ﷺ said:

الإسلام يجب ما قبله

Islam erases what came before it.[269]

But the one who sees himself as great in every deed, *'amal,* does not realize he must repent."

Friends of God have a lot of stories that they learn spiritually from heart to heart, or through *sīrat an-Nabī,* the biography of Prophet ﷺ. There are many Friends of God who receive confirmation of hadiths through their meditation and visions, in which they ask the Prophet ﷺ directly.

Grandshaykh ق, may Allah bless his soul, narrated this story.

One day there was a voice coming from Ka'bah of someone reciting Qur'an, and he said, *"min halāwata ṣawtihi, Sayyidina 'Alī qad kāna yaḍūb*. Sayyidina 'Alī ﷺ was nearly about to melt from the sweetness of the voice of the reciter."

On the other hand, we see in a hadith of Prophet ﷺ when Abū Mūsā al-Ash'arī ﷺ was reciting the Qur'an in a very beautiful voice and he didn't know the Prophet ﷺ was behind him listening,

---

[269] Muslim.

he looked and found Prophet ﷺ was happy with his recitation and he said, "By Allah, *Yā Rasūlullāh*, if I knew you were listening I would have recited in a more beautiful voice."

In that case, Abū Mūsā al-Ash'ari ؓ did not see himself as great, but he wanted to recite better for the pleasure of the Prophet ﷺ.

Grandshaykh ق continues:

From the sweetness of his voice, Sayyidina 'Alī ق was about to melt. Prophet ﷺ said to him, "Go and cut him in half." Sayyidina 'Alī ق hesitated, not due to disobedience, but because the Qur'an was near that man and he was afraid to cause blood to flow on the Qur'an, making it and the Ka'bah unclean.

The Old Woman and Her Basket

One day Sayyidina 'Alī ؓ saw an old woman carrying a basket with something heavy in it. She walked slowly, yet he didn't pass her.

He felt pity for that old woman and said, "O lady, please let me carry that basket."

She put it on the ground and said, "Yes, please help me."

He picked it up and it was so heavy, he could not raise it up to his knees. He was surprised at how that old lady was carrying something so extremely heavy. He went to Prophet ﷺ to inquire about this.

The Prophet ﷺ said, "*Yā* 'Alī, Allah ordered the whole of this world to be in that basket and sent it to earth to show that you are Asadullah al-ghalib—Allah's Victorious Lion. That is the weight of the whole of this world, and that old woman is a manifestation of our mother earth. Allah has granted to you to carry the whole of this world up to your knees."

This speaks to the power Allah granted Sayyidina 'Alī ☬, so just think, if he will cut that man with his sword, he will cut him from one side to the other with such force, he was worried the blood and intestines would be thrown on the Qur'an he was reading and on the Ka'bah.

Prophet ﷺ said, "Yā 'Alī, be careful! Satan hesitated one moment to make *sajda* and Allah threw him out of His Presence. Don't hesitate! Cut him!"

So trembling, Sayyidina 'Alī ☬ took his sword and immediately cut the man in half. Not one drop of blood appeared. The upper half of the person turned into a dog and ran out of Ka'bah, and the other half turned into a monkey and ran out from the other side.

Allah is showing the personality of that man; from one side he was like a barking dog, always complaining and backbiting, and from the other side he was like a monkey, always chasing his carnal desires.

The Prophet ﷺ said, "Anyone who sees himself better than others is of that kind; half of his personality is a dog and half is a monkey." Then he said, "Yā 'Alī, go home."

In Grandshaykh's notes, he has written, "yā'rifūn qira'at al-Qur'an, min ayn—they know how to recite Qur'an, from where? " They recite and they don't see themselves as great." Recite the Qur'an, but don't see your recitation as great or see yourself as better than others. That is like the character of the man whom Sayyidina 'Alī ☬ slew in the Ka'bah: one side a dog and the other side a monkey.

Grandshaykh ق adds, "No one has heard the recitation of Qur'an by Allah Himself, (which is the most superior!)"

If you consider whose recitation of Qur'an is most beautiful, Prophet ﷺ heard Archangel Gabriel ﷺ recite Qur'an; the Companions heard Prophet ﷺ recite Qur'an; the Tābiʿīn[270] heard Companions recite Qur'an; and, the Muslims of subsequent generations heard the recitation of their elders, at best! So in reality, no one has heard the reality of Qur'an, except Sayyidina Muhammad ﷺ.

Grandshaykh ق said:

> On the Day of Resurrection when God, the Exalted, will send believers to Paradise, He will be seen without any veil.
>
> Allah will manifest Himself to the believers and He will manifest himself under Ismullāh al-ʿadham, Allah's Greatest Name.
>
> With the power of that Beautiful Name, anyone can say to something "be" and it will come into being. Then in Paradise, Allah will manifest under that Greatest Name, and under that manifestation He will recite from Sūrat al-Anʿam. Whatever we are hearing in this world is under the manifestation of *Ismullāh ar-Raḥmān*—Allah's Name the Merciful. But in the hereafter, we will hear the authentic recitation under the manifestation of the Greatest Name, Allah's recitation of Sūrat al-Anʿam.

That is enough for all time. With a few lines of notes, Grandshaykh ق is showing us the consequence of bad characteristics is bad endings, and worst of all is to see the self as if we are better than others.

It made Satan disobey Allah's command. Prophet ﷺ said,

[270] Arabic: *Tābiʿīn*—the generation of descendants that immediately followed Sahaba.

فَلاَ تَكِلْنِي اِلَى نَفْسِي طَرْفَةَ عَيْنٍ

Yā Allah, don't leave me to myself for the blink of an eye.[271]

If the Prophet ﷺ with his superior manners and knowledge is saying this, how careful must we be?

Wa min Allāhi 't-tawfīq, bi ḥurmati 'l-Fātiḥah.

---

[271] Āḥmad, Abū Dāwūd, an-Nasāī and al-Bazzār and Ibn Ḥıbbān.

19: Illness and Mercy

Grandshaykh's Final Days

Awliyāullāh speak according to the *tajallīyāt,* manifestations, they experience, according to what Allah opens to them at that moment through His beloved Prophet, Sayyidina Muhammad ﷺ. When they are in that trance, the manifestation of that vision, then they say unexpected things that might be about themselves, about their private affairs, about their lives, about their followers or about a situation that occurs in this world.

Allah, the Exalted, gave them that ability to see what is written for them, and therefore Allah gave them a knowledge that He didn't give to His common servants. He gave them permission to inherit from the knowledge of the Prophet ﷺ and they take whatever He gives them, and they are very happy.

In 1973 Grandshaykh ق said:

> I have been sick for two months and I cannot do my private litanies daily; my heart is always connected to the presence of Prophet ﷺ and to the Divine Presence, but my body cannot perform every part of the daily private litanies.

Everyone becomes ill. Sayyidina Muhammad ﷺ endured a final illness, in which he had a high fever and was sweating profusely. According to their normal capacity, people become become ill. Don't think illness is from other than Allah's mercy. With that sickness you don't know how many difficulties Allah is removing from the ill person or from his descendants or ancestors. The Prophet's illness was on behalf of the entire Community. The Friends of God become ill to carry on behalf of their followers.

Recall the famous story of Sayyidina Khālid Baghdādī ق; when the plague was coming to Damascus. He was living on Jabal Qasiyun. So what did he do? He said, "O my Lord! I offer myself to carry this whole plague." So when he spoke those words, he became like a lightning rod, pulling the plague intended for all of Damascus to his body. After a few days he passed away.

His students, such as Sayyidina Ismā'īl an-Narānī and others, died from that plague as well, but the rest of the city was spared. Friends of God have immense love for Allah's creation and that special characteristic that they offer themselves to carry on behalf of the Community.

To return to Grandshaykh's story, he said:

Now I cannot perform my daily private litanies, but I am better off, moving higher and higher quickly, because I am not doing it.

لَيسَ عَلَى الْأَعْمَى حَرَجٌ وَلَا عَلَى الْأَعْرَجِ حَرَجٌ وَلَا عَلَى الْمَرِيضِ حَرَجٌ

It is no fault in the blind nor in one born lame, nor in one afflicted with illness... [272]

"*laysa 'alā al-maridi ḥaraj*—There is no responsibility or fault on the one who is ill" for not doing his daily private litanies. If you are ill and receiving treatment in the hospital, and you cannot pray due to illness, God, the Exalted, said in Holy Qur'an, you may pray after you are stronger or recovered.

He said:

I am better now despite my sickness, because angels are practicing on my behalf performing my daily private litanies

[272] Sūratu 'n-Nūr (the Light), 24:61.

better than I was doing, and more than I was doing by ten times[273].

Angels are *m'aṣūmīn,* pure and without sin, so when they perform *'ibādah,* worship, and the private litanies on your behalf, it is more accepted.

Grandshaykh ق continues:

By carrying the sickness and saving the Community of the Prophet ﷺ, al-Ummah, Allah rewarded me by sending these angels to perform my private litanies on my behalf. When I was relaxing and not sick, I used to do my private litanies every 24 hours, and now because I am sick, angels are ordered to do it. When someone gets sick, God, the Exalted, doesn't like anyone to oppress his physical body and put it in difficulties; angels will be worshipping on his behalf. Allah doesn't like anyone to be an oppressor, to oppress others or any of His creation.

He said:

Give importance to your body as you don't want it to fall apart. For every human being there are special angels created and all of them are sitting in the Jannat al-Muntahā in the farthest paradise. They are there, always waiting. If someone gets sick they were created for service of that human being—they go and perform that person's religious obligations of worship.

He said:

[273] This *suḥbat* was given by Grandshaykh in 1973 during the last days before he passed away, on 4th Ramadan).

Every day the Prophet ﷺ prays Ṣalāt aṣ-Ṣubḥ[274] in Paradise with his Companions, the prophets, the Friends of God, and those who died on *imān,* faith. There Sayyidina Bilal ؓ will call *adhān* and the Prophet ﷺ will stand and pray Ṣalāt al-Fajr with all those I mentioned. There I am standing with my soul, praying with them, and I am so much yearning for my body to be there, but my body is still here. And my body here is struggling and deterioriating, and my soul is happy and feeling stronger than before. Angels are preparing me to be in that meeting as soon as possible. They call me and present me in the presence of Prophet ﷺ and the Presence of God, the Exalted. I am waiting for that moment when Allah calls me.

It was nearly the end of Rajab, on the anniversary of the Night Journey and Ascension when he said this, and he remarked, "From this Shaʿbān to next Shaʿbān, during the course of one year, many major issues will occur, spiritually and physically."

According to their level, God, the Exalted, gives Friends of God knowledge of what will happen from 15th of Shaʿbān to the following 15th of Shaʿbān.

Grandshakh ق said:

With prayers and charity,[275] Allah prevents affliction to from falling on human beings. My words are not untrue, what I am saying is the truth. When you give charity for Allah's sake, He will give you more life. When you perform your private litanies daily, Allah will grant you higher and higher levels.

---

[274] Ṣalāt aṣ-Ṣubḥ, also more commonly knonwn as Ṣalāt aṣ-Fajr—the pre-dawn obligatory prayer.
[275] Arabic: *sadaqa* – voluntary charity.

From your charity and private litanies[276] your body and your soul will be given rewards. You are granted more or less life according to your *'amal,* actions[277]. God, the Exalted, makes it longer or less, or according to what you seek; if you want to follow the Prophet ﷺ and to be in presence of Allah, it depends on your ability and what you like. If you like this world, Allah will give you *dunyā*[278]. If you like *ākhirā,*[279] Allah will give you the hereafter.

Grandshaykh ق said, "Allah assigns every human being a life of 137 years."

You will be resurrected on Judgment Day as if you lived 137 years.

Lives: Long and Short

The Prophet ﷺ asked that you have a longer life to worship, not for enjoyment of this worldly life, but for your hereafter.

عن ابن مسعود رضي الله عنه قال : قال رسول الله صلى الله عليه وسلم :

"حياتي خير لكم تحدثون ويحدث لكم ووفاتي خير لكم تعرض علي اعمالكم فما

رأيت من خير حمدت الله وما رأيت من شر استغفرت الله لكم"

The Prophet ﷺ said, "...Your deeds are shown to me and if I see good, I praise Allah, and if I see bad, I repent and ask forgiveness on your behalf."[280]

When the Prophet ﷺ prays for us, he asks Allah to give us a longer life, as long as we are on *Ṣirāṭ al-mustaqīm,* the Straight Path, not oppressing our soul, not oppressing our body, not

---

[276] Arabic: *awrād* - private litanies

[277] Arabic:*'amal* - good actions, or more generally all deeds.

[278] Arabic: *dunyā* – this world

[279] Arabic: *ākhirā*—the Hereafter.

[280] Al-Bazzār and al-'Irāqī.

oppressing our brothers and sisters. If the Prophet ﷺ sees bad, he invokes God to take our souls, as there is no way to treat or cure us.

In the physical world there are illnesses from which we cannot recover from treatment, and the patient dies. Similarly in the spiritual world, some souls are ill and cannot be treated, so Prophet ﷺ asks Allah to let them die. Prophet ﷺ is given authority to ask for their lives to be longer if they are good and if they are not, then he asks to shorten their life. So always keep to the good, as we are always under supervision of Friends of God and the angels.

وَهُوَ مَعَكُمْ أَيْنَ مَا كُنتُمْ

And He is with you wherever you are.[281]

Don't say "Allah is not there." He is present, observing what you are doing, and also seeing your heart, and hearing what your heart is whispering to your mind. Allah said in Holy Qur'an:

قُلْ أَعُوذُ بِرَبِّ النَّاسِ

Say: "I seek refuge with the Lord of mankind,[282]

Satan also whispers in the mind, and some people are affected by that whispering and cannot find their way out of it, becoming what the medical profession calls "OCD" (obsessive compulsive disorder). Doctors have not been able to cure this condition. I was in Singapore, and they brought me a child diagnosed with OCD, and the doctors had prescribed medicine to

---

[281] Sūratu 'l-Ḥadīd (Iron), 57:4.

[282] The final chapter of Holy Qur'an, which begins, "*Say! I seek refuge in the Lord of Mankind.*"

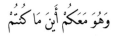

calm him. He goes to the bathroom to take *wuḍū*,[283] ablution, and it becomes a one-hour shower, then two hours; he washes, then washes again. He washes his head, then washes his head again. I told him to make ablution, and he demonstrated how he was doing it. We diminished his washing from one hour to two minutes.

When the heart is affected this way, it generates the disorder, from Satan whispering, "Do this, do this, do this!" and they not only do it, but they cannot come out of it until, in some cases, they get electric shock therapy. Then they wake up.

Mawlana ق said that problem is in the hands of people to help themselves, with Allah's permission. When the Prophet ﷺ and the Friends of God observe people and there is no way to resolve the problem through spiritual practices, Allah gives permission to try other means.

Wa min Allāhi 't-tawfiq, bi ḥurmati 'l-Fātiḥah.

---

[283] Arabic: *wuḍū*—Ritual ablution in preparation for worship.

20: GRANDSHAYKH'S RESPONSIBILITIES

The Generous Grocer

*W*Hen he was young, Grandshaykh's master often sent him on many errands throughout the village. Each task contained a special meaning.

He said there was a man in his village who resembled Sayyidina Abū Bakr ؓ in both physical and spiritual traits. Mawlana ق and many people liked to buy from that person.

Allah said:

وَأَقِيمُوا الْوَزْنَ بِالْقِسْطِ وَلَا تُخْسِرُوا الْمِيزَانَ

So establish weight with justice and fall not short in the balance. [284]

It means we must honor the actual balance and not decrease the weight—i.e. do not cheat. Also spiritually, Allah gave you a balance for your soul. You must be very careful how you balance the soul.

So this man put the groceries on one side of the scale and the weight on the other side, but he always put his hand under the weight and made the groceries lighter due to his love of God, the Exalted, and his love of the Prophet ﷺ and and because he knew customers will distribute the items in Allah's Way, so he sought to share in that reward. He was looking for the hereafter, and not for this world.

---

[284] Sūratu 'r-Raḥmān (the Merciful), 55:9.

> This grocer always examined the customers; if they were poor, he made the groceries lighter so he could give them more and take less of their money. Grandshaykh ق said, "He was a generous person, like Sayyidina Abū Bakr aṣ-Ṣiddīq ﷺ; he gave a lot without any account."

If one person is doing that, what do you think about Sayyidina Muhammad ﷺ? Of course he ﷺ will stop the Scale; even one *ṣalawāt*, praise on the Prophet ﷺ, will be heavier than all the *ʿamāl*, wrong actions of the Children of Adam from the first creation until Judgment Day.

What about God, the Exalted? For one goodness, *maʿrūf.*[285] He ﷻ will give without an account from us.

Mawlana Shaykh Nazim said that Grandshaykh ق often said to that man:

> I am coming here for your sake, not for my sake, because you give more. I come with the power of my shaykh, Shaykh Sharafuddīn… I come to buy more so you will be rewarded, as we are not taking for ourselves, but we are taking for the people in need.
>
> Mawlana explained:
>
> The Friends of God need a hook, by any small *ʿamal*, good action, to hook a person to the presence of Prophet ﷺ. That is how I hook you to the main wagon of Friends of God, so you become a wagon behind the engine, moving with fast speed in the train of Prophet ﷺ.

They are not taking to make themselves fat, but they are taking to feed others. These days people take from others in order

---

[285] Arabic: *maʿruf*—a good action, particularly in obedience to Divine Law.

to make themselves fat and they don't take to help the poor and homeless.

Grandshaykh ق said:

> My shaykh often sent me to places like that and many people, *ʿulamā,* [scholars who were in Shaykh Sharafuddīn's gathering] would say to me, "Where are you? We are not seeing you."
>
> He said, "I am in my job. I am fulfilling the orders of my shaykh."
>
> And they asked him, "We don't see where you are sleeping, a and we don't see you in the house."
>
> He answered, "No one knows where I am sleeping except my shaykh, as no one but him knows the responsibility on my shoulders."

At this point in the notes Grandshaykh ق describes *ṭayy,* how he folds or compresses time and space to reach areas where people are in need of his presence. That is why Sayyidina Bayāzīd al-Bistāmī sent his *ashkāl,* image, to at least 24,000 different places at the same time, depending on his duties and responsibilities, to address the needs of people.

Energy of Healing

One time, Grandshaykh ق said:

> There came to me the head of the scholars who was very ill, and my teacher told me to treat him. I saw he has a sickness that is very difficult to treat at that time. Now it is easy, but then it was not. Doctors told him there is no medicine for him, and he will die.
>
> Immediately I ordered an animal slaughtered, and without telling him what he was eating, I used the meat to make a

soup and gave him that with bread. I made that soup with my hand and I baked the bread.

He said:

My shaykh often sends me to such people around the world and I appear to them in various images. As *ṭabīb al-qulūb wa 'l-ajsām,* I treat their physical illnesses and their spiritual energy. If they need energy, I send them power. And if I see them physically ill, I look on the Preserved Tablets to find what is hidden there, with which to treat them.

Grandshaykh ق said:

His name was Bahauddin and I was treating him for three months, after which he became very strong and his sickness disappeared. He was the head of scholars so everyone knew him, and all the scholars and doctors who said he was going to die came to Shaykh Sharafuddīn and asked, "How did he recover and become strong?" He pointed to me and said, "Ask that doctor, the one who treated him."

Through gnosis[286], Allah granted his Prophet ﷺ two kinds of knowledge, physical healing and spiritual healing, and Friends of God inherited that. I saw what was written in the Preserved Tablet, "This person has to eat this for three months and he will be cured." So it is not according to what you have described, but it is as Allah has described on the Day of Promises, what Allah has written on the Preserved Tablet.

Today doctors can only guess regarding a treatment. They have hundreds of machines that they use to rule out this possibility and rule out that possibility, until they arrive at a certain illness for which a specific treatment is recommended.

---

[286] Arabic: *maʿrifah*—direct knowledge from Allah.

Friends of God do not do this type of analysis. They have their own "MRI" machine. They look on the Preserved Tablet[287] to see what cure may have been prescribed by God, the Exalted.

لكل دا دوا

The Prophet ﷺ said, "For every sickness there is a cure."[288]

Finished. You cannot have doubt in Allah's or Words. Some think this hadith means doctors can find the cure. No! It means that Friends of God can find the cure. They look, as Grandshaykh ق looked on the Preserved Tablets, and see it written, "That man needs to eat this meat for three months."

If you have cancer, Friends of God don't need to take a biopsy; they can give the *shifā'*, cure.[289] They say you have to cut off your feet or your hands, amputate the effected limb. They may say, "Recite 100 times *ṣalawāt,* prayers on the Prophet ﷺ," and the matter is finished, because with what they say Allah gives the cure. There is a cure for everything. From far away, Friends of God recite *Bismi'l-Lāhi 'r-Raḥmāni 'r-Raḥīm* for the patient and there is a cure in this.

So Grandshaykh ق saw on the Preserved Tablets that this man will be cured by eating the meat of this animal. What type of meat was it? It was the meat of a horse who itself had previously been cured of tuberculosis.

That is why people love horses and that is why horses are used for many purposes. You see today, people in Hollywood,

---

[287] Arabic: *al-Lawḥ al Maḥfūẓ*— the Preserved Tablet.

[288] Abū Dāwūd, 3857.

- حَدَّثَنَا حَفْصُ بْنُ عُمَرَ النَّمَرِيُّ، حَدَّثَنَا شُعْبَةُ، عَنْ زِيَادِ بْنِ عِلاَقَةَ، عَنْ أُسَامَةَ بْنِ شَرِيكٍ، قَالَ أَتَيْتُ النَّبِيَّ صلى الله عليه وسلم وَأَصْحَابُهُ كَأَنَّمَا عَلَى رُءُوسِهِمُ الطَّيْرُ فَسَلَّمْتُ ثُمَّ قَعَدْتُ فَجَاءَ الأَعْرَابُ مِنْ هَا هُنَا وَهَا هُنَا فَقَالُوا يَا رَسُولَ اللَّهِ أَنَتَدَاوَى فَقَالَ " تَدَاوَوْا فَإِنَّ اللَّهَ عَزَّ وَجَلَّ لَمْ يَضَعْ دَاءً إِلاَّ وَضَعَ لَهُ دَوَاءً غَيْرَ دَاءٍ وَاحِدٍ الْهَرَمُ " .

[289] Arabic: *shifā'*—cure; healing.

sometime Allah gives them an inspiration, and Allah knows what their spiritual condition is, but in order to give a hint to believers of the Prophet ﷺ, they make paintings of white horses with huge wings. Now that is a sign of respect for horses. They don't paint donkeys or mules with wings, but they paint horses that way. Why? Because it is significant.

Grandshaykh ق tells us:

> Allah created horses and left them in Paradise, and that is why people love horses. Horses were asked to leave Paradise, as were all animals at one time. But he refused, saying, "I am not going out, I am staying here. If you want to go out, go out; I am staying; I look beautiful here." So donkeys and other animals went out. Then angels told the horse, "Your meat is a cure for people with tuberculosis." The horse said, "If I am going to be of benefit for human beings I will go, because Allah created everything for the sake of Sayyidina Muhammad ﷺ and he is from the human race. I am sacrificing my Paradise stay for the sake of the Prophet ﷺ."

Look how animals have respect to Sayyidina Muhammad ﷺ while these extremists, the Wahabis, have no respect!

Grandshaykh ق said:

> At that time seven renowned doctors began to write articles on that cure and began treating their patients with horse meat. At that time they wrote about this cure in newspapers, urging to purchase extra horses to provide them to cure tuberculosis.

Today they no longer do that. But it may be the treatment they are giving for tuberculosis is made from horse meat, and they are not revealing that.

They said the meat of horses and donkeys is *makruh*—disliked in Shariʿah.[290] Why is it disliked, although it is a treatment for sick people? At that time there were no cars, so had they slaughtered horses, there would be no transportation for fighting the aggressors. When it is needed to cure sick people, you can slaughter horses and donkeys.

Grandshaykh ق related:

> That was my duty by my shaykh's orders, to go around the earth and help sick people.

He continued:

> There was a woman with tuberculosis my shaykh sent me to check; she was going to die. I looked at her with the hidden knowledge God, the Exalted, gave me from the Prophet's knowledge; it was written that if she eats dry raisins she will be cured. After three months the tuberculosis was gone.

So it depends on what kind of sickness you have and what Allah has written for you to cure that. Now they treat everyone with the same sickness with the same treatment, which is not correct. Friends of God they look, as the Prophet ﷺ said, "For every sickness there is a cure."

ʿItiqad, belief is crucial, as your faith will cure you. If you believe in what the shaykh is giving you, or in what the Prophet ﷺ has mentioned of prophetic medicine, God, the Exalted, will send that cure, your body will release hormones according to what you focus on, and you will be rejuvenated.

---

[290] Arabic: *makrūh*—Lawful, but disliked by Allah.

The Strange Cure

Once the foot of a student of Shaykh Sharafuddīn ق got gangrene. His name was Āḥmad. Doctors told him, "We must cut off your leg or you will die."

He told Shaykh Sharafuddīn ق, "They want to cut off my leg, but I would rather die."

Shaykh Sharafuddīn ق said, "Go to my son, ʿAbd Allāh."

Grandshaykh ق looked at the disciple's leg and saw that it was swollen.

Allah says:

الْخَبِيثَاتُ لِلْخَبِيثِينَ وَالْخَبِيثُونَ لِلْخَبِيثَاتِ وَالطَّيِّبَاتُ لِلطَّيِّبِينَ وَالطَّيِّبُونَ لِلطَّيِّبَاتِ أُوْلَئِكَ مُبَرَّؤُونَ مِمَّا يَقُولُونَ لَهُم مَّغْفِرَةٌ وَرِزْقٌ كَرِيمٌ

Impure women are for impure men, and impure men are for impure women, and women of purity are for men of purity, and men of purity are for women of purity. These are not affected by what people say: for them there is forgiveness, and a provision honorable.[291]

Grandshaykh ق said:

Anything that is disgusting, bad, or vile, goes with the vile. And what is good and sweet goes with the sweet. So if you have something that is bad, you treat it with a similar element.

That is why penicillin, a bacteria, becomes an antibiotic. Tuberculosis is cured by penicillin: something vile with something

[291] Sūratu 'n-Nūr (the Light), 24:26.

vile. That is why snake poison is used to cure some medical conditions: vile things are for the vile and the good is for the good.

> *Pure women for pure men, and impure women for impure men.*

> Grandshaykh ق said:

> I saw that is something vile, and it must be treated with something vile. So I looked at the letters of light that come like news scrollers from the Divine Presence, and I saw his treatment involves something very filthy, a wild pig. I sent for the hunter, and he went and got a pig, and skinned it. According to what I was instructed from the Divine Presence, I ordered the feet of the lamb and the intestine of the pig, with which we wrapped the affected area. After fifteen days, we brought the medical doctors, and pharmaceutical companies who never accept such a cure and we unwrapped his leg. And that story was written in the newspapers. All the bad blood and tissue that had turned black with gangrene was cured, and his leg had returned to normal. I told the doctors, "Now it is your duty to bandage him and our duty is finished." His feet came back as it was before with no deficiency, perfect.

> That man said, "I will give my life for my shaykh, for my teacher and what he did for me." He stood at Shaykh Sharafuddīn's door in service until the shaykh passed away. After that the student moved to Jordan, and passed away there in Amman.

Healing is in the hands of Friends of God and with permission they can cure any sickness, because Allah gave that secret to the Prophet ﷺ. With *ṣalawāt* any sickness can be cured, by saying:

اللهم على سيدنا محمد طب القلوب و دوائها و عافية الأبدان و شفائها و نور الأبصار و ضيائها، و على آله و صحبه و سلم

Allahumma ṣalli ʿalā Sayyidinā Muḥammad, ṭib al qulūbi wa dawā'ihā wa ʿafiyyat al-abdāni wa shifā'ihā wa nūr al-abṣāri wa ḍīyā'iha wa ʿalā ālihi wa ṣaḥibihi wa sallam.

O Allah exalt our master Muhammad, the physician of hearts and their cure, and the source of healing of bodies and their cure, and the light of vision and its brilliant lamp, and on his family and companions and send them peace.

Prophet Muhammad ﷺ is the source of healing, and there is a cure in praising him. Write that and it is cure for any kind of illness. Don't worry, with the love of Sayyidina Muhammad ﷺ Allah will cure every sick person and with *istighfār* cures every sick person.

Wa min Allāhi 't-tawfiq, bi ḥurmati 'l-Fātiḥah.

21: ISLAM—THE ART OF OBEDIENCE

Obedience Increases Faith

The Prophet ﷺ said:

كلمتان خفيفتان على اللسان, ثقيلتان في الميزان, حبيبتان الى الرحمن:

سبحان اللّه وبحمده, سبحان اللّه

Two words that are weighty on the Scale of Deeds, and very light on the tongue, beloved to the Most Merciful: Glory to Allah and His Praise and thanks. Glory be to Allah, the Greatest.[292]

And we complete it by asking forgiveness saying: *Istaghfirullāh*—May Allah forgive us."[293]

What is the benefit of God, the Exalted, having revealed the Holy Qur'an to Prophet ﷺ? What is the benefit of Allah having sent the Seal of Messengers, Sayyidina Muhammad ﷺ to mankind? What is the benefit of Allah having sent all the prophets and messengers into this world to guide us?

It all depends on one verse of the Qur'an. Like the head to the body, that verse is the head of all that God, the Exalted, has revealed to Prophet ﷺ, and all that Prophet has revealed in his sayings, hadith.

---

[292] The two *Saḥīḥ*s.

[293] Arabic: subḥanallāh wa bi-ḥamdihi subḥanallāhi 'l'adhīm, istaghfirullāh.

يَا أَيُّهَا الَّذِينَ آمَنُواْ أَطِيعُواْ اللّهَ وَأَطِيعُواْ الرَّسُولَ وَأُوْلِي الأَمْرِ مِنكُمْ فَإِن تَنَازَعْتُمْ فِي شَيْءٍ فَرُدُّوهُ إِلَى اللّهِ وَالرَّسُولِ إِن كُنتُمْ تُؤْمِنُونَ بِاللّهِ وَالْيَوْمِ الآخِرِ ذَلِكَ خَيْرٌ وَأَحْسَنُ تَأْوِيلاً

O believers! Obey Allah, obey the Prophet ﷺ, and obey those who are in authority. And if you have a dispute concerning any matter, refer it to Allah and the messenger, if you are (in truth) believers in Allah and the Last Day; that is better and more seemly in the end.[294]

Essentially, this is the religion and the message Allah conveyed to humanity. Allah doesn't want more than this from anyone, only obedience. If we obey we are safe, and if we disobey our safety is threatened.

God, the Exalted, said, *atiʿAllah—obey Allah,* and then He didn't stop. He said, *atiʿ ar-Rasūl—Obey My Prophet that I am sending to you."* If you don't obey the Prophet ﷺ it means you disobeyed God, the Exalted.

God, the Exalted, made it obligatory in our *ṣalāt* that when we recite the *Tashahhud,*[295] we say, "*ashhadu an lā ilāha illa 'Llāh*—I bear witness there is no God but Allah," then we must also say, "*wa ashhadu anna Muḥammadan ʿabduhu wa rasūluh*—and I bear witness that Muhammad is His servant and His messenger." If you exclude the second bearing witness, i.e. that Sayyidina Muhammad is Allah's messenger, Allah will reject your declaration and throw it in your face.

---

[294] Sūratu 'n-Nisā (Women), 4:59.

[295] *Tashahhud*—ordained supplication in the ritual Islamic prayer without which the prayer is not valid.

In the *tashshahud* we say: *"As-salāmu 'alayka ayyuhan-nabī*—I am sending saluations to you, Prophet ﷺ!" Without this declaration in *ṣalāt*, your prayer is not even looked at. It is not acceptable to stop after reciting *"ashadu an lā ilāha illa 'Llāh."* You can only stop after reciting *"ashadu anna Muḥammadan 'abduhu wa Rasūluh"* and stop; it is not obligatory to recite the rest, *"allāhumma ṣalli Muḥammadin..."*

In the *Tashahhud*, when we recite *"as-salām 'alayka ayyuhan nabīyyu... wa's-salāmu 'alaynā wa 'alā 'ibādillāhi 'ṣ-ṣāliḥīn*—Peace be on us and on all righteous servants of Allah." we are actually sending *salāms*, greetings of peace, upon ourselves (and the angels are accompanying us), and upon those in authority (the Friends of God).

In every action you must be careful and know who is in authority over you, or else you might mistakenly enter a way that leads to your punishment, or a way full of obstacles and thorns that sting you.

When you know who is in authority over you, you will go directly there, through one door only, and you are safe.

Sayyidina Muhammad ﷺ said, "I am the city of knowledge, and 'Alī is its gate."

Finished. Why are we looking here and there? Those who kept straight forward to that door reached and those who did not fell into obstacles.

Wa min Allāhi 't-tawfiq, bi ḥurmati 'l-Fātiḥah.

22: THE ENGRAVER AND THE ENGRAVED

Acceptance and Rejection

To disobey is to reject Allah's ﷻ command. You cannot reject any part of the *shahāda*; to recite the first part and not the second part. That is why we must say *"wa ashhadu anna Muḥammadan ʿabduhu wa rasūluh*—and I bear witness that Muhammad is His servant and His messenger" for without it, our prayers will not be accepted; they will be thrown in our face.

يَوْمَ يَرَوْنَ الْمَلَائِكَةَ لَا بُشْرَى يَوْمَئِذٍ لِّلْمُجْرِمِينَ وَيَقُولُونَ حِجْرًا مَّحْجُورًا وَقَدِمْنَا إِلَى مَا عَمِلُوا مِنْ عَمَلٍ فَجَعَلْنَاهُ هَبَاءً مَّنثُورًا

The Day they see the angels, no joy will there be to the sinners that Day. The (angels) will say: "There is a barrier forbidden (to you) altogether!" And We shall turn unto the work they did and make it scattered motes.[296]

The unbelievers rejected what Allah ordered them and they disobeyed, which led them to reject Sayyidina Muhammad ﷺ. Although they did many good things, Allah obliterated their good deeds and sent them to Hellfire.

In prayer, when you mention Allah's Name you must also mention the Prophet's ﷺ name else your prayer is not accepted.

---

[296] Sūratu 'l-Furqān (the Criterion) 25:22-23.

You also cannot reject the political (official) authority, but more importantly, you cannot reject the spiritual authority. Allah does not want us to reject any of his saints, and for this reason He also ordered the Prophet ﷺ and the Friends of God to accept everyone, because people need somewhere to go to ask for forgiveness and mercy without fear of rejection.

وَمَا أَرْسَلْنَاكَ إِلَّا رَحْمَةً لِّلْعَالَمِينَ

We sent you not(O Muhammad!) but as a Mercy for all creatures.[297]

وَمَا أَرْسَلْنَا مِن رَّسُولٍ إِلاَّ لِيُطَاعَ بِإِذْنِ اللهِ وَلَوْ أَنَّهُمْ إِذ ظَّلَمُوا أَنفُسَهُمْ جَآؤُوكَ
فَاسْتَغْفَرُوا اللهَ وَاسْتَغْفَرَ لَهُمُ الرَّسُولُ لَوَجَدُوا اللهَ تَوَّابًا رَّحِيمًا

We sent not a prophet, but to be obeyed, in accordance with the will of Allah. If they had only, when they were unjust to themselves, come unto you and asked Allah's forgiveness, and the Messenger had asked forgiveness for them, they would have found Allah indeed oft-returning, most Merciful.[298]

Allah is the Creator and everything else is His creation. In whatever He created, He manifested His Beautiful Names and Attributes which becomes like a shadow of these Beautiful Names and Attributes. That is the meaning of "*al-ʿibād dhilullāh*—human beings are the shadow of their Creator," and similarly, "*as-sulṭān dhilullāh ʿalā al-arḍ*—the king is the shadow of Allah on earth."

Physical terms are are used here only to give an understanding, for Allah has no form and hence, no shadow. We must be very careful here to understand that the meaning of *dhill*,

---

[297] Sūratu 'l-Anbīyā (the Prophets) 21:107.
[298] Sūratu 'n-Nisā (Women), 4:64.

shadow, is the manifestation of the Beautiful Names and Attributes on us.

From this we understand that as everyone is unique, for eacah person has been manifested under a different Divine Name.

> The absolute existence is for Allah and the servants of Allah are only appearances of His existence.
>
> No one exists except we are all appearances of that Divine existence, manifestations of the Beautiful Names and Attributes. If anyone rejects one of these appearances, it is as if he rejected the One that created the appearance. If you reject anyone of Allah's servants, that are appearances from Beautiful Names and Attributes, you are finding fault in the Master Engraver.

Obedience has to be perfect from every side. You must be like water in the river, flowing to the ocean. If a stone in the river bed creates a ripple or disrupts the flow, the water moves around it and continues to flow; it does not say, "This is a bad stone; who put it here? Throw it out!" We need to be like that water in a flowing river. However, we cannot be enlightened and reach our goal through contemplation alone. Religion is not merely exercises; it is wisdom.

Seek Spiritual Enlightment

The purpose of religion is to bring us to our Lord, to understand what Allah has prepared for those who obey Him, his Prophet ﷺ, and the guides (Friends of God). Creation is created to know the Creator. Allah wants us to be spiritually enlightened. So this kind of teaching is only with Friends of God, to whom Allah gave knowledge of His hidden treasures.

Those to whom Allah did not give these hidden treasures, what do they seek? They focus on energy and physical experiences, imagining this and that and focusing on it. This is kindergarten level. You must go beyond that, as demonstrated when the Prophet ﷺ said to Abū Hurayrah ؓ, "Yā Aba Hurayrah, did you contemplate on the verse:

إِنَّ فِي خَلْقِ السَّمَاوَاتِ وَالأَرْضِ وَاخْتِلاَفِ اللَّيْلِ وَالنَّهَارِ لآيَاتٍ لِّأُوْلِي الألْبَابِ الَّذِينَ
يَذْكُرُونَ اللّهَ قِيَامًا وَقُعُودًا وَعَلَىَ جُنُوبِهِمْ وَيَتَفَكَّرُونَ فِي خَلْقِ السَّمَاوَاتِ وَالأَرْضِ
رَبَّنَا مَا خَلَقْتَ هَذا بَاطِلاً سُبْحَانَكَ فَقِنَا عَذَابَ النَّارِ

Behold in the creation of the heavens and the earth, and the alternation of night and day, there are indeed signs for men of understanding; men who celebrate the praises of Allah standing, sitting, and lying down on their sides, and who contemplate the (wonders of) creation in the heavens and the earth (with the thought): "Our Lord! Not for the non-existent have You created (all) this! Glory to You! Give us salvation from the penalty of the Fire."[299]

Those who are remembering Allah day and night, standing and sitting and laying down, and they contemplate and meditate on the creation of heavens and earth. They think on all that is other than Allah; they meditate on heavens and earth. They don't meditate on the Creator as they are still in kindergarten and need authority to do that, they need *ūli 'l-amr*, Friends of God who have the authority to take them to that higher level.

When Grandshaykh ق was granted this authorization, he said, "I accept only on the condition that I am given authority to raise my students to the level of the saints about whom I speak."

[299] Sūrat Āli-ʿImrān (the Family of ʿImrān), 3:190-191.

That is the level of Friends of God, not kindergarten; that is for instructors. To graduate beyond kindergarten you need a Friend of God.

Abu Hurayrah ﷺ answered, "Yes, I am thinking about the stars, the moon, the sun and planets, how they are and how they orbit."

تفكر ساعة خير من قيام ليلة.

The Prophet ﷺ said, "Your contemplation of one hour is equal to one night standing in worship."[300]

He was meditating on the atmosphere above us. Today many people meditate on the energy of the cosmos. The Prophet ﷺ is teaching us such contemplation is a form of worship.

Then the Prophet ﷺ passed by Sayyidina ibn 'Abbās ﷺ, who explained the Qur'an, and asked him, "What do you think about that verse?"
He answered, "When I hear that, I contemplate on Allah's greatness."

تفكر ساعة خير من عبادة سنة

The Prophet ﷺ said, "Such contemplation is equal to one year of worship. Khayran min 'ibādat sannah."[301]
Then he passed by Sayyidina Abū Bakr aṣ-Ṣiddīq ﷺ and asked him, "What do you think about that verse?"
He said, "Yā Rasūlullāh, whenever I think about that verse I contemplate that Allah's greatness is so huge, and it is bad for anyone to reject obedience to their Lord."
And I say, 'O my Lord! Let me be the one to be punished and let all of them go to Paradise."

---

300 Al-Qurṭubī.

301 a renowned *athar*, similar to the hadith, "The meditation of one hour is better than the worship of sixty years." Related by Abū ash-Shaykh.

تفكر ساعة خير من عبادة سبعين سنة

The Prophet ﷺ said, "Such contemplation is equal to seventy years of worship. Khayran min ʿibādat sabaʿīn sannah."[302]

Companions experienced the Prophet's words as if they were living them, just as (Prophet Abraham ﷺ?) says he felt the intense heat of the fire through which he carried the burden of the whole Community, that it could be cleaned and saved from Hellfire. That is the kind of teaching and wisdom we need. Friends of God are not going to waste their students' time to keep them in kindergarten; they raise their students to soar in heavens!

كُنْتُ كَنْزاً لاَ أُعْرَفُ فَأَحْبَبْتُ أَنْ أُعْرَفَ، فَخَلَقْتُ خَلْقا فعرفتهم بي ؛ فعرفوني

Allah said, "I was a hidden treasure and I wanted to be known, so I created creation, and through that creation they knew Me."[303]

We seek these precious treasures. Friends of God prepare people to receive Mahdi ﷺ, who is present with everyone. If the eyes of the heart are open, anyone can see Mahdi ﷺ in his heart. It only needs clarity and transparency in everything we do. When we reach that state we will be raised, all of us together. We don't want one to be higher and one to be lower. We are after these treasures.

So Grandshaykh ق took a guarantee that whatever he speaks of higher levels, we will be raised up to that authority, so when heavenly support comes we are ready. We like to appear in the

---

[302] This is a famous *athar* (tradition related back to a Companion or Successor).

[303] Arabic: *ḥadīth qudsī*—a Divine saying whose meaning directly reflects the meaning God intended but whose expression is not Divine Speech as in the Qur'an, rather is the speech of the Prophet ﷺ it thus differs from a hadith *nabawī* (*see* above).

presence of Prophet ﷺ as peaceful people standing out like stars on a dark night.

Mawlana says you cannot find fault in Allah's creation, as it is perfect. There is wisdom in the way anyone is created: learn the wisdom. Scientists know there is wisdom in every creation. And they try to investigate through these pharmacy companies to find the benefit of these different creations. Let us accept the equality of all people, with no hatred and or anger in our hearts. Then our shaykh will be pleased to introduce us in the presence of Prophet ﷺ and not ashamed of our bad manners and bad character.

Grandshaykh ق said there is a group of people that rejects the existence of Allah (atheists). But our problem is, in every moment, through our deeds we deny God, the Exalted, by rejecting His servants. Anything Allah created is His servant; they are exacting the way He wants them to be. You cannot reject anyone; you must show humility. God, the Exalted, has honored human beings. Respect also the angels that are with them. Don't reject that nice picture, that Allah created that person.

مرت جنازة برسول الله صلى الله عليه وسلم فقام فقيل إنها جنازة يهودي فقال إنما قمنا للملائكة"

One day a funeral procession passed by the Prophet ﷺ and he stood up.

The Companions asked, "Why did you stand?"

He said, "Is it wrong to stand?"

They said, "He is a Jew [i.e. not Muslim]."

The Prophet ﷺ answered, "We stood for the honor of the angels accompanying him."[304]

---

304 An-Nasā'ī.

In reality, the Prophet ﷺ stood to honor a son of Adam.

وَلَقَدْ كَرَّمْنَا بَنِي آدَمَ

We have honored the sons of Adam.[305]

إِنَّا لِلَّهِ وَإِنَّا إِلَيْهِ رَاجِعونَ

From Allah we come and to Him is our return.[306]

So that is why Grandshaykh ق and Mawlana Shaykh Nazim said, we are appearances of Allah's Beautiful Names and Attributes, so how can we criticize others?

Allah wanted his hidden treasures to be known, so He invited Prophet ﷺ on The Night Journey and Ascension to give him the secrets. He didn't invite any other prophets to His Presence except Sayyidina Muhammad ﷺ. He invited the Prophet ﷺ in body and soul to receive these hidden treasures as a trust, which are the creation. Allah is not in need of creation; creation is in need of Allah. He wanted to give these treasures to the one He made responsible for them.

Wa min Allāhi 't-tawfiq, bi ḥurmati 'l-Fātiḥah.

---

[305] Sūratu 'l-Isrā (the Night Journey), 17:70.
[306] Sūratu 'l-Baqara (the Heifer), 2:156.

23: Secrets of the Holy Qur'an

The Holy Ascension

Grandshaykh ق said

In that holy journey, as the Prophet ﷺ ascended the heavens beyond the station of Archangel Gabriel ﷷ to the Divine Presence, Allah was revealing to him the secrets of the Holy Qur'an. From the station of Gabriel ﷷ and below is the contents of the Qur'an and the ahadith of Prophet ﷺ. From that level come the different explanations of Qur'an. From the station of Gabriel ﷷ and above, Allah revealed to Prophet ﷺ the secret of every letter of the Qur'an, each of which is an ocean so huge one cannot dive in it. God, the Exalted, also opened to him station of the manifestation of the 99 Names, a station in which he has no partner.

That is why the Friends of God say the only true *muwwaḥid*, monotheist, the one who testified to the Oneness of God, the Exalted, is Sayyidina Muhammad ﷺ. He saw the revelation of the manifestations of the 99 Names and from that he understood the reality of Allah's Oneness. Nothing exists except Allah's Existence. So the genuine *muwwaḥid* testifies *ash-hadu an lā ilāha illa 'Llāh.*

We are *muwwaḥid* according to the station we are in. Currently, our station is *thumma āmanū thumma kafarū,* one day in belief, one day in unbelief.[307] Only Sayyidina Muhammad ﷺ has reached the level of absolute belief.

During the holy ascension, God, the Exalted, did not speak to Prophet ﷺ in his capacity of "*rasūlullāh*", the one carrying Allah's

[307] C.f. Sūratu 'n-Nisā (Women), 4:137.

message to humanity; that is from the station of Gabriel ﷺ and down. Allah has granted Prophet something even higher: from Khamis al-Qur'an—the inner Secret of the Qur'an. He spoke to the Prophet in his capacity as guardian of these secrets, which are above the station of Archangel Gabriel ﷺ. God, the Exalted, said, "*wa lā yushrik fihī āḥada,* it is only for him and he has no partner in it." No one can be partner to Sayyidina Muhammad ﷺ in that knowledge. Everything the Prophet ﷺ received is between himself and Allah; no one else knows the secret given by Allah to the Prophet except Sayyidina Muhammad ﷺ.

As contemporary scholars such as Shaykh Shaʿrawi and Imam an-Nawawī have written, "The Prophet ﷺ saw his Lord with the eyes of his head."

When Sayyidina al-Mahdi ﷺ comes, traces of that secret of the Holy Qur'an will be given to the Community.

> That is why Sayyidina 'Umar ؓ asked the Prophet ﷺ, "Are those people going to be prophets?"
>
> The Prophet ﷺ said, "No, they are not prophets. They are normal people."

They are such that they forget even how many *rakaʿats* they have prayed, thinking, "Did I pray two or three *rakaʿats*?" then they add one or two and it becomes six. Then they are distracted and they forgot how many *rakaʿats* they prayed.

Allah does not place a burden on anyone greater than they can carry. That is why humanity took only a little knowledge during that holy ascension, up to the level of Gabriel ﷺ. Since we were unable to take more, what ever that amount, was not more than the manifestation of the Beautiful Names and Attributes ar-Raḥmān.

The Mirror of Knowledge

Grandshaykh ق said:

The Prophet ﷺ was ordered to open only from the Name ar-Raḥmān. He was ordered to reveal those verses of Holy Qur'an in that capacity, at that level. But what he received at the level of the 99 Names that is above Archangel Gabriel ﷺ, the Prophet ﷺ did not open to the Community, and was not ordered to reveal it, and he spoke according to what our hearts can carry. If that knowledge is opened, our hearts cannot carry it and they will break, and everyone will faint, and there will be no more life left on earth nor in the universe. A little bit will be opened in the time of Mahdi ﷺ, and all of it will be opened in Paradise.

Grandshaykh ق continues:

In that holy ascension, the third knowledge Allah gave to Prophet ﷺ was to show him all Friends of God that Allah ever created.

مِنَ الْمُؤْمِنِينَ رِجَالٌ صَدَقُوا مَا عَاهَدُوا اللَّهَ عَلَيْهِ فَمِنْهُم مَّن قَضَى نَحْبَهُ وَمِنْهُم مَّن يَنتَظِرُ وَمَا بَدَّلُوا تَبْدِيلًا

Among the Believers are men who have been true to their covenant with Allah. of them some have completed their vow (to the extreme), and some (still) wait: but they have never changed (their determination) in the least.[308]

They are the assistants to the Prophet ﷺ. Allah gave him the sanctified power from pre-eternity to post-eternity. That power adorns the Prophet ﷺ and from the Prophet ﷺ it adorns saints that are in this presence. Allah ﷻ said to him: "These are your assistants. Dress them from that sanctified

[308] Sūratu 'l-Aḥzāb (the Confederates), 33:23.

power. If you don't dress them, they cannot carry that work. They must assume that power."

Grandshaykh ق continues:

When Allah gave him permission to use that power, Prophet ﷺ dressed every Friend of God individually, and that is why we see different levels for the Friends of God. You cannot say that the only Friend of God is your shaykh; there are numerous Friend of Gods around the world. You focus on your shaykh alone, which is your connection and that is where your duty lies.

When Allah dressed Prophet ﷺ with what He gave him, and Prophet dressed the Friends of God, then Allah opened to him the meaning of the verse:

وَلَقَدْ كَرَّمْنَا بَنِي آدَمَ

We have honored the human beings. [309]

When that verse was revealed, Prophet ﷺ was brought inside to be shown what Allah has honored them with. The Friends of God were astonished and stunned with what they saw there: the real honor Allah bestowed on human beings, and who will appear under that verse and manifestation of the Holy Qur'an. They could not say anything. Then after that third level, Prophet ﷺ dressed the Friends of God and took them into that ocean, and Prophet ﷺ took all the atoms and offspring of human beings in a state of absolute purity, as on the Day of Promises.

كل مولود يولد على الفطرة فأبواه يهودانه وينصرانه ويشركانه

[309] Sūratu 'l-Isrā (the Night Journey), 17:70.

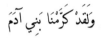

Every Human being is born on the natural state of purity. Then either their two parents will make them Jewish or make them Christian or make them Zoroastrian or make them idolaters.[310]

He showed them the state of purity in which human beings are born. And he showed them to Sayyidina Muhammad ﷺ and said, "They are clean. Will you keep them for Me as a trust?" He said, "Yes, *yā Rabbī*." And Allah gave them.

That is why Allah gave the Prophet ﷺ *shafaʿa*, to intercede for the Community.

Wa min Allāhi 't-tawfiq, bi ḥurmati 'l-Fātiḥah.

[310] Tirmidhī; a similar narration is related by Bukhārī and Muslim.

24: GUARDIAN OF HUMANITY

Earthly Sleep

The third wisdom of Allah bringing Sayyidina Muhammad ﷺ on *Laylatu 'l-Isrā wa 'l-Miʿrāj,* the Blessed Night Journey and Ascension, was to show him all the saints of the Community and to carry their responsibilities.

Grandshaykh ʿAbd Allāh ق relates:

> God, the Exalted, also brought all the progeny of Sayyidina Adam ؑ, and Prophet took them as a trust which he must return to Allah in their pure state, clean and free of sin.
>
> When Allah asked him do you accept to take all of Banī Ādam as a trust the Prophet ﷺ said "yes, *Yā Rabbī*—O my Lord."
>
> When the Prophet ﷺ answered "yes, O my Lord," God, the Exalted, revealed to him all kinds of bad characteristics of human beings: how much they will conspire, make tyranny in the land, doing things Allah has forbidden, and how they will be veiled with the darkness of those characteristics.
>
> The Prophet ﷺ then became afraid and said, "O my Lord! that is too much. Send me some of Your sincere ones to guide the Community after me, to inherit from me some of my power, to guide human beings on my way, the Sunnah and on the Straight Path, *aṣ-ṣirāt al-mustaqīm*."
>
> When God, the Exalted, assembled the atoms of the Children of Adam ؑ on the Day of Promises and said, "Who am I?" a group of them answered, "You are our Lord and we are Your servants." And another group said, "You are what You are

and we are what we are," and a third group said, "We are what we are."

The first group consists of Allah's sincere servants, the guides and teachers. The second group Allah took and sent to the *Baḥr aẓ-ẓulmah,* the Ocean of Darkness, because they needed to be cleaned and polished. There they will fight their egos and struggle; this world is a reflection of what happened there for 80,000 of Allah's years. When we come to this world we don't recall any of that, but it exists. We will see on Judgment Day how much we have disobeyed, and we will regret.

Here in this world, we are anesthetised and cannot see what we did then. On Judgment Day that will appear and we will see it. Friends of God can see that now. They are from the ones who said, "You are our Lord and we are Your servants."

And the rest are those who said, "We are what we are and You are what You are."

And so Allah brought them after 80,000 years and asked them a second time. Some of them, after so much struggle, responded, "You are our Lord and we are Your servants." The others said, "You are what You are and we are what we are," and Allah sent them for 80,000 additional years in the Ocean of Darkness.

Those in this world who are obedient are the ones who after 80,000 years said, "You are our Lord and we are Your servants." Those who were stubborn and didn't accept God, the Exalted, are the disbelievers, corrupt people and atheists. Grandshaykh ق said that there are unbelievers who do not yet believe, and stubborn unbelievers who will never believe.

Those who are not stubborn from that group will one day find guidance and find the right way and convert. They are not stubborn; they know the truth when they hear it, and come quickly running to it.

So the Prophet ﷺ saw the bad characters in men and said, "O my Lord! this is too much; give me some supporters," and Allah gave him the Friends of God.

Grandshaykh ق is teaching us something very important. Allah is demonstrating that even with the enormous levels of power he bestowed on Sayyidina Muhammad ﷺ, still the Prophet is in need of God, the Exalted, at every moment. He wants to show the Prophet ﷺ "you cannot bring everyone to belief. Your power is limited to an extent. You can have everyone but I want to keep some to show you I am the Creator; you are not the creator." So he left some people unguided, like Abū Jahl and Abū Lahab, and they were enemies to Prophet ﷺ.

إِنَّكَ لَا تَهْدِي مَنْ أَحْبَبْتَ وَلَكِنَّ اللَّهَ يَهْدِي مَن يَشَاءُ وَهُوَ أَعْلَمُ بِالْمُهْتَدِينَ

It is true you will not be able to guide all whom you love, but Allah guides those whom He wills, and He knows best those who receive guidance.[311]

Protection of the Prophet

Those who follow the religion must know they are protected and they are under the guidance of Friends of God, who will guide them to Sayyidina Muhammad ﷺ and his blessings. They are accepting Islam and accepting the Prophet ﷺ, and although we are full of shortcomings, we are under his *shafaʿa*.

---

[311] Sūratu 'l-Qaṣaṣ (the Narrations), 28:56.

وَاكْتُبْ لَنَا فِي هَـٰذِهِ الدُّنْيَا حَسَنَةً وَفِي الآخِرَةِ إِنَّا هُدْنَا إِلَيْكَ قَالَ عَذَابِي أُصِيبُ بِهِ مَنْ أَشَاء وَرَحْمَتِي وَسِعَتْ كُلَّ شَيْءٍ فَسَأَكْتُبُهَا لِلَّذِينَ يَتَّقُونَ وَيُؤْتُونَ الزَّكَاةَ وَالَّذِينَ هُم بِآيَاتِنَا يُؤْمِنُونَ

"And ordain for us that which is good, in this life and in the Hereafter: for we have turned unto You." He said: "With My punishment I visit whom I will; but My mercy extends to all things. That I shall ordain for those who do right and practise regular charity, and those who believe in Our signs.[312]

Allah is telling us, "My mercy has encompassed everything and wrapped everything. I am going to write it for the people who are accepting, who are devoted, who are not hoarding what Allah gave them, and who give in the way of Allah."

As they give, Allah gives more. If you give *ʿibādah*, worship, Allah gives more rewards; when you fast more, He will give you more power; when you pray more, He gives more blessings; and if you are a generous person, giving of your wealth, He will send more.

If you give all your possessions, like Sayyidina Abū Bakr ﷺ, your faith will grow strong. If you give half, as Sayyidina ʿUmar ؓ gave, you will get half of what Abū Bakr ؓ got. Some give and regret it. Others give, but their hands tremble.

We are always struggling.

So when Allah showed this to the Prophet ﷺ, and showed him, "My power is unlimited while your power is limited."

---

[312] Sūratu 'l-ʿArāf (the Heights), 7:156.

Friends of God look at the students whom God, the Exalted, has assigned to be their followers. They can have followers from the stubborn ones, from unbelievers who aren't stubborn, from those who were thrown into *Baḥr aẓ-ẓulmah* and then came back and acknowledged Allah is their lord, and even from *munāfiqīn*, hypocrites who are stubborn and corrupt.

قُلْ يَا عِبَادِيَ الَّذِينَ أَسْرَفُوا عَلَى أَنفُسِهِمْ لَا تَقْنَطُوا مِن رَّحْمَةِ اللَّهِ إِنَّ اللَّهَ يَغْفِرُ الذُّنُوبَ جَمِيعًا إِنَّهُ هُوَ الْغَفُورُ الرَّحِيمُ

Say: O my servants who have transgressed against their souls! Despair not of the Mercy of Allah, for Allah forgives all sins, for He is Oft-Forgiving, Most Merciful. [313]

On the Day of Promises, Allah assigned a group to each Friend of God and at that time the heart of Prophet ﷺ relaxed, as Allah had given supporters to assist him in guiding people to Him. In this world, Friends of God are trying their best to guide people as much as they can. Some people are not able to be guided, even when they are assigned to a Friend of God, who refers them back to the Prophet ﷺ. They come under the hadith:

> *My intercession is for those from my Nation who commit grave sins.*

And those who even the Prophet ﷺ cannot clean and guide, that to teach everyone that even he has a limit and only Allah has no limits.

Grandshaykh ق said:

> There is a special mercy that Allah will open on the Day of Judgment and that Friends of God know about, but there is

[313] Sūratu 'z-Zumar (the Groups), 39:53.

no permission to speak about it. That *raḥmat*[314] is to save Ummat an-Nabī ﷺ completely from any hellfire or punishment. These knowledges and this particular *raḥmat* have been rooted and planted in the hearts of Friends of God. There is no permission to talk about it and their tongues are frozen. That will not come until the secret of Qur'an appears and runs like a waterfall in the hearts of everyone. At that time, that *raḥmat* will appear and the people will know about it. That is only when the secrets of Qur'an will appear, and that will happen soon, and what I am talking is like drizzle before the big rainstorm, like a tornado that appears on the horizon, that will come suddenly and take everything with it. Those who have a solid cement foundation will not be affected by the tornado, but those who don't have a solid structure will be blown away by it.

Grandshaykh ق continues:

Some who are also preparing for that big event will be safe, like that lady in the time of Prophet Noah ﷺ; although the flood overtook the world, she never experienced it because she was a believer.

He said, "Oh my students, I have good tidings for you!" Grandshaykh ق explained the great level that Allah gave to Sayyidina Muhammad ﷺ although he is limited to some extent, yet compared to other prophets, Friends of God, prophets, and other human beings, the Prophet's knowledge is like a huge ocean.

Grandshaykh ق said:

Don't think after Allah called the Prophet ﷺ on al-Isra wa 'l-Mi'rāj, the Night Journey and Ascension, and showed him

---

[314] Arabic: *raḥma*—mercy.

secrets of the manifestation of the 99 Names and the Greatest Name, *Ismallāh al-ʿaẓam,* don't think after all that was manifested to him that Prophet ﷺ came back to us. That is impossible, as this world at that time cannot carry Sayyidina Muhammad ﷺ. What appeared to us after The Night Journey and Ascension was only a reflection of the full reality which stayed there, because this world cannot carry that power. The entire world will break into pieces. The Prophet ﷺ became like a huge voltage distributor that you cannot approach.

With all these manifestations of the Beautiful Names and Attributes this whole universe cannot carry the Prophet ﷺ and so Allah kept the reality of the Prophet in His Divine Presence, always giving, giving and giving. He sent only one reflection of that back to earth and the rest remains with Allah.

Wa min Allāhi 't-tawfiq, bi ḥurmati 'l-Fātiḥah.

25: MASTERING THE EGO THROUGH HUMILITY

Our Clever Egoes

The strategy of our ego is to make something wrong look correct, and it supplies us with many excuses to do the wrong thing, tricking us into believing what we are doing is permissible and good. Allah said in Holy Qur'an:

فَلَا تُزَكُّوا أَنفُسَكُمْ

Therefore justify not yourselves;[315]

It means "Don't give yourself excuses and don't praise yourself." Allah doesn't look at your pictures. He doesn't see you as ugly, beautiful, etc., but He looks at the condition of your heart; is it pure, without anger or hatred, without jealousy?

We all pray and fast, but what distinguishes us from others? The only thing that differs us is if we do our best and struggle against the wildness in our nature, by practicing discipline. We are wild horses. If we give the reins to our egos, they will go out of control so fast that no one can catch them. That is why we adhere to the science of Sufism.

Sufism: Price and Practice

Everything has its positive and negative. You cannot use Sufism without respecting Shariah; you must uphold the law or you

---

[315] Sūratu 'n-Najm (the Star), 53:32.

would go to the negative side. You cannot declare you are a high level Sufi, but pray like a rooster, without respecting the *ṣalāt,* the formal prayer.

I see many people bow in *rukū*ʿ[316] and don't come up all the way in *qiyām* (stand with a straight back), and go down immediately in *sajda,* prostration. You cannot do that. You cannot use the spirituality of Sufism trying to get the maximum benefit and discard or ignore legal principles. Today many people take the name "Sufi" without looking deeply into Shariʿah, which is the support or foundation of Sufism. They speak Sufi terminology without applying its truest principles.

Why did Allah send His messenger? Other religions have spiritual teachings, but we are Muslims; we follow Islam. Therefore, we must keep the principles of Shariʿah, or we deviate from the right way and a new generation will be lost from our bad examples.

In the past when Sufis were trying to develop that science in themselves, what did they do? They wore woolen clothes[317]. You can make cotton clothes the same thickness as wool, even the same texture. Why weren't they wearing cotton clothes, why wool? To remind them that their characters are like wild animals. To get rid of something, you must first remember it exists. So by wearing wool, you remember you are an animal.

We say, "*al-insānu ḥaywānun nāṭiq*—humans are a talking animal." If we don't polish that wild character, it will lead us to disaster, pulling us into the traps of Satan from where we will unable to pull ourselves out. We must focus on that.

---

[316] Arabic: *rukū*ʿ—bowing posture of the prayer.

[317] The root of the word *taṣawwuf* is *ṣūf,* wool.

The Prophet ﷺ mentioned many times that he feared for his Community that there are people who can speak very well and persuade us to follow the wrong way, and there are others who cannot speak well, but through their good character and good examples they can guide people to the best way.

قال صلى الله عليه وسلم: اخوف ما اخاف على امتي كل منافق عليم اللسان.

(رواه احمد)

The Prophet ﷺ said, "The thing I fear most for my nation is every hypocrite eloquent of tongue."[318]

It means, "Be careful of those who speak nicely and you are grabbed by the eloquence of their words, thinking this is what you need to follow, and you end up in the trap of Satan."

The Friends of God take care for their students to avoid the trap of Satan. In our contemporary world there are different cultures, ideologies, and different ways of understanding religion. If you go from Morocco to Egypt, the understanding changes. Egyptian culture differs from the Gulf and the Persian Gulf area, which is different from Pakistani culture, and Pakistan is different from India, and Indian culture is different from Central Asia, which is different from Southeast Asian culture. And those cultures are different from Western culture. Every culture has its own style and tastes. You cannot blend them together, or else they will be lost.

It is a Sunnah of Prophet ﷺ to speak to people according to their understanding. If the audience is multicultural, you must speak in general, not to something specific. If you want to speak to a Pakistani or Bangladeshi, it is different from speaking to a Frenchman, Englishman, or to a European.

---

[318] Āḥmad.

You can understand this point from the narration in Qur'an about Prophet Jacob ﵇[319]. He sent them to Egypt during a drought when there was no more food, after Prophet Joseph ﵇ was saved by Allah from the schemes of his brother, and after many trials, was put in charge of the food of Egypt.

وَقَالَ يَا بَنِيَّ لاَ تَدْخُلُواْ مِن بَابٍ وَاحِدٍ وَادْخُلُواْ مِنْ أَبْوَابٍ مُّتَفَرِّقَةٍ وَمَا أُغْنِي عَنكُم مِّنَ اللّهِ مِن شَيْءٍ إِنِ الْحُكْمُ إِلاَّ لِلّهِ عَلَيْهِ تَوَكَّلْتُ وَعَلَيْهِ فَلْيَتَوَكَّلِ الْمُتَوَكِّلُونَ

Further (Jacob) said: "O my sons! Enter not all by one gate: enter by different gates. Not that I can profit you against Allah (with my advice). None can command except Allah. On Him do I put my trust, and let all that trust put their trust on Him." [320]

Prophet Jacob ﵇ had twelve sons and all of them eventually became prophets of the Children of Israel. From them came the twelve tribes. So the Prophet Jacob ﵇ told his sons, "Go and get the food they are giving, but do not enter from one door; enter from different doors. "

In the spiritual meaning, "Don't enter from one door, but enter from different doors" means that he, Prophet Jacob ﵇, the father, is the main door, but he told his sons to enter by many doors.

The Many Doors

Here it is as if Grandshaykh ق is describing to us that the shaykh or those who are authorized to give *dhikr* must have many doors, depending on the background of every culture or every community.

---

[319] Arabic: Yaʿqūb ﵇.

[320] Sūrah Yūsūf (Joseph), 12:67.

Grandshaykh ق says:

> Allah said, "Enter from different doors," and no one knew the wisdom behind that. Allah said it was something in the heart of Y'aqūb ﷺ that he asked them to enter through different doors.

وَلَمَّا دَخَلُواْ مِنْ حَيْثُ أَمَرَهُمْ أَبُوهُم مَّا كَانَ يُغْنِي عَنْهُم مِّنَ اللّهِ مِن شَيْءٍ إِلاَّ حَاجَةً فِي نَفْسِ يَعْقُوبَ قَضَاهَا وَإِنَّهُ لَذُو عِلْمٍ لِّمَا عَلَّمْنَاهُ وَلَكِنَّ أَكْثَرَ النَّاسِ لاَ يَعْلَمُونَ

And when they entered in the manner which their father had enjoined, it would have naught availed them as against Allah; it was but a need of Jacob's soul which he thus satisfied; and lo! he was a lord of knowledge because We had taught him; but most of mankind know not.

That means we must approach people from their own backgrounds and assign to each culture someone who can speak to them. You cannot bring someone from Southeast Asia to speak to people from Morocco, for they see things differently. That is why we must be very careful to understand the issues as they relate to one and another. That is why it is good to assign people from their own communities for they understand them.

Blurred Visions

So what is important coming here tonight is, we must carry that woolen skin to clean ourselves of the characters that prevent us from progressing. Now if you see something in the Naqshbandi *ṭarīqah* that makes you advance, you must not say it, or else they will stop all of that from appearing. At first you might see something a bit blurry, like shadows—not hallucinations. It might be correct and it might not, so don't follow it or you might end up in mistake for you and those who follow you. Keep that to yourself and do not reveal it. Then traps of Satan will open and catch you. So leave it and keep it hidden. Don't let yourself speak about it.

When Grandshaykh 'Abd Allāh ق complete his five-year seclusion, Shaykh Sharafuddīn ق told him, "What you have seen of miracles, you must now divorce as one divorces his wife three times."

Many people say, "I saw this" or "I saw that." We always advise them to leave it; don't follow it up. In the Naqshbandi *ṭarīqah* what is important is not what you are seeing, which means nothing. It is important when you don't see. When you don't see anything, you feel guilty and assume you are not making any progress, so you try harder. When you see something and you assume it is important, you think you reached a higher level and become misguided because what you saw is not real. Which is stronger, the sun or the moon?

The moon has very nice, soft light you can observe and even stare at its surface. What happens when you look at the sun? You burn your eyes. Look directly at sun and then look away; all you can see is a blackout. When you reach sunlight you are in the ocean of nothingness, in the ocean of reality. Looking at the moon, as when you begin to see with your spiritual eyes, that is for beginners. But when you don't see, you are already in the ocean, swimming, and that is a higher level.

In seclusion, the first thing the shaykh instructs you is, "Don't look into what you see. If you go after it, you are feeding your ego candy, something to be happy with, and it will stop in its place, because you think you are progressing."

In reality, you are not progressing, but you are trapped. That is why when you look at the sun everything becomes dark. That means this world is dark in your eyes. Look at the sun and then look at where you are standing, for example, say you are in a rose garden. You no longer see that rose garden. For you, this world becomes black, meaning your heart is not there. But when you look at the moon, which is for beginners, you will be happy with it, and fall into problems and mistakes.

So we dress in wool to remind us we are carrying that animal on our backs, until we purify our hearts. The most important step is to remove anger and jealousy.[321] That animal nature is reinforced in you since childhood, and can only be removed by reciting daily 500 times *Yā Ṣamad.*[322]

These are remedies for such traits. So make sure you keep observing Ṣalāt an-Najāt. If you don't pray before Fajr, pray it at anytime—make those two *rakaʿat*s and that *sajda*. Similarly, you can pray Ṣalāt ash-Shukr and Ṣalāt at-Tasbīḥ at anytime. Recite 500 times *Yā Ṣamad* every day; that will purify you.

Some people are seeing dogs in dreams; that represents the ego, always barking, wanting to say something.

Grandshaykh ق said:

> If you left a dog in a room and gave it a little bit of smoke in the room, it will not be able to continue barking, and if you leave it like that it will explode (from not releasing that energy).

If you don't feed the blurry visions as candy to your ego, it will blow up and die, and then you will be inspired. At that time, when shaykhs come in your dream, that is a true dream. If they tell you something in a dream, go and fulfill it as that is guidance, and they have permission to guide their followers through dreams.

Wa min Allāhi 't-tawfiq, bi ḥurmati 'l-Fātiḥah.

---

[321] To achieve this, pray *Ṣalāt an-Najāt*.
[322] Aṣ-Ṣamad, of the 99 Beautiful Names, meaning "The Everlasting."

GLOSSARY

'abd (pl. *'Ibād*): lit. slave, servant.

'Abd Allāh: Lit., "servant of God"

Abū Bakr aṣ-Ṣiddīq ⚭: one the closest Companions to the Prophet ⚭, his father-in-law, who shared the Hijrah with him. After the Prophet's death, he was elected as the first caliph (successor) to the Prophet ⚭. He is known as one of the most saintly of the Prophet's Companions.

Abū Yazīd/Bayāzīd Bistāmī: A great ninth century *walī* and master in the Naqshbandi Golden Chain.

adab: good manners, proper etiquette.

adhān: call to prayer.

al: Arabic definite article, "the"

'alamīn: world; universes.

alḥamdūlillāh: Praise God.

'Alī ibn Abī Ṭālib ⚭: the cousin of the Prophet ⚭, married to his daughter Fāṭimah and fourth caliph of the Prophet ⚭.

alif: first letter of Arabic alphabet ا.

'Alīm, al-: the Knower, a divine attribute

Allāh: proper name for God in Arabic.

Allāhu Akbar: God is Greater.

'amal: good deed (pl. *'amāl*).

amīr (pl., *umarā*): chief, leader, head of a nation or people.

anā: first person singular pronoun

'aql: intellect, reason; from the root *'aqila*, lit., "to fetter."

'Arafah: a plain near Mecca where pilgrims gather for the principal rite of Hajj.

'arif: knower, gnostic; one who has reached spiritual knowledge of his Lord.

'ārifūn' bi 'l-Lāh: knowers of God

Ar-Raḥīm: The Mercy-Giving, Merciful, Munificent, one of Allah's ninety-nine Holy Names

Ar-Raḥmān: The Most Merciful, Compassionate, Beneficent, the most often repeated of Allah's Holy Names.

'arsh, al-: Divine Throne

aṣl: root, origin, basis.

astaghfirullāh: lit. "I seek Allah's forgiveness."

awliyāullāh: saints of Allah (sing. *walī*).

āyah/āyāt (pl. Ayāt): a verse of the Holy Qur'an.

Āyat al-Kursī: the Verse of the Throne, a well-known verse from the Qur'an (2:255).

Badī' al-: The Innovator; a Divine Name.

Banī Ādam: Children of Ādam; humanity.

Bayt al-Maqdis: the Sacred Mosque in Jerusalem, built at the site where Solomon's Temple was later erected.

Bayt al-Ma'mūr: much-frequented house; this refers to the Ka'bah of the heavens, which is the prototype of the Ka'bah on earth and is circumambulated by the angels.

baya': pledge; in the context of this book, the pledge of initiation of a disciple (*murid*) to a shaykh.

bismi'l-Lāhi 'r-Raḥmāni 'r-Raḥīm: "In the name of the All-Merciful, the Compassionate"; this is the introductory verse to all the chapters of the Qur'an except the ninth.

Dajjāl: the False Messiah (Antichrist) whom the Prophet ﷺ foretold as coming at the end-time of this world, who will deceive mankind with pretensions of being divine.

dalālah: evidence

dhāt: self / selfhood

dhawq (pl. adhwāq): tasting; technical term referring to the experiential aspect of gnosis.

dhikr: remembrance, mention of God through His Holy Names or phrases of glorification.

ḍīyā: light.

Diwān al-Awlīyā—the gathering of saints with the Prophet ﷺ in the spiritual realm. This takes place every night.

du'a: supplication.

dunyā: world; worldly life.

'eid: festival; the two major festivals of Islam are 'Eid al-Fitr, marking the completion of Ramadan, and 'Eid al-Adha, the Festival of Sacrifice during the time of Hajj.

farḍ: obligatory worship.

Fātiḥah: Sūratu 'l-Fātiḥah; the opening surah of the Qur'an.

Ghafūr, al-: The Forgiver; a Divine Name.

ghawth: lit. "Helper"; the highest ranking saint the in hierarchy of saints.

ghaybu' l-muṭlaq, al-: the absolute unknown, known only to God.

ghusl: full shower/bath obligated by a state of ritual impurity prior to worship.

Grandshaykh: generally, a *walī* of great stature. In this text, where spelled with a capital G, "Grandshaykh" refers to Mawlana 'Abd Allāh ad-Daghestani (d. 1973), Mawlana Shaykh Nazim's master.

hā': letter ه

ḥadīth nabawī (pl., ahadith): prophetic hadith whose meaning and linguistic expression are those of the Prophet Muḥammad ﷺ.

ḥadith qudsī: divine saying whose meaning directly reflects the meaning God intended but whose linguistic expression is not Divine Speech as in the Qur'an, it thus differs from a hadith *nabawī* (*see* above).

ḥaḍr: present

ḥaywān: animal.

ḥajj: the sacred pilgrimage of Islam obligatory on every mature Muslim once in his/her life.

ḥalāl: permitted, lawful according to the Islamic Shari'ah.

ḥaqīqah, al-: reality of existence; ultimate truth.

ḥaqq: truth

Ḥaqq, al-: the Divine Reality, one of the 99 Divine Names.

ḥarām: forbidden, unlawful.

hāshā: God forbid!

ḥarf (pl. *ḥurūf*): letter; Arabic root "edge."

hijrah: emigration.

ḥikmah: wisdom

ḥujjah: proof

hūwa: the pronoun "he," made up of the letters *hā'* and *wāw* in Arabic.

'ibādu 'l-Lāh: servants of God

iḥsān: doing good, "It is to worship God as though you see Him; for if you are not seeing Him, He sees you."

ikhlāṣ, al-: sincere devotion

ilāh (pl. *āliha):* idols or god(s)

ilāhīyya: divinity

ilhām—Divine inspiration sent to *awlīyāullah.*

'ilm: knowledge, science.

ʿilmu 'l-awrāq: knowledge of papers

ʿilmu 'l-adhwāq: knowledge of taste

ʿilmu 'l-ḥurūf: science of letters

ʿilmu 'l-kalām: scholastic theology.

ʿilmun ladunnī: "Divinely-inspired" knowledge

imān: faith, belief.

imām: leader of congregational prayer; an advanced scholar followed by a large community.

insān: humanity; pupil of the eye.

insānu 'l-kāmil, al-: the Perfect Man; the Prophet Muhammad ﷺ.

irādatullāh: the Will of God.

irshād: spiritual guidance

ism: name

isma-Llāh: name of God

isrā': night journey; used here in reference to the night journey of the Prophet Muḥammad ﷺ.

jalāl: majesty

jamāl: beauty

jamaʿa: group, congregation.

jihād: to struggle in God's Path.

Jinn: a species of living beings, created out of fire, invisible to most humans. Jinn can be Muslims or non-Muslims.

Jumuʿah: Friday congregational prayer, held in a large mosque.

Kaʿbah: the first House of God, located in Mecca, Saudi Arabia to which pilgrimage is made and which is faced in the five daily prayers.

kāfir: unbeliever.

Kalāmullāh al-Qadīm : lit. Allah's Ancient Words, viz. the Holy Qur'an.

kalimat at-tawḥīd: lā ilāha illa-Llāh: "There is no god but Allah (the God)."

khalīfah: deputy

Khāliq, al-: the Creator, one of the 99 Divine Names.

khalq: creation

khuluq: conduct, manners.

lā: no; not; not existent; the particle of negation.

lā ilāha illa-Llāh Muḥammadun rasūlullāh: there is no deity except Allah, Muhammad is the Messenger of Allah.

lām: Arabic letter ل

al-Lawḥ al Maḥfūẓ: the Preserved Tablets.

laylat al-isrā' wa 'l-miʿrāj: the Night Journey and Ascension of the Prophet Muḥammad ﷺ to Jerusalem and to the seven heavens.

Madīnātu 'l-Munawwarah: the Illuminated city; city of Prophet Muḥammad ﷺ. Referred to as Madina.

mahr: dowry given by the groom to the bride.

malakūt: divine kingdom.

Malik, al-: the Sovereign, a Divine Name.

maqām: spiritual station; tomb of a prophet, messenger or saint.

maʿrifah: gnosis.

māshāAllāh: it is as Allah Wills.

Mawlānā: lit. "our master" or "our patron," referring to an esteemed person.

maẓhar: place of disclosure.

mīzān: the Scale which weighs the actions of human beings on Judgment Day.

mīm: Arabic letter م

miʿrāj: the ascension of the Prophet Muḥammad ﷺ from Jerusalem to the seven heavens.

Muḥammadun rasūlu 'l-Lāh: Muḥammad is the Messenger of God.

mulk, al-: the World of dominion

Mu'min, al-: Guardian of Faith, one of the 99 Names of God.

mu'min: a believer.

munājāt: invocation to God in very intímate form.

murīd: disciple, student, follower.

murshid: spiritual guide, *pir*.

mushāhadah: direct witnessing

mushrik (pl. *mushrikūn):* idolater, polytheist.

muwwaḥid (pl. *muwaḥḥidūn*): those affiriming God's Oneness.

nabī: a prophet of God

nafs: lower self, ego.

nūr: light

Nūḥ: the prophet Noah ﷺ.

Nūr, an-: The Source of Light, a Divine Name.

Qādir, al-: the Powerful, a Divine Name.

qalam, al-: the Pen.

qiblah: direction, specifically, the direction faced by Muslims during prayer and other worship towards the Sacred House in Mecca.

Quddūs, al-: the Holy One, a Divine Name.

qurb: nearness

quṭb (pl. *aqṭāb*): axis or pole. Among the poles are:

Quṭb al-bilād: Pole of the Lands

Quṭb al-irshād: Pole of Guidance

Quṭbu 'l-aqṭāb: Pole of Poles

Quṭbu 'l-a'ẓam: Highest Pole

Quṭbu 't-tasarruf: Pole of Affairs

al-quṭbīyyatu 'l-kubrā: the highest station of poleship

Rabb, ar-: the Lord

Raḥīm, ar-: the Most Compassionate, a Divine Name.

Raḥmān, ar-: the All-Merciful, a Divine Name.

raḥma: mercy.

raka'at: one full set of prescribed motions in prayer. Each prayer consists of a one or more *raka'ats*.

Ramaḍān: the ninth month of the Islamic lunar calendar, the month of fasting.

rasūl: a messenger of God

Rasūlullāh: the Prophet of God, Muhammad ﷺ.

Ra'ūf, ar-: the Most Kind, a Divine Name.

Razzāq, ar-: the Provider

rawḥānīyyah: spirituality, spiritual essence of something.

rizq: provision, sustenance.

rūḥ: spirit. Ar-Rūḥ is the name of a great angel.

rukū': bowing posture of the prayer.

ṣaḥīḥ: authentic; term certifying validity of a hadith of the Prophet ﷺ.

ṣāim: fasting person (pl. *ṣāimūn*)

salām: peace.

Salām, as-: the Peaceful, a Divine Name.

as-salāmu 'alaykum: peace be upon you (Islamic greeting)

ṣalāt: Islam's ritual prayer.

Ṣalāt an-Najāt: prayer of salvation, done in the wee hours of the night.

Ṣamad, aṣ-: Self-Sufficient, upon whom creatures depend.

Saḥābah (sing., sahabi): the Companions of the Prophet, the first Muslims.

sajda (pl. *sujūd*): prostration.

ṣalāt: prayer, one of the five obligatory pillars of Islam. Also to invoke blessing on the Prophet ﷺ.

ṣalawāt (sing. *salāt*): invoking blessings and peace upon the Prophet ﷺ.

ṣawm, ṣiyām: fasting.

sayyid: leader; also, a descendant of Prophet Muhammad ﷺ.

Sayyidinā/ sayyidunā: our master (fem. *sayyidatunā:* our mistress).

shahādah: lit. testimony; the testimony of Islamic faith: *Lā ilāha illa 'l-Lāh wa Muḥammadun rasūlu 'l-Lāh* or "There is no god but Allah, the One God, and Muḥammad is the Messenger of God."

Shah Naqshband: Grandshaykh Muhammad Bahauddin Shah-Naqshband, a great eighth century *walī*, the founder of the Naqshbandi *Ṭarīqah*.

shaykh: lit. "old man," a religious guide, teacher; master of spiritual discipline.

shifā': cure.

shirk: polytheism, idolatry, ascribing partners to God

ṣiffāt: attributes; term referring to Divine Attributes.

Silsilat adh-dhahabīyya: "golden chain" of spiritual authority in Islam

sohbet (Arabic *suḥba):* association: the assembly or discourse of a shaykh.

subḥanallāh: glory be to God.

sulṭān/sulṭānah: ruler, monarch.

Sulṭān al-Awlīyā: lit., "the king of the *awlīyā*,"; the highest-ranking saint.

sunnah: the practice of the Prophet ﷺ; that is, what he did, said, recommended or approved of in his Companions.

sūrah: a chapter of the Qur'an; picture, image.

Sūratu 'l- Ikhlāṣ: the Chapter of Sincerity, 114.

ṭabīb: doctor.

tābi'īn: the Successors, generation after the Prophet's Companions.

tafsīr: to explain, expound, explicate, or interpret; technical term for commentary or exegesis of the Holy Qur'ān.

tajallī (pl. tajallīyāt): theophanies, God's self-disclosures, Divine Self-manifestation.

takbīr: lit. "Allāhu Akbar," God is Great.

tarawīḥ: the special nightly prayers of Ramadan.

ṭarīqat/ṭarīqah: literally, way, road or path. An Islamic order or path of discipline and devotion under a guide or shaykh; Islamic Sufism.

tasbīḥ: recitation glorifying or praising God.

tawāḍa': humbleness.

tawāf: the rite of circumambulating the Ka'bah while glorifying God during Hajj and 'Umrah.

tawḥīd: unity; universal or primordial Islam, submission to God, as the sole Master of destiny and ultimate Reality.

'ubūdīyyah: state of worshipfulness. Servanthood

'ulamā (sing. *'Alīm*): scholars.

'ulūmu 'l-awwalīna wa 'l-ākhirīn: knowledge of the "Firsts" and the "Lasts" refers to the knowledge that God poured into the heart of Muḥammad ﷺ during his ascension to the Divine Presence.

'ulūm al-Islāmī: Islamic religious sciences.

ummah: faith community, nation.

'Umar ibn al-Khaṭṭāb ؓ: an eminent Companion of the Prophet ﷺ and second caliph of Islam.

'umrah: the minor pilgrimage to Mecca, performed at any time of the year.

'Uthmān ibn 'Affān ؓ: an eminent Companion of the Prophet ﷺ and his son-in-law, who became third caliph of Islam. Renowned for compiling the Qur'an.

walad: a child

waladī: my child

walāyah: proximity or closeness; sainthood.

walī (pl. *awliyā'*): saint, or "he who assists,"; guardian; protector.

wasīlah: a means; a special station granted to the Prophet Muḥammad ﷺ as intermediary to God in the granting the petitioner's supplications.

wāw: Arabic letter و

wujūd, al-: existence; "to find," "the act
of finding," as well as "being
found".

Y'aqūb: the prophet Jacob ⚶.

yamīn: the right hand, used to mean
"oath."

yawm al-'ahdi wa'l-mīthāq: day of oath
and covenant, a heavenly event
before this life, when the souls of
mankind were present before
God where He took from each
soul the promise to accept His
Sovereignty as Lord.

yawm al-qiyāmah: Day of Judgment.

Yūsūf: the prophet Joseph ⚶.

Printed in the United States
122694LV00004B/67-90/P